THE POLITICAL THEORY OF
JOHN DEWEY

A. H. SOMJEE

TEACHERS COLLEGE PRESS

Teachers College, Columbia University
New York, New York

13589

To the memory of my mother

FOREWORD

IN HIS GIFFORD LECTURES in 1929, published as
The Quest for Certainty: A Study of Knowledge and Action, John
Dewey described the final stage of a revolution that he called, in
words of the last chapter of his book, "the Copernican Revolution in
philosophy." The phrase was borrowed from Kant, with the observation that the consequences of Kant's treatment of the world and our
knowledge of the world, from the standpoint of the knowing subject,
were Ptolemaic rather than Copernican. The revolution which Dewey
described was a reversal of traditional ideas about the mind, reason,
conceptions, and mental processes, in which the opposition between
knowing and doing, theory and practice was abandoned in the actual
enterprise of scientific inquiry in which knowing goes forward by doing. The old center was mind knowing an external material; the new
center, indefinite interactions taking place within a course of nature
subject to alteration and direction by intentional operations. Dewey
had contributed to the revolution he described in *The Quest for
Certainty.* His early studies in psychology, ethics, and experimental
logic laid the grounds for the detailed reorientation of approach to
all philosophical problems in *Reconstruction in Philosophy* in 1920.
The change of perspective was not only from an old traditional approach to a new one, but from the limits of one cultural tradition to
an inclusive orientation to all men in interaction with their physical,
biological and cultural circumstances. *Reconstruction in Philosophy*

was written from lectures given in China and Japan. On his return to the United States he turned his attention to human action and its circumstances—to human nature and conduct, to experience and nature, and to the public, to civilization, to culture, and to social action.

Dewey's political philosophy has received rather less attention than other parts of his philosophy, perhaps because the destruction of the old political philosophy has overshadowed the experimental search for the public and inquiry into the nature and consequences of political action initiated by Dewey. When Peter Laslett edited a collection of essays in *Philosophy, Politics and Society* (New York: Macmillan, 1956), he wrote emphatically in his *Introduction* (p. vii), "For the moment, anyway, political philosophy is dead." However, he later qualified that judgment because "the mood is very different and very much more favorable than it was six years ago" *(Philosophy, Politics and Society*, 2nd series, p. vii).

Dewey was critical of the abstract, metaphysical concept of the state, but his inquiry concerning the public and the consequences of public action placed political action in a context of actions of other associations of men and of actions of individuals, and it related politics to economics, technology, society, and culture. He lived to see the development of international politics and the United Nations after the second World War, and doubtless reflected on the vindication of his analysis of the formation of the public in the development of new nations and the extension of the consequences of public action in the relations of nations. In the revolution of philosophy, political thought and action has taken on a new architectonic function which is preparing the way for a new philosophy of culture for all men.

It is appropriate that the significance of Dewey's political philosophy should be perceived by an Indian scholar of political science, sociology, and anthropology. A. H. Somjee lived through the period of the separation of India from Great Britain. The problems faced by the new independent nation, which took its place in the British Commonwealth and the United Nations while it formed its constitution, set up new political institutions, and faced problems of economic, social and educational reform, made vividly apparent the need to clarify the philosophic foundations of political action and change. Professor Somjee had made his first studies of Dewey in London at a time when Dewey's instrumentalist and experimental mode of inquiry had had little influence on rival views of existence and experience. Somjee later consulted Americans who had studied with Dewey but who had not yet seen the important place which his political theory occupies in the Copernican Revolution. I first talked with Professor Somjee about Dewey when I was Visiting Professor at Baroda University. I had been a student of Dewey's when he returned from China and Japan, and I had studied and taught *The Public and Its Problems*. When I read Professor Somjee's manuscript and discussed its chapters with him, I was convinced that he was right in presenting Dewey's political theory as a major stage not only in the evolution of Dewey's thought but also in the development of modern views of political thought and action. Somjee had presented the philosophical grounding of Dewey's political theory and in so doing he had clarified the development of Dewey's philosophy.

Professor Somjee relates Dewey's political theory to the framework and the foundation provided by Dewey's broader philosophy by relating it to "experience" and "inquiry." Experience, as Dewey conceived it and used it, was not the epistemological "experience" of British empiricists but the source of knowledge and the realm of action, more akin to culture, which determines man and his circumstances, than to mind, which forms ideas from impressions. Inquiry is the method of science applied to the solution of all problematic situations. Somjee's analysis of experience and inquiry are valuable not only for the light which they throw on Dewey's political philosophy but also for the insight which they give into the central place they have come to occupy in twentieth century philosophy. Professor Somjee also places Dewey's political philosophy in the history of the development of political thought, and he analyzes Dewey's reaction to the theories of his predecessors, in particular Kant, T. H. Green, Maine, Austin, and Hobbes. Finally, and most important, Professor Somjee presents a comprehensive and specific statement of Dewey's view of scientific method as it is applied in political philosophy. In carrying out these three analyses, Professor Somjee has not only made available a needed study of Dewey's political philosophy but has given new vigor and relevance to the basic philosophy by which Dewey prepared the way for much that is new in modern philosophic thought.

RICHARD MCKEON

University of Chicago
February 26, 1968

ix

PREFACE

IN RECENT POLITICAL THEORY, few books have had
the impact on the formulation of essential problems of the discipline
of David Easton's *Political System* (New York: Knopf, 1953), effectively discriminates which functions of political theory from those of
political philosophy, and succeeds in bringing the former closer to
theory in the more developed social sciences such as economics, psychology, and sociology. It also has sought to crystallize functions of
political theory in the light of the role of theory in the natural
sciences and has emphasized the need to formulate adequate concepts to illuminate complexities of phenomenon in question, to
undertake empirical investigation based on propositions drawn from
them, and to lay down rigorous standards of reasoning and testability of arguments and statements about politics.

Today all these are, more or less, accepted canons of the discipline of political theory. The bulk of works published each year in
the field address themselves, by and large, to these as well as other
related problems. This then has become a living tradition in political theory.

Inspiration for this effort has come from various sources, not
many of which have been adequately identified. In political theory
proper this tradition can be traced back to the writings of Harold
Lasswell, Charles Merriam, and George Catlin. Together with these,
however, few works of psychologists and sociologists have been

emphasized. Little or no credit has been given to philosophers and philosophers of science.

A few years ago, I decided to undertake an examination of philosophical and social ideas of John Dewey with a view to find out whether they could be regarded as one of the sources of this tradition. The more I analyzed those ideas, the more I began to feel that they not only constituted a vital source of this tradition, but that Dewey himself could be regarded as one of the precursors of the new approach to political theory. I have written this book with a view to substantiating this contention. It is my feeling that the American obsession with novelty coupled with the postwar reaction against Dewey's educational theories have prevented American scholars from recognizing his contribution to the new approach to political theory.

Dewey's ideas on political theory are mainly significant in the following respects: the scientific approach, the range of empirically oriented concepts, and the manipulative function of all knowledge, including theories about politics. In trying to discover the significance of science for the social sciences, Dewey no doubt moved too close to the natural sciences for our taste. Nevertheless, we ought not to forget the fact that he belonged to that generation of thinkers who made many-sided efforts to establish a transmission belt between the two branches of knowledge, leaving us in a vantage position of having attained a more balanced perspective. With Dewey, it was the thrill and excitement of the availability of new knowledge with all its dazzling consequences that moved him. His excessive emphasis on science is, in a sense, similar to that of Marx. The range of possible concepts towards the formulation of empirically oriented theory of politics, as presented by Dewey, doubtless has an antiquarian air about it; nevertheless, his discussion is stimulating and not wholly devoid of relevance to our ways of setting about the subject. Finally, with regard to the manipulative aspect of his theory, no matter how very critical we may become of his philosophy of instrumentalism, he certainly focused his attention on a nagging question in social sciences, namely, the obligation to influence social policy. Writings of Dewey perhaps give bad conscience even to those who have convinced themselves that social investigators and social policy indicators or makers are two *distinct* groups. Dewey compels us to question such a demarcation of convenience on our part and think in terms of the social consequences of our abstruse theoretical formulations.

The main drift of political theory today is in the direction of the general theory of politics, the use of political models as analytic systems referring to concrete political systems, problems of measurement of empirical knowledge, the problems of valid inference, and so forth. The roots of these concerns no doubt are in problems which Dewey addressed himself to. In the final analysis, they all deal with the basic question of the relationship between facts and ideas. In that sense, going back to Dewey does not mean returning to the remote past of social sciences but discovering the relevant, going to the very foundation on which contemporary thinking in political theory rests.

I have repeatedly been asked by friends as to why I, an Indian with graduate training in Britain, have taken an interest in Dewey. In my attempted answers, so far I have convinced neither them nor myself. Some of these have been as follows: Tremendous emphasis on social and economic reconstruction, which my generation in India has known, might have been responsible for my interest in a thinker who always ends up on a note of *reconstruction*. But I am not very sure. My initial attraction to him, as I remember, was largely due to his extraordinary faith in the possibility of human growth. This too, however, could be traced back to my native background, where growth has become an ideal in a society which stagnated for centuries. Having been initially attracted to him, what sustained my interest in Dewey was his refreshingly equal emphasis on theory and practice. How much that too was due to my native background, I would leave my readers to judge.

In my study of Dewey, I was assisted by a number of scholars. I owe a debt of gratitude to my mentor at the London School of Economics, Prof. Michael Oakeshott. I had the temerity to write my doctoral dissertation under his supervision, knowing full well what he thought of John Dewey. His sense of fairness, unfailing generosity and civilized scepticism helped me to go deep into Dewey's ideas. Prof. Herbert Schneider during his years at UNESCO, Paris, was a source of constant encouragement. Prof. Richard McKeon, whose debt I cannot sufficiently acknowledge, made very valuable suggestions for the revision of my manuscript. Dr. Allan Milne and Prof. John Chapman read the manuscript. Needless to say that whatever shortcomings there are in this manuscript, I alone am responsible. I am grateful to the University of London for their kind permission to incorporate parts of my doctoral dissertation in this volume. My thanks are also due to my wife for her constant help and reminder that a simple book *can* be written on a difficult thinker and therefore ought to be attempted.

A. H. Somjee

North Vancouver
January 1967

CONTENTS

INTRODUCTION

THIS BOOK IS AN ATTEMPT to understand John Dewey's political ideas against the background of his philosophy in general. It attempts to substantiate the contention that his writings on politics, when considered against the background of his philosophy, are mainly significant in respect of the light they throw on the problems of political inquiry.

Dewey's political ideas have received much less attention than his ideas on the philosophy of science, logic, psychology, and education. A number of factors may be said to be responsible for this. His political ideas reveal their significance only when analyzed in the light of two of the principal elements in his system of thought, namely, his concept of experience and his theory of "common inquiry." His highly obscure manner of expressing his ideas, moreover, has usually encouraged his readers to look no further than necessary in his writings. Readers trained in technical philosophy have grappled with the excessive qualifications in his statements and the diverse undercurrents of idealism, naturalism, and physicalism in his arguments. Others interested in his philosophy of education and in his psychology have been immensely helped by Dewey himself with an enormous number of more readable popular articles, papers, and commentaries. But those readers interested in his social and political philosophy have scarcely got beyond its central and simple idea, the close relationship of political theory to political practice. His reputation as *practical* philosopher, furthermore, has predisposed a majority of those interested in his social and political philosophy to look only for his concrete proposals for the redressing of social evils and maladjustments: pragmatists are notorious for making reflective thought instrumental in the solution of practical problems. Consequently, the various interpretations of the methodological elements in Dewey's political writings have come to be restricted to examinations of one or another form of functionalism.

Such is the tone of two of the important papers written on Dewey's political philosophy—"Dewey's Social and Political Philosophy" (1939) by G. R. Geiger[1] and "The Political Philosophy of Experimentalism" (1940) by Hu Shih.[2] Dr. Geiger has rightly suggested that Dewey's political philosophy is a plea for the adoption of the experimental attitude in political thinking and acting. However, he does not inquire into its philosophical basis.

Dewey's experimental attitude was based on the significance of science to his general theory of inquiry, or his attempt to embody in philosophy the investigatory as well as the manipulative significance of the procedure of science. This was therefore of a great relevance to the problems he raised in his political philosophy. By taking the experimental attitude that Dewey advocated at its face value, Dr. Geiger deprives himself of recognizing the significance of Dewey's theory of inquiry to the problems of political analysis and reconstruction.

In the other paper, Mr. Hu Shih interprets Dewey's political ideas with reference to the historical circumstances in which they were expressed. Dewey's mature political ideas were expressed during the inter-war years, and his emphasis on the function of the state at this time reflects the condition of the American economy and the role of the state in fighting the Depression. Mr. Hu Shih's interpretation of Dewey's political philosophy is restricted accordingly. What Mr. Shih does not take into account is the "intellectual machinery," to use Dewey's phrase, involved in the treatment of contemporary problems. In such works from this period as *The Public and Its Problems* (1927), *Individualism, Old and New* (1930), *Liberalism and Social Action* (1935), and *Freedom and Culture* (1939), Dewey did not conceal the inspiration and guidance which he had received from science in suggesting and investigating the possibilities for manipulating various social, economic, and political situations. His ideas in all these works were directly or indirectly connected with his own theory of inquiry, and their significance cannot be fully appreciated without taking this into account.

Two other interpretations of Dewey's political philosophy, especially of his views on democracy, are *John Dewey: The Reconstruction of the Democratic Life* (1951) by Jerome Nathanson and *Intelligence in Politics* (1931) by Paul Ward. Mr. Nathanson's book is more or less an exposition of Dewey's views on the possibilities of human nature and of democratic participation in government as the necessary condition for the fullest development of human potentialities. Professor Ward's book makes use of Dewey's ideas in order to provide what may be said to be the pragmatic justification of democracy as a desire for peaceful change and a means for preventing the stresses and strains of revolution on the body politic.[3] For Dewey, however, the only sanction for democracy lies in the fact that, like science, democracy has institutionalized the procedure of trial and error. Consequently, as a form of government it provides both the rulers and the ruled with the opportunity for putting into practice their ideas and policies and for learning from the results of their "experiment." Dewey's approach to democracy is therefore much more positive and much more profound than one would gather from Professor Ward's book. Professor Ward has also analyzed Dewey's emphasis on the situation which lies behind every specific problem. He has not, however, fully brought out the unique and dynamic character that Dewey ascribes to specific problems and to the possibilities of manipulating them.

To some extent, Dewey himself was responsible for the lack of adequate attention to his political ideas. Although in all his political writings there is some indication of the methodological framework which he had in mind, in none of them, excepting *The Public and Its Problems*, are its salient features fully embodied. This no doubt is one reason why Dewey regarded *The Public and Its Problems* as his best work. Unfortunately, the obscurity of his style, as far as his social and political writings are concerned, reached its greatest extreme in this book. Consequently, neither its reviewers nor those of Dewey's readers who otherwise showed a great interest in his writings[4] could do justice to this seminal work. Nor is it surprising to see the limited references made to this book in the various papers written in the past few years on the social and political philosophy of Dewey.

In order that the significance of Dewey's political ideas may be fully appreciated, this book presents in the first two chapters an account of his principal philosophical ideas. Their exposition centers around two of his basic concepts, *experience* and *common inquiry*. The concept of experience fully brings out Dewey's emphasis on the functional character of all thinking and of all reflective inquiry, and his concept of common inquiry attempts to bridge the gulf, as far as he is concerned, between physical inquiry and social inquiry. This he achieves by pointing out that there is only one kind of inquiry, namely the experimental inquiry that operates differently in different subject matters. Operations of experimental inquiry call for experimentation under the direction of ideas or hypotheses. Since beliefs, values, and subjectivity appear to conflict with the operations of experimental inquiry, Dewey attempts to restate them so as to avoid this conflict.

Before undertaking an examination of Dewey's political ideas against the background of his philosophy, we must take into account those of his political ideas that were either vitally influenced by his philosophy or that stemmed directly from it. From this point of view his writings on Kant and Green are important. His criticism of Kant can be divided into two phases: the first, derived from the neo-Hegelians in Britain and America, and the second, largely based on his mature philosophical ideas. The former phase left behind deposits of Hegelian organisicm and activism in his thought. Both organicism and activism remained a permanent influence on his conception of political activity. Organicism transformed his conception of political activity into some form of a concerted activity, and activism provided a dynamic character for the problems of politics and consequently demanded equally dynamic and flexible manipulative efforts to solve them. The latter phase of his criticism of Kant provided him with the material for the development of his ideas on the problems of political investigation, the functions of political organization, the conception of cooperative authority, trial-and-error procedure and so forth. His views on Green's ethics of self-realization became the source of his subsequent views on self-realization through the cultural medium and democratic participation. The task of discovering the philosophical roots of Dewey's political ideas, together with an analysis of his earlier political writings, which indicate his search for a new attitude in political theory, has been undertaken in Chapter Three.

Dewey's mature political ideas, when considered against the background of his philosophy, especially his theory of knowledge, tend to fall into three main divisions, each with special characteristics that are implicit in his theory of knowledge. The first characteristic of his theory of knowledge is to be found in his attribution of a directive function to ideas or concepts. They direct our operations

4

of knowing. Such a directive function was later attributed, in his philosophy, to political ideas or political concepts. An analysis of the directive functions of political ideas or political concepts has been undertaken in the section on the epistemological aspect of Dewey's political theory. It groups together his views on the uses and merits of various concepts in the understanding of political phenomena. The second characteristic of his theory of knowledge is his view that reflection or thinking takes place when a problematic situation is present. Its approximate counterpart in his political writings is to be found in his emphasis on specific problems in politics. His views on investigations and causal determination of specific problems in politics have been examined under the heading of the analytical aspect of Dewey's political theory. The third characteristic of his theory of knowledge is his contention that an inquiry begins with the presence of a problematic situation and that it terminates when the problematic situation is existentially resolved or empirically reconstructed. The political counterpart of this characteristic is to be found in his ideas on manipulation. They are grouped together and their significance to his political theory pointed out in the section on the manipulative aspect of Dewey's political theory. The epistemological, analytical and manipulative aspects of his theory that are dealt with in Chapter Four are therefore some sort of political counterparts of the three main characteristics of his theory of knowledge.

Although this book is essentially confined to the task of analysis and evaluation of those ideas of Dewey that are significant, directly or indirectly, to the problems of political inquiry, it would not be out of place to outline in a few words the philsophical framework in which he has discussed these problems.

In his political writings Dewey repeatedly attacked the concept of the state. His attack ought not to be confused with the attacks on the *authority* of the state of political pluralists like Barker, Laski, and Cole, who at the turn of the century were engaged in restating political philosophy in the light of the important part played by various associations in society. They attacked the state for unjustfiably receiving the credit for the services rendered by various voluntary associations. Dewey's attack, in contrast with that of political pluralists, was on the *concept* of the state rather than its authority. He rejected the concept of the state on the following two grounds: Firstly, the universal features of this concept tend to obliterate the differences which exist between one political organization and another.

5

Secondly, the concept of the state inevitably draws us into a historical controversy over its nature. Such a controversy cannot be termi-
nated with the help of any empirical data, and is therefore not worth
pursuing.

Dewey believed that the concept of the state becomes some sort
of obstacle in our understanding of the complexities of the political
phenomena that surround us. By its very nature it cannot become a
tool of inquiry, and as long as it continues to receive attention, it is
not likely to encourage the formulation of alternative concepts of investigation.

His primary emphasis thus fell on the need to understand phenomena with the help of a consciously formulated conceptual framework. In this respect, to my mind, Dewey becomes the pioneer of the
contemporary movement in scientific political theory headed by
thinkers like George Catlin, Charles Merriam, Harold Lasswell, and
David Easton. These four political scientists have formulated far
more sophisticated conceptual frameworks than Dewey. Nevertheless, these pages would substantiate the view that Dewey is the
forerunner of them all. Although Dewey's mature political work, *The
Public and Its Problems* (1927), was published at the same time as
George Catlin's *Science and Method of Politics* (1927), his standpoint
in political theory evolved earlier. His paper, "Austin's Theory of
Sovereignty," published as early as 1894, already indicates his emphasis on conceptual framework in empirical investigation.

For Dewey, however, the understanding of the phenomena was
not an end in itself. It was something he tried to make instrumental
to the realization of his own political values, which may be summarized as follows.

Along with Graham Wallas, Dewey believed that the society in
which we live today is completely disorganized as a result of the
impact of industrialization. Not only is it disorganized, but even
the communication among its constituent units has broken down as
a result of the lack of common intellectual symbols. The new and
well-organized society can come into existence only when common
intellectual symbols are provided to its members. In order to attain
this goal the new society has to have an adequate knowledge of
itself. Its knowledge of itself forges new bonds and brings into
existence a new community.

Such a community, Dewey believed, would provide an adequate
background for the pursuit of enlightened politics. In that respect,

Dewey shared the optimistic ideas of the youthful Walter Lippmann regarding the use of intelligence bureaus to supply impartial information to baffled citizens on all topics. Unlike Lippmann, who later on became skeptical of his earlier ideas, Dewey remained an unrepentant enlightenist until the end of his career.

Within the community based on constantly enriched knowledge of itself, Dewey visualized a cooperative conception of authority that enabled individuals to have the greatest degree of participation at all levels. He believed that individuals must contribute to the making of all those decisions which affect their well-being. The model of cooperative authority that Dewey had for politics was largely borrowed from science. It was, as we shall see later on, both weak and unrealistic. Nevertheless, it indicates Dewey's profound conception of democracy.

Dewey had a great faith in the boundless growth of human potentialities. He believed that they are likely to grow more in an environment that gives them maximum scope for expression and action. Consequently, he laid great emphasis on the creation of an environment conducive to continuous growth.

Finally, Dewey put a great premium on social and political experimentation. According to him, the spirit of experimentation had made science rich and dynamic. A similar spirit could be cultivated in the social and political field provided all dogmas were to be rejected. By bold experimentation a society can find solutions for all its problems—and only a democratic form of government, he maintained, would permit experimentation.

These, then, are some of the principal political values that form the basis of Dewey's political philosophy. We shall now examine in detail his philosophical and political ideas and discover their significance to the problems of political inquiry.

1

THE CONCEPT
OF EXPERIENCE

IN ORDER FULLY TO UNDERSTAND the significance of Dewey's political ideas, it is necessary to examine them against the background of his philosophy. His philosophical ideas can be fruitfully considered in terms of two of his basic concepts—namely, the concept of experience and the concept of common inquiry. We shall examine the former in this chapter and the latter in the next. As these two concepts are Dewey's alternative suggestions to the points of view taken in historical philosophies, it would be proper to begin with an examination of his criticism of these philosophies.

Historical Philosophies

Dewey's treatment of the historical philosophies is selective. In his major philosophical writings, he repeatedly refers to two main human intellectual developments: the philosophical speculations of classical Greece and the seventeenth-century revolution in science. The restriction of his attention to these two phases indicates the basis of his criticism. He believes that our present attitudes towards our moral and political problems are, in a large measure, those which we have inherited from classical Greece. On the other hand, our attitudes towards physical phenomena are largely a product of the seventeenth-century revolution in science and its subsequent development. He then goes on to compare the respective achievements of social and physical inquiry. His selection of these two periods of human thought and his attempt to judge one inquiry in the light of the other predisposes him to the task of what he has called the "reconstruction in philosophy."

Dewey's treatment of the historical philosophies is also interpretive:

> . . . *philosophy, like politics, literature and plastic arts, is itself a phenomenon of human culture. Its connection with social history, with civilization, is intrinsic.*[1]

He finds philosophical problems ultimately connected not only with social history but also with the existential situation in which they occur. Let us examine this contention in some detail.

Contexts of thought, says Dewey, are spatio-temporal.[2] The spatial background of thought "covers all the contemporary settings within which the course of thinking emerges," whereas the temporal background may be said to consist of the existing customs and intellectual traditions.[3] Hence a philosophical controversy at any time is more than a mere verbal debate; it has, on the contrary, a certain social or economic interest to defend or justify.[4] Dewey's entire treatment of Greek philosophy is from this point of view: he interprets Greek rationalism as an attempt to take the moral kernel out of the traditions and customs being challenged by the Sophists, and to place them on an intellectual footing.[5] Likewise Aristotle seemed to have transferred the notion of *hierarchy* from the existing social structure into the realm of logic. Even the independence of the rational technique possessed by thinkers like Bacon, Descartes, and Kant is called into question. These thinkers either provided a rational basis for an existing set of beliefs, or they adjusted

> . . . *that body of traditions which constitute the actual mind of man to scientific tendencies and political aspirations which are novel and incompatible with received authorities.*[6]

Dewey draws an important conclusion from his social-contextual interpretation of the historical philosophies. This conclusion is that all that goes in the name of eternal truths and values is, properly speaking, neither universal nor timeless. On the contrary, the entire content of eternal truths and values is derived from contemporary experience. Therefore whatever value they have is limited to their own time.

In denying the status of universal truths to the fundamental values of historical philosophies, Dewey prepares the ground for his

10

own thesis on the relation of values and existence. The actual human predicament and particular situation becomes, for him, the source of ethical ideas.[7] As far as the logical character of these ideas is concerned, Dewey made it both subordinate to and inseparable from the actual content of these ideas. Later on, we shall examine his view that all logical forms accrue within the process of inquiry.[8]

Continuing our examination of Dewey's treatment of the historical philosophies, we also find that he discovers a strong escapist element in historical philosophies in general, and in Greek philosophy in particular. Greek philosophy, says Dewey, acquired unity of thought by turning its back on actual experience, which is far too diverse and chaotic to suggest any neatly drawn lines of thought. The Greek thinkers also separated theory from practice, for practical activity deals with "individualized and unique situations which are never exactly duplicable and about which accordingly, no complete assurance is possible,"[9] and even looked down upon practical activity because it is full of changes. Their notion of the Universal Being, developed with the help of syllogistic logic, was fixed and immutable. Therefore, they considered change to be the mark of an inferior being. Thus Greek philosophy, instead of working within the situation, provided an escape from the painful diversities of concrete experience.

Greek philosophy, according to Dewey, treated thought as an inner activity, intrinsic to mind only. This, in turn, was instrumental in developing a notion of mind that was self-sufficient and complete.[10] The Greek philosophers conceived reality to be something antecedently existent, eternal and unalterable, which the mind tries to know but not to alter. They took for granted a "complete correspondence between knowledge in its true meaning and what is real."[11] The objects of knowledge, they thought, provide standards by which to judge the objects of experience. As the objects of knowledge were taken by them to be fixed, they declared the objects of experience to be unreal, because they were varied and changeable. The mind, like a spectator, was supposed to know and register the antecedently existent reality.

Experience

Following this brief analysis of Dewey's treatment of the historical philosophies, we shall now examine what he means by the

11

term "experience." Its four main characteristics are the following.

(1) Experience is objective.

(2) Experience concerns the entire existence.

(3) Experience includes ideas.

(4) Experience is a guiding method for philosophy.

Let us examine each of them separately.

◢━━━◣ *Experience is objective.*

Experience of the environment. At the very outset Dewey discards subjectivist attempts to explain experience in terms of private psychic states of consciousness. Hegel and James are, properly speaking, the two principal sources of Dewey's objectivistic concept of experience. Dewey studied philosophy under G. S. Morris, a Hegelian who was examining Kant and the English empiricists. Morris succeeded in converting Dewey to the antidualistic attitude of Hegel, and Dewey remained antidualist to the end of his life. With the help of Hegel's philosophy, Dewey rejected Kantian epistemology on the one hand and the dualism of subject and object on the other. Dewey learned from Hegel that only within "self-consciousness can object and subject be distinguished."[12] However, according to Hegel, the source of self-consciousness was "the Absolute mind," which he maintained expresses itself in social institutions as "the objective mind." To this Hegelian objectivism, which was largely metaphysical, Dewey gave an empirical turn with the help of the physiological psychologists. This he achieved particularly with the help of the ambivalent note on consciousness in the Jamesian psychology:

> *There is a double strain in the* Principles of Psychology *of William James. One strain is official acceptance of epistemological dualism. According to this view, the science of psychology centers about a* subject *which is "mental" just as physics centers about an* object *which is material. But James's analysis of special topics tends, on the contrary, to reduction of the subject to a vanishing point, save as "subject" is identified with the organism, the latter, moreover, having no existence save in interaction with environing conditions. According to the latter strain, subject and object do not stand for separate orders or kinds of existence but at most for certain distinctions made for a definite purpose within* experience.[13]

12

This latter view of James acted as a "ferment," says Dewey, in transforming his old beliefs regarding consciousness.[14] But he did not stop at the "objective biological approach" of the Jamesian psychology.[15] He made use of it in giving an empirical turn to the Hegelian metaphysical conception that the absolute mind expresses itself in social institutions. James thus naturalized for Dewey what Hegel had already socially objectified:

The metaphysical idea that an absolute mind is manifested in social institutions dropped out; the idea, upon an empirical basis, of the power exercised by cultural environment in shaping the ideas, beliefs, and intellectual attitudes of individuals remained.[16]

Later on, this became the basis of Dewey's contention that the only possible psychology, as distinct from a biological account of behavior, is a social psychology.[17]

Dewey does not use the term "experience" in a possessive sense, as in "*my* experience" or "*your* experience." Instead, he regarded experience to be experience *of* the environment. An experience *of* the environment is commonly shared by all in the environment. And when we say "my experience" we only identify ourselves with a *part* of that experience.

By regarding experience as experience *of* the environment, Dewey removed the logical difficulty of relating subject with object. He took for granted the unity of the experiencing subject and the experienced object. With Hegel subject and object could be distinguished within self-consciousness, so with Dewey they could be distinguished within the total experience.

To Dewey, the scope of experience is coextensive with all that the human organism does or undergoes in its environment: as a matter of fact, it extends to the entire human existence. What we see in experience, then, is an active, adjusting, and reconstructive organism, trying to overcome obstacles in a given environment. Any account of experience, says Dewey, must . . .

fit into the consideration that experiencing means living; and that living goes on in and because of an environing medium, not in a vacuum.[18]

Nevertheless, human existence itself is not "a peaceful exhalation of the environment." On the contrary, it is a life of struggle against

13

innumerable obstacles. It is a struggle which requires the human organism

> *to employ the direct support given by the environment in order indirectly to effect changes that would not otherwise occur. In this sense, life goes on by means of controlling the environment. Its activities must change the changes going on around it; they must neutralize hostile occurrences; they must transform neutral events into co-operative factors or into an efflorescence of new features.*[19]

In such an environment where the human organism has to "neutralize hostile occurrences" and seek support from those forces which are favorable to its existence, the human organism develops a few arts, ranging from complicated technological mechanisms to human habits. Habits, to Dewey, are the tools of self-survival. Like mechanical tools and implements, they equip us with instruments for adjusting and mastering the environment.[20]

Objective qualities. We shall now examine Dewey's views on the qualities of objects and the way in which we experience them. Dewey believed that objects have their own qualities ingrained in them. Whereas Locke attributed secondary qualities like "hot" or "blue" to the objects, Dewey combined these qualities with the objects themselves. "Hot" or "blue," when taken along with the objects of which they are qualities, thus become "hot oven" or "blue sky." Furthermore, Dewey maintained that the qualities of objects create corresponding reactions of feelings in us, and this is how we come to know about them.

What is important for us to note here is that Dewey combines with the object what Santayana called "tertiary qualities." In other words, "ugly," "beautiful," and all that which inspires religious devotion are essentially our reactions to certain qualities demonstrated in the object itself. Thus, he tried to remove the element of subjectivity from aesthetic or religious experience.[21]

At the same time, Dewey also believed that the qualities of an object enable us to understand its nature and to bring it under our control. In this way, then, our reactions to the qualities of an object do not terminate in our exclamatory pronouncements, which are only initial reactions. They are followed, later on, by our cognitive operations.

By attributing tertiary qualities to the objects of experience, Dewey prepared the ground for his objectivistic, naturalistic ethics and politics. Objective tertiary qualities enabled him to reduce the element of subjectivity to a minimum.[22]

"Experience," then, meant to Dewey all that the organism undergoes in its environment in its "simultaneous doings and sufferings," when not "slipping along into a path fixed by inner consciousness." He thus rejected the subjectivistic position that private consciousness is the source of experience; to him, it is an "incidental outcome of experience of a vital objective sort."[23]

◄━━━► *Experience is existential.*

As we have already seen, Dewey considered "experience" an experience of the environment—an environment that is physical, biological, and cultural. The biological and cultural aspects of our environment rest on the physical, but all form one single existential whole. It is within the existential whole that problems arise. For the sake of convenience we classify existential problems as physical, biological, and cultural. Existential problems give rise to thinking, which terminates when it has existentially solved those problems. Let us therefore examine the nature of this existential whole and the kind of thinking that it gives rise to.

> *We live in a world which is an impressive and irresistible mixture of sufficiencies, tight completenesses, order, recurrences which make possible prediction and control, and singularities, ambiguities, uncertain possibilities, processes going on to consequences as yet indeterminate.*[24]

In such a world, "ambiguities" provide a scope for human action, whereas "order" and "recurrences" make possible "prediction and control." Contingent elements are singular and highly individualized, neither uniform nor predictable: they become, therefore, the source of freedom in the natural world.

The existential whole that we call by the name "environment," full of contingencies and possibilities, is neither perfect nor finished. There are some conditions in it which are favorable to human existence and others which are not. Their simultaneity makes human existence extremely precarious, the very precariousness of which is yet responsible for the development of human intelligence. With the help of magic, superstition, religion, and science, men have tried either to pacify or to conquer the forces that are hostile to human existence.

The alternative to pacifying or conquering hostile forces in the face of such precariousness of existence is the creation of a corresponding world of ideas that is taken to be the real world. The creation of such a world provides an escape but not a solution. This is what has been done, says Dewey, in the moral and political theories of classical Greece. He finds a turning away from the existential problems of the time in a search for eternal and unchangeable reality, an attitude considerably influencing subsequent moral and political theories.

From Dewey's point of view, thinkers who create a corresponding world of ideas overlook two main considerations: that reflective thought has an existential source, coming into existence because of the element of doubt or conflict, and that reflective thought must resolve the element of doubt or conflict that gives rise to it. This functional character of reflective thought we will now examine.

In order to establish the functional character of reflective thought, Dewey rejects, at the very outset, all divisions in the forms of thought. His basic contention is that reflective thought arises in a situation which is "problematic." The "problematic" element that gives rise to reflective thought resides in some actual and specifiable situation.[25] In his writings on logic, Dewey attempts to establish what he calls the existential origin of the valid cognitive perceptions.[26]

Furthermore Dewey does not consider logic to be an independent intellectual exercise. To him, even logic shares the functional character of reflective thought. This is because "logical forms" accrue within the process of inquiry undertaken to remove elements of doubt or conflict. The functional character of "logical forms" lies in the fact that they "are concerned with control of inquiry so that it may yield warranted assertions."[27]

Reflective thought, then, is both a product of the problematic situation and an instrument in resolving it. Since the problematic situation is existential, reflective thought is supposed to detect the causal factors of a problematic situation. This brings us to Dewey's views on causality. Dewey builds his defense of the principle of causality with the help of commonsense experience.[28] To him commonsense experience presents no difficulty for the acceptance of the principle of causality.

Dewey believes that logical difficulties in the acceptance of the principle of causality can be overcome if we can correctly define the term "end." To the Greeks, ends were essentially fixed, and a changing event or object could only be known with reference to its fixed ends. Dewey, on his part, prefers to speak of an "end" as an "ending" or as a terminal point of a thing.[29] Furthermore, a thing that has an ending, has, by logical inference, a "beginning" also.[30] Beginning and ending may therefore be connected with each other by some kind of sequential order. It is in the sequential order that causality resides. In Dewey's words, "causality is another name for the sequential order itself."[31]

In order to resolve a problematic situation, reflective thought must be able to discriminate between two types of ends that we find in our experience, *natural* ends, or termini of certain processes, and *practical* ends that we prescribe to ourselves as targets. Practical ends are, in other words, ends-in-view. The Greeks, says Dewey, could not see this difference on account of their bias concerning fixed ends. Practical ends in ethics and politics are not given to us in advance but are discovered in actual situations. Their discovery is essentially the product of the operations of reflective thought. They are the suggestions that reflective thought offers in order to resolve problematic situations.

Experience includes ideas.

This brings us to the examination of the third characteristic of experience. Dewey believes that experience includes ideas as well as sensations. In this respect, his position is radically different from that of the English empiricists, for whom the dichotomy of sensations and ideas was complete. Let us, therefore, examine the meaning and function that Dewey gives to ideas.

To Dewey existence itself is the source of ideas. We formulate ideas *about* experienced objects. Having formulated them, we use ideas as substitutes for experienced objects themselves. We can constantly test their value as substitutes in the course of actual practice when we put them to use.

Ideas by their very nature imply the following: As substitutes, ideas enable us to analyze and recapture whatever we undergo in the form of experience. At the same time, they also indicate a direction for us to take. This is what Dewey means when he says that "ideas are plans of operation."

The foregoing analysis clearly suggests that Dewey took ideas and hypotheses to be identical. They are instituted in the same way as hypotheses. No ideas come into existence without deliberate effort. In other words, Dewey ascribes to ideas the meaning and function of hypotheses.

We shall now examine the function of abstract ideas. Their source, as we have seen, is existence. Dewey shows this in two connections. On the one hand he maintains that abstract ideas, such as mathematical ideas, have their occasional "existential" reference. On the other hand he emphasizes that mathematical ideas can be put to "existential use" in the form of symbols. Thus he considers mathematical ideas in their applied form only. Mathematical ideas, he says, enable us to perform certain operations symbolically that we would otherwise perform overtly;[32] nevertheless, symbols are ultimately derived from actual experience. As symbols, they are detached from their existential reference; and the more these symbols are detached from their existential reference, the greater is the scope of their application.[33] Mathematical ideas, says Dewey, are an extremely powerful tool for overcoming the limitations of observation. However, it would be incorrect if their independence from any specified application is taken to mean independence from application as such. In short, Dewey argues against a position that ideas or even abstract ideas belong to a world of their own. To him, they stand only in functional relation to existence itself, which as we have seen is also their source.

As to the relation of ideas to sensations or sense data, Dewey is in complete agreement with the Kantian dictum that "perception without conception is blind, conception without perception is empty." However, what he rejects in the Kantian position is the independent character of both perception and conception. From his point of view, ". . . the distinction of sense and thought occurs *within* the process of reflective inquiry."[34] To Dewey, therefore, their distinction is not "given," but is deliberately "instituted" in a reflective inquiry. Furthermore, the way in which both perception and conception are discriminated within reflective inquiry is such that they remain functionally and operationally connected with each other.

> *In logical fact, perceptual and conceptual materials are instituted in functional correlativity with each other, in such a manner that the former locates and describes the problem while the latter represents a possible method of solution.*[35]

To Dewey this "correlativity" is very important, because conception and perception test each other's functional character. Facts may rectify a few ideas which are presented in the form of meanings and relations, whereas ideas may make possible a fresh arrangement of facts through the discovery of new relationships. Finally, in relation to each other, neither facts nor ideas are fixed: both are tentative. Their functional correlativity has been demonstrated very effectively in physical inquiry and, as we shall see in the next chapter, Dewey recommends the adoption of the same method in social inquiry.

━━━━━ *Experience is a guiding method for philosophy.*

This brings us to the examination of the fourth and last characteristic of experience. Dewey believes that philosophy, in its preoccupation with consistency and logic, leaves out much that we experience in everyday life and, to that extent, tends to be remote. His own suggestion in this connection is that philosophy must take into consideration the entirety of experience in order to correct its own partialities and abstractions.

In order to grasp the entirety of experience we must go beyond the "distinct" and "clearly evident," making use of what Dewey calls "denotation." He points out that we experience things at two different levels. At the *primary* level, things are encountered, undergone, suffered, enjoyed, but not known. At the *cognitive* level, there is an effort to "know" what is undergone, and to that extent, it is abstracted. As much is lost at this level, Dewey suggests "experience" as a philosophic method for returning to the primary level. This is made possible by going back to what is "pointed" or "denoted," either empirically or by logical analysis. Of the two, Dewey shows his preference for empirical denotation.[36]

Traditional philosophies, says Dewey, confuse the two levels of experience. They equate the "statement of things" with their "existential equivalents." This is not confined to philosophical concepts. In his political theory, Dewey singles out the concept of the state as the supreme example of this practice. Over and above this, traditional philosophies miss the significance of the fact that all statements, even sense data, are, by their very nature, abstractions. No description or statement can describe everything about an object without reducing its specific features to what figures in the description itself.

It should be noted that Dewey's definition of abstraction is far too inclusive to allow any understanding of what the first level of experience is. Even consciousness of what we undergo may introduce certain selective operations and hence may limit our experience. If we cannot be conscious at the primary level of experience, then how do we come to know it? Dewey, as we shall see, abandons "denotation" and moves on to the problem of "controlling" the primary level of experience. The fact of controlling, therefore, plays a very important part in his theory of knowledge. He believes that whatever we control, we "know."

To Dewey, as we have seen, the cognitive level of experience has only one character, and that is functional. We encounter problematic situations in our first level of experience, and it is the function of the cognitive element to resolve them by bringing them under control. Thus our "knowing" of the primary level of experience is confined, according to Dewey, to the question of "controlling" it. Such an approach alters the very problem of knowledge. Dewey is no longer interested in the epistemological controversy about whether knowledge is possible or not. Rather, it is the problem of knowledge that connects the cognitive aspect of experience with the experiental. In Dewey's own words:

> . . . reference to the primary and ultimacy of the material of ordinary experience protects us, in the first place, from creating artificial problems which deflect the energy and attention of philosophers from the real problems that arise out of actual subject-matter. In the second place, it provides a check or test for the conclusions of philosophic inquiry; it is a constant reminder that we must replace them, *as secondary reflective products, in the experience out of which they arose, so that they may be confirmed or modified by the new order and clarity they introduce into it . . .*[37]

In short, we know only when we discover the ways and means of controlling what we experience. Later on we shall examine whether or not in the political field the cognitive element of our experience is also functional in this particular sense.

Before we go on to examine the scope and nature of the inquiry that may be said to emerge out of Dewey's concept of experience, let us examine a few difficulties which arise in Dewey's position.

The concept of experience that we have analyzed in the foregoing pages is both incapable of any general definition and vague in its scope. Nor is it systematic. On the whole it appears that Dewey has tried to bring together his attitudes towards different philosophical problems under one common heading.

Difficulties, both metaphysical and commonsense, arise in Dewey's attempt to make "experience" objective. As we have seen, "experience," to Dewey, is essentially the experience *of* the environment. The totality of experience is not possessed by any single individual, whose "experience" is only a part of this totality. This creates a metaphysical difficulty. How can the totality exist by itself? Experience itself is not, like the concrete external world, capable of an independent existence. The concrete external world is only the object of experience. Experience itself is nothing but human reaction to, or reception of, the external world. As experience is essentially human reaction to, or reception of, the external world, it is necessarily *somebody's* reaction to, and *somebody's* reception of, the external world. Now the totality of experience of which Dewey speaks has no human agency to sustain it. Such a difficulty did not arise in Hegel's position, because Hegel postulated the Absolute mind which could sustain all his holistic categories. Difficulty arises only when Dewey retains a holistic Hegelian category like "experience" and claims to be a naturalist at the same time.

Dewey attributed tertiary qualities to the objects of experience. He maintained, as we have seen, that our aesthetic or religious feelings are nothing but our reactions to tertiary qualities of certain objects. Such an interpretation of religious and aesthetic experience has its own commonsense difficulties. For instance, two persons looking at the same object of artistic achievement will not be in complete agreement in their opinions about the object, in spite of the fact that both react to its "tertiary qualities." Much of our emotional experience is, as a matter of fact, the product of our own interpretation of general reactions to certain objects or situations. Emotional or aesthetic experiences are dominated by an interpretive element, which becomes the source of disagreement and variety in opinion.

Secondly, the concept of causality occupies an important position in Dewey's philosophy. According to Dewey, reflective thought is capable of finding the efficient cause of a problematic situation by analyzing all the factors that go to produce the problematic situation. The efficient cause and the problematic situation are connected with each other by a simple sequential order. Now there may not be any difficulty as long as Dewey maintains that cause and effect are connected by a sequential order, because innumerable examples from practical experience can be used to illustrate this. But difficulties arise when one goes on to make an inductive generalization from these practical examples. Dewey, on his part, identifies causality with sequential order and takes both causality and sequential order to be

21

self-evident. He therefore has no answer to give to the critics of causality.

Thirdly, Dewey prescribes extremely limited and precise functions to ideas, as combining a kind of retrospective analysis of experience with plans for future operations. The correctness of ideas is confirmed for Dewey when they are put into actual use. Therefore, the same meaning and function is given to ideas that is normally given to hypotheses: ideas are supposed and tested in the same manner as hypotheses. Thus Dewey fails to recognize the fact that all ideas are not hypotheses in the sense of being deliberately supposed and tested. A hypothesis is at best only one kind of idea.

Furthermore, Dewey finds the source of all ideas, including abstract ideas, in existence itself. We have seen that Dewey emphasizes the occasional existential reference of abstract ideas, on the one hand, and their "existential use" on the other. Dewey puts a great emphasis on the fact that abstract ideas or symbols exist for some kind of existential use only. His emphasis on existential use is very clear in the following passage:

> . . . the liberation afforded by the free use of symbolism of mathematics is often a means of ulterior return to existential operation.

Now if we consider this in the light of Dewey's condemnation of formal rationalism, it may appear that the liberated symbols are not often put to the existential use of which Dewey speaks. This admission then may considerably weaken Dewey's contention that reflective thought and ideas have only one function, that of resolving problematic situations.

Fourthly, the idea of two levels of experience, of which Dewey speaks, is itself open to doubt. He takes for granted that in the primary level no ideas, opinions, or judgments are involved: things are suffered, or enjoyed, but not known. Now to what extent is it correct to say that what is not known in our experience is "pure" experience, devoid of ideas, opinions, and judgments? We can find an answer to this question only when we examine the experience of a particular individual. Any particular individual is, as a matter of fact, a creature of opinions, prejudices, and habits.[38] In his contact with the external world, which to Dewey is the source of experience, all these elements play an active part: thus there is no level of personal experience which may be said to be devoid of them. In the light of this criticism, the two levels of experience become an impossibility.

2

THE CONCEPT OF
COMMON INQUIRY

IN THIS CHAPTER WE SHALL EXAMINE Dewey's thesis on common inquiry, which mainly derives its inspiration from the pattern of physical inquiry. He claims that only one kind of scientific inquiry is possible, and that is experimental inquiry. Dewey's thesis on common inquiry can be divided into three separate parts: the growth of nonqualitative physical inquiry; the experimental theory of knowledge; and the need to reconsider certain ethical problems in the light of his thesis on common inquiry.

The Growth of Nonqualitative Physical Inquiry

The Greeks derived their observations of physical phenomena from commonsense experience. However, their observations were largely aesthetic and couched in terms of "qualities." With the help of their "logos," they conferred upon the material of their observation aesthetic forms like harmony, proportion or measure, and symmetry. Above all, their notion of *change* was qualitatively and teleologically characterized. According to the Greeks, *change* took place in the realm of imperfect being—a qualitative distinction—and was a movement towards a fixed end that was itself changeless.

Galileo may be said to be responsible for introducing radical changes into Greek physical science. The Greeks described as qualitative alterations "movements" such as warm things becoming cold or growth from embryo to adult form. They never conceived of them as mere "motions," that is, "changes of position in homogeneous space." Galileo, on the other hand, maintained that the force of a "movement" at a stage spends itself up and comes to rest. It is not inferior because it moves, nor does it move with a purpose to reach a fixed goal. Galileo, therefore, may be said to have taken change or "movement" out of the realm of qualities.[1]

Furthermore, Galileo also radically altered the treatment of qualities of objects of scientific knowledge. The "antique science" spoke of qualities precisely in the same manner "as those possessed by works of art, the properties which are one with beauty and with all that is admirable." Galileo, on the other hand, made a quantitative statement of the qualities of objects. The work of Galileo to Dewey, therefore, was:

> . . . not a development but a revolution. It marked a change from the qualitative to the quantitative or metric; from the heterogeneous to the homogeneous; from intrinsic forms to relations; from aesthetic harmonies to mathematical formulae; from contemplative enjoyment to active manipulation and control; from rest to change; from eternal objects to temporal sequence.[2]

The net result of the change brought about by the contributions of Galileo and subsequent thinkers was that it stripped from objects all qualities, in the ethical and teleological sense, given to them by Greek science, particularly by Aristotle. In short, it substituted the term "data" for the term "objects." The term "data" signifies that the subject matter is "for further interpretation," that it is "something to be thought about." Objects, on the other hand:

> . . . are finalities; they are complete, finished; they call for thought only in the way of definition, classification, logical arrangement, subsumption in syllogisms, etc. But data signify "material to serve"; they are indications, evidence, signs, clues to and of something still to be reached; they are intermediate, not ultimate, not finalities.[3]

Before Galileo, qualities of objects were essentially features of ethical and aesthetic use or enjoyment; in the post-Galilean physical science, qualities such as hot and cold or wet and dry came to be considered as "problems" in connection with the object to be understood. In other words, the qualities of an object came to be considered as its "relations," which could be stated in homogeneous terms. We can exercise control over an object only when we know its internal and external relations; in the words of Dewey, when

. . . water is treated not as the glistening, rippling object with the variety of qualities that delight the eye, ear, and palate, but as something symbolized by H_2O, something from which these qualities are completely absent, it becomes amenable to all sorts of other modes of control and adapted to other uses.[4]

Thus H_2O is not a rival for the position of water that we see or use, but it is something that is reduced to its necessary relations, on which further operations and control are possible.

Dewey's notion of quality becomes clearer when we try to understand it in the light of his basic thesis of two levels of experience. Water as we "have" it belongs to the noncognitive level of experience, but water as "understood" in its relations, H_2O, is essentially cognitive and to that extent abstracted from the primary level of experience. However, it is the cognitive operation, H_2O, which both "knows" and "controls" water at the primary level of experience.

The Experimental Theory of Knowledge

At the very outset, Dewey acknowledges that his theory of knowledge has been framed after the general pattern of "experimental knowing."[5] He also acknowledges the support given to his theory by Heisenberg's principle of indeterminacy. The three main characteristics of his experimental theory of knowledge are as follows:

(1) Knowing is a kind of activity.
(2) It results in the reconstruction of an empirical situation.
(3) The activity of knowing is directed by general ideas or hypotheses.

We shall examine each of these characteristics separately.

Knowing is an activity.

According to Dewey, one of the major defects of traditional theories is the separation of "knowing" from "doing," or of theory from practice. The Greeks were the first to separate theory from practice. This is because their philosophy was a product of a leisure class that looked down upon the practical arts and crafts. Dewey saw the separation of theory from practice in later times as representing a docile following of the Greek tradition.

The net results of the separation of knowing from doing were as follows. First, the object of knowledge came to be some form of ultimate Being, which was both "antecedent to reflective inquiry and independent of it."[6] Secondly, the process of "knowing" was reduced to the mere registering of the traits of an antecedently existent reality. Third, the conception of "mind" was created, the function of which was to know, and not alter, the antecedently existent reality. Dewey grouped all theories that separated knowing from doing under the heading of "the spectator theory of knowledge." His own theory, Dewey claims, is diametrically opposed to it.

Dewey conceived the activity of knowing in two different senses: activity in the sense of overt doing, and activity in the sense of an operation. Since activity as an overt doing is connected with the second characteristic of Dewey's theory of knowledge, namely, that knowing results in the construction of new empirical situations, we shall consider it later.

Problems for knowing. In order to understand what Dewey means by the term "knowing" as an activity or operation, we must first of all know the place of objects of knowledge in his theory. Dewey, as a matter of fact, rejects the very term "object of knowledge." To him there are only "problems for knowing." This is what makes all the difference in his conception of reality and the character of knowing.

Dewey does not reject sense impressions, but he does reject the passive recipient "mind," which at best provides "categories," in the Kantian sense, for chaotic sense impressions. His own position is as follows:

> *Original objects of experience are produced by the natural interactions of organism and environment, and in themselves are neither sensible, conceptual nor a mixture of the two. They are precisely the qualitative material of all our ordinary untested experiences.*[7]

This "qualitative material" is further reduced into sense data by the operations of knowing. In being reduced to sense data, the qualitative material is removed from its original position. Sense data, then, are not "given" but "abstracted."

Sense data, which are a product of what Dewey calls "the original perception," or primary operations of knowing, present themselves to us as problems for knowing:

> *In reality the original perception furnishes the* problem *for knowing; it is something* to be *known, not an object of knowing. And*

in knowing, the first thing to be done is to select from the mass of presented qualities those which, in distinction from other qualities, throw light upon the nature of the trouble. As they are deliberately selected, being discriminated by special technical operations, they become data; these are called sensible simply because of the role of sense organs in their generation. They may then be formulated as the subject matter of primitive existential propositions.[8]

The operation of knowing, therefore, may be said to provide its own problems.

Knowing and the known. What is most important in Dewey's theory of knowledge is the fact that he conceives of knowing not only as an activity, but also as a partner in what is finally known. The fact that knowing is a *partner* in what is finally "known" is explained by Dewey as follows: The active operations of knowing *interact* with the subject matter. What comes to be known, then, is a product of the *interaction* of subject matter on the one hand and active operations of knowing on the other. In other words, what comes to be finally known is not something that existed before, but something to which this interaction has made "the needed difference."[9] Reality thus ceases, with Dewey, to be something that is antecedently existent. It becomes, instead, that which each operation of knowing creates by way of interaction with the subject matter.[10]

◄► *Knowing as an overt doing results in reconstruction of the empirical situation.*

In order to establish the point that knowing results in an overt doing and hence in the reconstruction of the empirical situation, what Dewey must refute is the conception of knowing as an activity confined to the inner recess of a mysterious entity called "mind." He achieves this by making a behavioristic analysis of thinking. "Thinking" in his vocabulary is nothing but a deferred action.[11] Bodily movements within an environment are suddenly held up in the presence of an obstacle or a problem, and when thinking provides a solution, these movements are resumed. Thinking is a privilege of animate beings only, because they alone are capable of considering a problematic situation *as* problematic, and "in the degree that responses take place to the doubtful *as* the doubtful, they acquire *mental* quality."[12] There is no mind apart from certain acts in which the quality of what Dewey calls "intelligence" is revealed. He does not interpret "mind" in terms of behavior; he merely calls certain acts "intellectual or mental," provided they are "such as to have a directed tendency to change the precarious and problematic into the secure and resolved."[13] We may say, then, that with reference to his situational contextualism, Dewey understands "mind" as a particular sort of "doing."

What follows this assertion is one of the most ambitious attempts of Dewey, the behaviorist, to explain what we call "mental behavior" in terms of reactions that certain external situations bring forth from the human organism. This response of the human organism for Dewey is something public, observable, and verifiable, and not inner or hidden in the recesses of the human mind. This response may be emotional, volitional, or intellectual; but into whatever category it falls, it has common characteristics. The emotional phase is confined to the reactions to "immediate quality." Different emotions are aroused by different conditions present in the "indeterminateness" of the situation. In the volitional phase, the indeterminateness of a situation crystallizes itself in the direction of a preferred object or the qualities of a preferred object. Finally, in the intellectual phase:

> . . . mental action is identical with an indirect mode of response, one whose purpose is to locate the nature of the trouble and form an idea of how it may be dealt with—so that operations may be directed in view of an intended solution.[14]

Dewey's position that "knowing" results in the reconstruction of an empirical situation has its source in the existential or situational source of problems, on the one hand, and his conception of "knowing" as an "overt doing," on the other. We have already seen that to Dewey problems that give rise to thinking are essentially existential. He prefers to refer to a problem as a "problematic situation" and to say that thinking terminates only when the problematic situation is existentially resolved, in other words, empirically reconstructed. Such a conception of thinking is further supported by Dewey's conclusions that "knowing" is "overt doing."

The fact that thinking terminates in the reconstruction of an empirical situation also offers a solution to the problem of novelty offered neither by the Platonic theory of knowledge as "remembering" nor by the most plausible of the "empirical" theories that assert

the identification of the acquired knowledge with an antecedent condition of things. According to Dewey's theory of knowledge, what
"exists" cannot, in fact, be "reconstructed" unless something is
added to what previously existed. Thus each grain of genuine knowledge recreates material that becomes, at once, both "novel" and
"known." Properly speaking, Dewey works out only the logic of how
the reconstructed situation alone is capable of being known; he takes
for granted the extremely dialectical equation of the reconstructed
and the novel.

In Dewey's theory of knowledge, knowing as an overt doing and
the reconstruction of empirical situations occupies an important
place. It would, therefore, be appropriate to examine here the weaknesses of his position.

The three phases of mental life of which Dewey speaks—namely
the emotional, the volitional, and the intellectual—do not necessarily
have overt manifestations, even when they are taken to be reactions
to existential problems. Dewey does not prove what he asserts, namely, that these three phases are behavioral in the sense of being "public, observable, and verifiable." As a matter of fact, there is no way of
interpreting responsive behavior in terms of these three phases
except by interpreting our own experience of them. The fact that, in
indeterminate situations, such processes go on in the minds of others
can only be inferred. At best these are intersubjective interpretations.

What is unacceptable in Dewey's position is the fact that knowing is an *overt doing* and not the fact that knowing is an *operation*.
To repeat this position in Dewey's words, ". . . if knowing is one
mode of doing, then it, as well as other modes of doing, properly involves bodily instruments."[15] If these bodily instruments mean the
physical mechanism, then the difficulty is not so great as when it is
made to mean "overt doing."

Furthermore, in asserting that "knowing is a form of doing,"
Dewey has inadvertently transferred the causal connection from one
doubtful sequence to another. Thinking, we are told, is a "deferred
action." When a problematic situation is recognized as problematic,
thinking in the form of certain intellectual operations like location,
deliberation, suggestion, reasoning, and so forth, takes place. Within
Dewey's own definition, the interaction of the problematic situation
with cognitive effort results in certain consequences, which possess
the properties of being known. But what Dewey actually does is to
continue this chain of causality into overt action. Now this may or

may not be its continued sequence; it would be true only of an act already performed. But this does not happen in all the situations in which "indeterminateness" calls for thinking.

◄══════ *The activity of knowing is directed by general ideas or hypotheses.*

This brings us to the third characteristic of Dewey's theory of knowledge, namely, that the operations of knowing are conducted with the help of directive ideas. To this character of ideas Dewey gives the name "operational." Ideas, in his theory, do have an empirical origin. They are supposed to be ideational representations of what exists or what is performed, but in themselves they are only intermediary, because they are also drawn out as plans of further operation. The idealists, says Dewey, no doubt ascribe a "constitutive" character to ideas, but this they confine to the realm of transcendental and *a priori* ideas, whereas the empiricists reduce ideas to the status of illusion. According to Dewey, both groups fail to understand what he calls the "operational" character of ideas. Only within experimental inquiry does the significance of ideas as directing operations come to the surface. Ideas, then, are not conceived by Dewey in any psychological sense, but only in the operational sense, as they are conceived in the natural sciences.

Common Inquiry and Different Subject Matter

The foregoing analysis clearly suggests that Dewey interprets physical inquiry as "a typical nature of knowing." It is to him the most dependable form of "knowing," and that is why he frames his theory of knowledge on the basis of it.

Furthermore, Dewey's theory of knowledge is also the basis of his thesis on common inquiry. It is not the technique of experimentation, says Dewey, that stands in the way of the development of common inquiry. This technique, on the contrary, is a common characteristic of all inquiry. Some sort of experimentation is inherent in all inquiry that is conducted on the basis of certain hypotheses, and it is difficult to think of any inquiry that does not involve hypotheses. These hypotheses differ in the degree of their confirmation. What stands in the way of the development of common inquiry is the fact that the social sciences still treat their subject matter in the same "qualitative" terms that the natural sciences used until the seventeenth century.

◼▬▬◼ *The difficulty of isolating a problem*

According to Dewey, there is a difference between the subject matter of the social sciences and the physical sciences, but this difference arises only within a common inquiry. Their greatest single difference lies in the fact that the problems of the physical sciences can be isolated while the inquiry is in progress.[16] Problems that are either difficult or impossible to isolate call for different categories for their inquiry;[17] nevertheless, the "difference in the subject-matters is not incompatible with the existence of a common pattern (of inquiry) in both types."[18]

Subject matter whose relative isolation is difficult to achieve is described by Dewey as "complex." In his analysis of complex subject matter, Dewey suggests means of isolating some of its features where the technique and conclusions of physical science are applicable. The subject matter of the social sciences, says Dewey, is a product of the interaction of physical and social factors; it would be incorrect to say that it is a product of purely human or psychological factors.[19] To the extent that physical elements are involved in complex subject matter, the conclusions of physical and biological sciences become helpful in isolating the social problem.

However, Dewey's emphasis on "isolation" goes directly against some of his earlier conclusions. In trying to work out the applicability of a common inquiry for all the branches of study, Dewey had to make much of the possibility of isolation. Nevertheless, in trying to found ethics and politics on an objective basis, Dewey laboriously built up an existential notion of experience and inquiry, in so doing, conceiving of them in an "existential continuum." On this account critics have called his philosophy holistic.[20] Consequently, the conclusions of his naturalistic objectivism, which transform different elements into a continuous whole, go directly against his prime concern in inquiry, namely, the search for what can be isolated in a problem in question.

◼▬▬◼ *The absence of a pragmatic test*

Inquiry into social subject matter is also faced with a procedural difficulty. In the absence of any pragmatic tests of the hypotheses, controversies in social inquiry do not easily terminate as do controversies concerning physical subject matter. Dewey therefore suggests that difficulties in testing hypotheses in social inquiry can be considerably reduced by considering problems in their existential framework and by putting hypotheses to a pragmatic test of transforming the empirical situation.

Dewey takes for granted that all hypotheses in social inquiry can undergo empirical transformation. This position springs from his earlier contention that "knowing" results in "overt doing" and hence in the reconstruction of empirical situations. But we have already examined the unsatisfactory position of this particular claim. In other words, if we mean by the term "pragmatic test" the capacity of hypotheses actually to control or transform the empirical situation, then all social hypotheses are incapable of undergoing that test. Hence controversy in social inquiry cannot be narrowed down on this account.

The application of a common inquiry to complex social subject matter involves, then, the possibility of making the necessary "isolation," on the one hand, and existentially or pragmatically testing its hypothesis, wherever that is possible, on the other. But a common inquiry based on the pattern of physical inquiry cannot operate unless the nonqualitative treatment of objects in the physical sciences is reproduced for objects in the social sciences. This, then, is the next problem to be considered.

Re-examination of Certain Ethical Problems

◄═══➤ *Moral problems*

Dewey begins his re-examination of moral problems by stating that social inquiry now finds itself in the same crude qualitative state as physical inquiry before Galileo.[21] The physical sciences now are in a position to exercise control over their problems because they do not state their problems in terms of qualitative use and enjoyment, but in terms of quantitative relations. The question for Dewey, then, is how to formulate moral problems in nonqualitative terms.

Dewey does not deny that situations have *moral* causes or consequences, but he demands that situations, when considered as problems, be totally devoid of "the qualities of sin and righteousness, of vicious and virtuous motives."[22] In other words, a "moral problem" must be considered, in the first place, as simply a "problem." Its moral qualities are not destroyed, because with reference to its own existential situation it remains a "moral problem." In other words, "moral problems" are not *sui generis*.

⟞⟞⟞ *Reconstructive judgments*

The other obstacle to the nonqualitative treatment of moral problems is the way in which judgments are passed on the conduct of men. In traditional ethics, apart from profound disagreement about the norms for judging the conduct of men, the standards themselves have been arrived at with the help of *a priori* reasoning and therefore have no relation to the problems faced in an actual situation. Such *a priori* rationalist norms not only fail to exert a normative influence on the conduct of men, but result in what Dewey calls "evaluative judgments."[23] Evaluative judgments, to Dewey, are the greatest obstacles to the scientific treatment of moral problems. First of all, it is in the nature of evaluative judgments to be concerned with what is already done, with moral worthiness, and not with solutions. The standards are arrived at in advance. Thus, what is banished from the field of moral inquiry is the element of "consequences," and that is why so much emphasis is put on "motives" in traditional ethics.[24] For, as soon as consequences are taken into account, standards proclaimed in advance appear to be external to the process of judgment. Evaluative judgments also cannot be what Dewey calls "judgments of practice," or "reconstructive judgments," but are more or less confined to praise or condemnation. Nowhere else is the separation of thought and activity so severely felt as in the case of evaluative judgments, where moral obligation, divorced from its actual or existential reference, is reduced to the level of academic discussion. Judgment, in order to be reconstructive, must occupy an intermediary position. It must at once become a report of what actually takes place and a program for the "reconstruction" of that situation.

⟞⟞⟞ *Standards, ends, and means*

Next we come to examine the place of standards in Dewey's ethical theory. Dewey has put a great emphasis on the fact that the standards of judgment should not be external to the situation judged. In order to discover standards within the situation, Dewey undertakes an analysis of the relation of means and ends on the one hand,[25] and ends and standards on the other.[26] Ends, he asserts, are ends-in-view, or the ends of processes that we make for ourselves, and in order to realize these ends we have to take into consideration the means that realize them. But ends are tempered by the means that realize them and by their social reception, or by social approbation and disapprobation. In reflecting whether or not an act would be approved by the group, the agent judges the ends that he pursues by the standards created in this reflection. Later on, says Dewey:

> *The thought of the reaction of favor or disfavor of a particular social group or a particular person tends to recede to the background. An* ideal *spectator is projected and the doer of the act looks at his proposed act through the eyes of this impartial and farseeing objective judge.*[27]

Thus the standards are nothing but the results of reflection on the ends to be pursued. Reflection may either create a new end or endow the end pursued with a new quality. Obligation towards it is generated by its ideality in reflection.

However, in raising ends to the level of standards, Dewey added to them two not necessarily related elements. These unrelated elements are reflection on the one hand and social approbation on the other. Both are supposed to transform ends into standards. Reflection converts ends into standards by creating an ideal end in which the shortcomings of actual ends do not exist, whereas social approbation converts ends into standards by calculating their worth in terms of "general wellbeing." These two ways of transforming ends into standards remain diverse, and Dewey does not unify them.

Good and right

Next we go on to examine the conceptions of "good" and "right." In Deweyan ethics, desire is the source of good. But a desire does not become a good unless reflective thought has added a qualitative or social reference to it. The term "good" to Dewey remains meaningless unless we indicate what it is "good for." In other words, certain things appear to be or become good only with reference to certain other things. Now the question of "right" comes in where "good" is in doubt. However, the *concept* of right cannot act as an arbiter between two contending goods. As Dewey says:

> *. . . while Right as an idea is an independent moral conception or "category," this fact does not solve the question of what is right in particular.*[28]

In order to know what "right" in particular is, we have to go to the existing system of laws which embodies it. In the words of Dewey:

> *... the supposition of complete isolation (of good) is contrary to fact. Others do not leave us alone. They actively express their estimates of good in demands made upon each one of us. ... And these demands of others are not just so many special demands of different individuals. They are generalized into laws; they are formulated as standing claims of the 'society' in distinction from those of individuals in their isolated severalty. When considered as claims and expectations, they constitute the Right in distinction from the Good. But their ultimate function and effect is to lead the individual to broaden his conception of the Good; they operate to induce the individual to feel that nothing is good for himself which is not also a good for others. They are stimuli to a widening of the area of consequences to be taken into account in forming ends and deciding what is Good.*[29]

In other words, in every society the society's own conception of good is embodied in its system of laws, but there is another way of looking at a system of laws. When it is looked at from the point of view of claims and expectations of individuals, it also helps to determine what is right.

Subjectivity, belief, and value

We now come to examine Dewey's views on subjectivity. Dewey rejects the view that our subjectivity is the source of beliefs and values. For him, the ultimate source of values is the entire "human predicament." We are surrounded by nature, which is a profound mixture of "qualities and relations, individualities and uniformities, finalities and efficacies, contingencies and necessities."[30] We reflect on these diversities of nature in order to discover its meaning and enduring aspects. But even when we reflect on its diversity or reconstruct its contingency, we do not introduce anything extraneous, because we ourselves are a part of it:

> *... the striving of man for objects of imagination is a continuation of natural processes; it is something man has learned from the world in which he occurs, not something which he arbitrarily injects into that world. When he adds perception and ideas to these endeavors it is not after all he who adds; the addition is again the doing of nature and a further complication of its own domain.*[31]

35

In such a concrete and objective world in which everything is *given*, including what to reflect on, Dewey reduces men to the status of agents, in the Hegelian sense, who fall in line with those processes in nature that ceaselessly go on.

Knowledge of this whole becomes, with Dewey, the source of beliefs and values, for men do not passively accept the consequences of their living and acting in the environment. They also reflect and discriminate among them. Their reflections and discriminations are directed towards the knowledge that may enhance what is directed and mitigate what is shunned. Ultimately it is our knowledge which acquaints us with the causal relationships of different objects and events, and through knowledge alone do we come to secure what is desired and avoid what is distasteful. Hence what effectively helps us to discriminate is knowledge. Any alternative to knowledge is either an "uninformed belief" or a prejudice or predisposition.

The universe and objects in it are far too complex to be known at a glance. The very notion that beliefs are subjective arises from a notion that the universe is a "block" universe which can be seen from inside out at a glance. What this notion overlooks is the fact that very complex elements, such as "individualized qualities, status arrests, limiting 'ends,' and contingent changes,"[32] compose our universe. Knowledge of them requires considerable effort on our part, and beliefs regarding them cannot be formed without knowing them. Whatever is not informed is not a belief but a preconception or a prejudice. The nucleus of traditional ethics is the subjectivity of belief. Consequently, traditional ethics reduce moral belief to some kind of "personal affair" or a "matters of arbitrary and undiscussable preference."[33] Standards, which ought to be a guide to values, become in traditional ethics a matter of taste and conscience.

It is not the theory of value that helps us to solve the problems of value that we face in actual situations. Values are essentially the values *of* certain objects, which acquire value because of their capacity to remove the deficiency in a given situation. That is to say, individuals do not automatically regard certain objects to be valuable: they attach values to certain objects (in rational conduct) only after critically examining the differing capacities of different objects to fulfil the deficiency of a given situation.

Three factors are involved, then, in the process of valuation. They are (1) the situation of deficiency, (2) the capacity of an object to fulfil it, and (3) the "critical" examination of the situation and the object by the agent.

This brings us once again to the question of subjectivity, that is, to whether the deficiency in a situation and the capacity of an object to fulfil it is in any sense a subjective judgment. Dewey's answer is that it is not a subjective judgment: both the situation of deficiency and the capacity of an object to fulfil it are capable of empirical verification and refutation. Besides, nothing that is preconceived or extraneous guides the judgment of value:

> *Judgments about values are judgments about the conditions and the results of experienced objects; judgments about that which should regulate the formation of desires, affections and enjoyments.*[34]

What Dewey emphasizes thereby is the part that *knowledge* plays in the judgment about values.[35] The more we know about the connections and interactions, "the more we *know* the object in question."[36]

In the discovery of the value-quality of an object, both situation and reflection, or critical intelligence, play important parts. Values are not antecedently existent, but are discovered operationally in the situation. Like the object of knowledge in Dewey's theory of knowledge, values are also arrived at by a process of interaction between situation and critical intelligence.

Let us now consider a few objections to Dewey's naturalistic treatment of ethical problems. Dewey, as we have seen, does not consider moral problems to be *sui generis*; they stand on the same ground in his naturalistic ethics as do physical problems and are considered in the same situational context. Now moral problems cannot be considered to be existential in the same sense in which physical problems are considered to be existential. For example, two individuals, an adult and a child, want to cross a highway which has no pedestrian crossing. The adult can manage to get across safely, but he is not sure of his copedestrian child. The adult is also in a great hurry. Now here is a *moral* problem that the adult is faced with, and that is whether to leave the child to its own fate or to wait for some time and escort the child across the road. The problem is no doubt existential, but it is not physical. The situation is "problematic" because an obligation is involved and not because an obstacle is present.

Secondly, in his treatment of ethical problems, Dewey puts a great emphasis on reflection. Concepts like "good," "value," "standard," and so forth, are to him, as we have seen, nothing but products of reflection on the situation. Now reflection on the situation may suggest all these ethical values, but the question is whether reflection alone is sufficient. Reflection, psychologically speaking, is not always impartial. Quite often, it is a mere rationalization of self-interest or a point of view taken in advance.

Thirdly, even if we grant reflection to be the oracle of impartiality, reflective judgments themselves cannot command obligation. This is because all reflective judgments are not necessarily normative, although every normative judgment essentially involves reflection. Judgments which involve obligation are, then, a particular class of "reflective judgments."

Fourthly, in Dewey's ethical theory there is no definite indication of what might be said to be a criterion of judgment. His emphasis on the uniqueness of every situation is so great that he rejects the possibility of any absolute criterion. His own standpoint is that a situation of deficiency and the efficacy of an object or an act to overcome it, together with our reflection on the situation, help us to discover the criterion within the existential situation. In actual effect, Dewey looks forward to the consequences of every act, and hence to the future. In this he shares the weakness of all the pragmatists:

Future as such *is elected as a criterion of truth, and . . . when this criterion is considered it turns out to be no criterion at all. The problem has been postponed, not solved.*[37]

Dewey, in short, has no answer to provide to this kind of criticism. His own explanation swings back and forth from the extreme subjectivity of reflection to an equally extreme objectivity of consequences.

This brings us to the end of our examination of Dewey's thesis on common inquiry. Our criticism of Dewey's theory has been twofold. First, we have questioned Dewey's contention that inquiries result in the transformation of the empirical situation. We have pointed out that there are inquiries that involve only cognitive operations, and that hence bring about no existential transformation. Second, we have pointed out some difficulties in Dewey's naturalistic treatment of ethical problems, specially with regard to a criterion of judgment.

3

ANTECEDENTS OF DEWEY'S
POLITICAL THEORY

THIS CHAPTER IS DEVOTED to the task of elucidating
some of the philosophical and political views of Dewey which were
antecedents in the development of his political theory. His systematic views on political theory appeared with the publication of *The
Public and Its Problems* (1927). We shall therefore examine his earlier political writings in the light of the position taken up in this
work. The more important of these writings are concerned with his
views on Kant and Green.

In the writings of most critics of Dewey, considerable attention
has been paid to the influence of Hegel. As Dewey remained a consistent opponent of Kant, it has been commonly supposed that the
ideas of Kant did not exercise any significant influence on him. Our
contention in this connection would be that in spite of Dewey's expressed criticism of the ideas and the philosophic standpoint of Kant,
there exists in the end an intrinsic relationship between his ideas and
those of Kant. This contention is partly substantiated in this chapter
and partly in the next. An examination of Dewey's views on Green's
moral philosophy, on the other hand, enables us to appreciate the
methodological shift that occurs in his subsequent writings, especially in the statement of his political ideas.

Like all other American philosophers of the nineteenth century,
Dewey began his philosophical career by taking a keen interest in the
problems raised by late eighteenth and early nineteenth century German philosophy. At the same time, Dewey also acquainted himself
with the French reaction to German philosophy and the continuation
of the French rationalist tradition of the encyclopedists, in the form
of positivism.[1] In spite of the fact that his mature philosophical ideas

39

regarding the functional nature of reflective thought were similar to those of the positivists, French positivism left no effect on Dewey whatsoever. Like Dewey, the positivists were inspired by the natural sciences of their own times and were engaged in making a philosophical statement of what came to be regarded as "scientific method" in their own time.[2] The social and political significance of the positivists' philosophical ideas was considerable, and there were broad similarities to Dewey's temperament and attitude revealed in their science-inspired political philosophy. Nevertheless, on the whole, Dewey remained largely indifferent to them. Before turning to science, Dewey had come under the influence, first, of the idealists and, second, of the physiological psychologists. His own philosophical background coupled with the radically different science of his time, by which he was inspired, may be said to be responsible for his indifference to the positivists. He neither supported them nor criticized them. In a vague way, he took Marx to be the representative of the nineteenth century science-inspired social philosophy,[3] and by criticizing Marx's philosophy of science, Dewey felt that he had done away with all those schools in social and political philosophy that owed their allegiance to nineteenth-century science.

Equally negligible had been the influence of the ideas of the British empiricists and utilitarians on Dewey's political philosophy. His earlier Hegelian training made him extremely critical of the dichotomy of sensations and ideas that existed in British empiricism, and his lack of philosophical sympathy towards them prevented him from taking any interest in their political ideas. Moreover, their conception of the self-sufficient atomistic individual, for which Dewey admitted only a partial justification,[4] was in direct contravention to the social organicist attitude that he had inherited from Hegel. It was precisely his lack of agreement with Mill on the conception of the individual that was responsible for his total indifference to Mill's scientific attempt to deduce the laws of social behavior from the laws of individual behavior.[5]

Bentham's emphasis on judging the merits of political and judicial measures with reference to their "consequences" to the happiness of the individual was regarded by Dewey as a right attitude to adopt.[6] But there, too, Dewey remained intensely suspicious of the individual as Bentham conceived him: pleasure-seeking and self-sufficient. It was this defective conception of the individual, Dewey believed, that stood in Bentham's way of advocating collective social measures on the basis of "consequences."[7] Dewey's excessive criticism of the individualists in psychology and in social philosophy, together with his community-building philosophy of education and bold collectivistic social planning—in spite of the innumerable safeguards in his philosophy—pushed his nebulous conception of the individual to a vanishing point. In 1939, on the eve of the Second World War, with two great totalitarian experiments in front of him, Dewey was prepared to undo all his criticisms of the individual in social philosophy:

> *I shall now wish to emphasize more than I formerly did that individuals are the finally decisive factors of the nature and movement of associated life.*
>
> *The cause of this shift of emphasis is the events of the intervening years. The rise of dictatorships and totalitarian states and the decline of democracy have been accompanied with loud proclamation of the idea that only the state, the political organization of society, can give security to individuals . . .*
>
> *In rethinking this issue in the light of the rise of totalitarian states, I am led to emphasize the idea that only the voluntary initiative and voluntary co-operation of individuals can produce social institutions that will protect the liberties necessary for achieving development of genuine individuality.*[8]

But such a statement came only at the tag end of Dewey's philosophical career, when it was much too late to alter the structure of his ideas. Consequently, Dewey's social and political point of view remained associated with a type of anti-individualism that he himself was willing to give up.

Dewey and Kant

As far as the problems raised by German philosophy of the late eighteenth and early nineteenth century are concerned, Dewey's main interest is Kant: Kantian epistemology and the influence of Kantian epistemology on morals and politics of post-Kantian Germany. But Dewey's approach to Kant, through which he viewed German morals and politics, was not a unified approach. It consisted of two different kinds of reactions to the ideas of Kant, to which two different expressions were given. His first reaction to the ideas of Kant acquired its form from the climate of philosophical opinion, dominated by the

41

neo-Hegelians both in America and in Britain, that existed towards the close of the last century. His second reaction to the ideas of Kant resulted in the publication of his *German Philosophy and Politics* (1915), the philosophical form of which was largely derived from ideas drawn from his logic and theory of knowledge. Consequently, in order fully to appreciate his attitude towards the problems raised by German philosophy of the late eighteenth and early nineteenth century, we must disassociate his two different reactions to Kant and consider their respective influences on his political philosophy.

◄━━━━► *Dewey's earlier reaction to Kant*

Dewey wrote his doctoral thesis on the psychology of Kant in the year 1884 for Johns Hopkins University. Although this thesis was not published, we can guess Dewey's critical approach to Kant from the tone of a paper published in the same year under the title of "Kant and Philosophical Method."[9] This paper was greatly critical of Kantian formalism and expressed grave doubts over Kant's attempt to make the organic unity of categories, as found in consciousness, the criterion of experience.[10] In his criticism of Kantian formalism, Dewey drew heavily at this stage from the ideas of Hegel as popularized by the neo-Hegelians, and not from science or genetic logic, as he did in his subsequent criticism of Kant. Hegel's logic appeared to him to be more satisfactory than Kant's organic unity of categories, which represented Kant's conception of the self and which could not be objectively viewed. The Hegelian negative, Dewey felt, provided an unlimited scope for reason to operate constructively in contrast to Kant's formal reason, which interpreted sense impressions. Lastly, Hegelian dialectic seemed to make all the laws of mind and history comprehensible and therefore offered a possibility of unifying mind with history. Dewey's first paper on Kant thus ended with the expression of his conviction that Hegel had more satisfactory answers to offer to problems raised by Kant concerning the nature of the self and the function of reason.

Such, then, was the starting point of Dewey's attitude towards Kant. It was an attitude that he had inherited from such neo-Hegelians as G. S. Morris, the Cairds, Wallace, and Lord Haldane. Neo-Hegelianism was one of the strongest movements in philosophy towards the end of the last century.[11] T. H. Green, who was more a Kantian than a Hegelian, indirectly strengthened the movement by attacking the empiricists and the utilitarians. However, with the

Cairds, Wallace, and, above all, Bosanquet (especially in his political philosophy), British idealism took a completely Hegelian turn. But of all the neo-Hegelians, the influence on Dewey of G. S. Morris, through his writings and personal contact both at Johns Hopkins and at Michigan, was about the greatest and most enduring.[12]

Two years after the publication of his first paper on Kant, Dewey published two more papers, "The Psychological Standpoint" and "Psychology as Philosophic Method,"[13] in which he extended his criticism of Kant with the help of the ideas of the idealists. The thesis that Dewey expounded in these two papers was that *consciousness* is the proper subject matter of psychology. The type of psychology that Dewey subscribed to at this stage was rational psychology, with its technique of introspection.[14] Dewey's thesis on consciousness as the proper subject matter of psychology was an attack on psychological philosophy from Locke to Spencer—in which subject is separated from object. It was also an attack on Kant for treating the self as an end in itself, thereby preventing the self from becoming a subject of psychological analysis. In his attack, Dewey largely depended on the logical tools of transcendental idealists like Hegel and Green. The ability to discriminate subject and object, he argued, presupposed the presence of one more factor, namely self-consciousness, but that was not all. If the knowledge of subject and object is relative to self-consciousness, then self-consciousness itself is dependent on and relative to something else. This something else, said Dewey, is the universal consciousness: the presupposition of self-consciousness in the same manner as self-consciousness is the presupposition of our ability to discriminate subject from object.[15] If these presuppositions were to be recognized, then the self cannot be regarded a thing in itself. Nor does any difficulty arise in uniting subject with object, because the real problem is their discrimination, not their unification.

This, then, in a nutshell, was the reaction of the young Dewey to Kant as it acquired philosophical expression under the influence of the dominant ideas of the neo-Hegelians. His criticism of Kant at this stage exhibits the unmistakable marks of the wave of anti-Kantianism of the last quarter of the last century. The attitude of the youthful Dewey towards Kant was, we may conclude, only a reflection of the philosophical *Zeitgeist* of the period in which he came to intellectual maturity.

But this, however, must not lead us into a belief that his earlier attitude towards Kant, which was later on replaced by a more original as well as a more critical attitude, had no influence on his social and political philosophy. The neo-Hegelians, who helped him to criticize Kant, also provided him with a metaphysical framework that subsequently became the matrix within which his social and political philosophy developed. Thus, even when he grew out of the framework of anti-Kantianism, he could never completely shake off the neo-Hegelian influence, and it existed side by side with his subsequent attitude to Kant in the shaping of his social and political outlook. The following are the two principal features of his inheritance from the neo-Hegelians: they are, first, organicism, and, second, activism.

Organicism

Dewey's earlier acceptance of the thesis of the neo-Hegelians on transcendental organicism—consisting of universal consciousness as well as individual consciousness, of the reconciliation of the subject with object, and of making the self the subject of logical and psychological inquiries—produced a rich crop of organicism in his own writings on psychology, politics, education, and even methodology. There are two possible ways of reviewing the organicist element in Dewey. It may be reviewed, first, in terms of the stages through which his organicism evolved. Broadly speaking, these stages were three in number: transcendental organicism, which accepted the metaphysics of universal consciousness and tried to view the place of the individual consciousness within it; cultural and social organicism, which considered the physical environment and social institutions as a whole and tried to analyze their determining influence on human behavior; and intellectualist organicism, which considered knowledge as embodied in the various techniques and institutions that human beings have been able to evolve, as a social possession to be used for the purpose of directing human activities as well as for the purpose of organizing the consequences of their activities.

The organicist element can also be presented in terms of various premises in Dewey's writings leading to his organicist conclusions. As our thesis makes limited reference to the various stages through which Dewey's thought developed, it would be proper for us to adopt this latter point of view.

His organicist premises are most conspicuously felt in his psychology, politics, and methodology. Each one of these topics will receive detailed consideration in the next chapter.[16] Here we shall mention briefly what these organicist premises and conclusions are.

The organicist premise in Dewey's psychology is to be found in his examination of human behavior against the background of the physical and cultural environment. As far as the determining influences on human behavior are concerned, physical and cultural factors form one single environment, in which human beings are able to survive by building up certain psychophysical patterns of behavior which the physical aspect of the environment demands and which the cultural aspect of the environment approves. The building up of these patterns is the function of *habit*, but such patterns built up by different individuals are not similar, in spite of the fact that individuals in a social group are exposed to more or less similar determining influences. Here, Dewey's notion of habit is comprehensive enough to account for the variations that arise as a result of the exercise of will or intelligence. Dewey's psychology based on habit is then as organicistically comprehensive as his notion of the behavior-determining environment.

In politics, Dewey's emphasis falls on the other aspect of organicism, namely interdependence, as opposed to the emphasis on holistic aspect in his psychology. This is to be found in his consideration of the fact of association as the universal law. The fact of association is, then, the organicist premise of his political analysis. In other words, coexistence and conjoint activity are given as facts of ordinary experience which do not call for any philosophical explanation. Dewey's premise of coexistence and conjoint activity make him interpret the nature of political activity in corporate terms. He remains very emphatic in his assertion that political activities are not pursued for the sake of individuals, but for the sake of groups or societies through the agency of individuals. The task of political inquiry for him becomes the discovery of problems of common concern, on whose solution the general well-being of the society depends. With Dewey, political activity remains, therefore, some kind of concerted activity undertaken by the representatives of the public, who promise to look after its interests.

The organicist premise in Dewey's methodology is to be found in his attempt to frame a comprehensive theory of inquiry based on science. The particular organicist element that he emphasizes is to be found in his treatment of science as the consummatory stage in the evolution of human knowledge. Like self-consciousness in Hegel

45

—realizing itself through art, religion, and philosophy—human intelligence in Dewey comes to realize itself in science, evolving the techniques of trial and error, of making hypotheses, and of confirming them after a prolonged search for a dependable form of knowledge. The technique that science embodies can be said to be the most dependable technique that human beings have been able to develop so far. In science, human intelligence becomes self-conscious and discovers its own mission and sphere of responsibilities. Its mission comes to be that of widening the range of human control over those forces on which human existence and well-being depends. Its sphere of responsibilities extends to the realms of means as well as ends.

▭ *Activism*

The other enduring influence of neo-Hegelianism on Dewey's social and political philosophy was the influence of what may be called, for the want of a better term, activism. With the help of the ideas of the neo-Hegelians, Dewey was able to criticize Kantian formal rationalism. Dewey felt that Kant had limited the functions of reason by making it an interpreter of sense impressions. As opposed to this, the dynamics of Hegelian reason, realizing and manifesting itself in various institutions, had much greater appeal for him. Within the framework of Dewey's subsequent naturalism, the dynamic reason of Hegel transformed his conception of physical and social objects and events into processes. After this, all forms of reality came to acquire for Dewey some sort of a processive character.

Hegelian rationalism on the one hand converted Dewey's conception of objects and events into processes. On the other hand, it influenced him towards the formation of a conception of the individual that was active, reconstructive, and self-realizing. Together they presented a new metaphysical basis for his theory of political organization. The processive character of reality made the problems of political organization *unique* as well as *dynamic*. Consequently, in his political analysis Dewey laid considerable emphasis on the generic discrimination of phenomena and the specific problems that arise within them. On the organizational side, his emphasis fell on the flexibility of manipulative machinery necessary for coping with dynamic problems. This in turn gave birth to new political values—constant observation, communication of the results of observation, experimental programs for political action, and so forth. Dewey's political writings are full of emphasis on such values.

These then, in brief, are some of the far-reaching effects on his political philosophy of Dewey's early contact with the idealists, especially the neo-Hegelians. As we examine the second phase of Dewey's reaction to Kant, we shall see these effects continuing side by side with the political implications of his later attitude towards Kant.

Dewey's subsequent reaction to Kant

Normally speaking, there are two possible reactions to a system of thought in philosophy: reaction to the form and reaction to the content. Innumerable illustrations of such reactions can be cited from the history of philosophy. For the sake of appreciating the peculiarities of Dewey's reaction to Kant, which falls into neither classification, let us illustrate the usual reactions to philosophical systems.

Very few philosophers of his intellectual stature have taken their predecessors as seriously as did Kant. He showed a good deal of respect[17] for his predecessors by reconsidering the philosophical problems they had raised. Such was his attitude towards British empirical philosophy, which reached its climax in Hume's skepticism. Instead of showing contempt towards the empiricists for having created a crisis in philosophy, Kant devoted his life and energy to the task of re-examining the premises from which their conclusions were derived. Such a re-examination of their premises helped Kant to assimilate their empiricism within the framework of his own theory of knowledge. Assimilation of the principal ideas of empiricists like Locke, Berkley, and Hume within his own theory of knowledge shows that the reaction of Kant to these thinkers was a reaction to the *form* of their ideas.

The reaction of Marx to the ideas of Hegel appears on the surface to be similar to Kant's reaction to the epistemological form of the empiricists. It was in actual fact very different. The basic methodological form in Marx, in spite of his claim to scientific materialism, was not very different from Hegel's. Marx had inverted Hegel's priority of logic over historical process by making thought process the outcome of material existence, or by turning the Hegelian dialectic on its head; nevertheless, he could not get rid of the methodological form that was implicit in Hegel's philosophy of history. The three-beat rhythm of Hegel's historical process continued with Marx. So did the Hegelian conception of the historical necessity. Very little difference remained between the spellbound spectators of Hegel, watching the great drama of history, and the agents of Marx, individuals serving in the historical conflicts between the productive and nonproductive forces of society. The historical process, both in Hegel and in Marx, was conceived in terms of inevitability. To that extent, the methodological form belonging to one was not very different from the other's. And to that extent also, the reaction of Marx to Hegel was a reaction to the *content* of the system of thought rather than to its form.

But Dewey's reaction is a reaction neither to the form nor contents of the Kantian system of thought. Kant and Dewey must be regarded as two disputants who present rival points of view over certain common problems. The gap of a hundred and fifty years does not prevent the dispute from becoming a living dispute, for from Dewey's point of view, the theories of morals and politics, having become the victims of methodological aberrations of Kantian epistemology, have hardly made any substantial progress since the days of Kant. As far as Dewey's political philosophy is concerned, the dispute with Kant is centered around the following three problems raised by the Kantian system of thought: epistemological dualism, the Kantian principle of reason and authority, and the moral state and economic society. We shall now examine the criticisms and the alternatives that Dewey has to offer in his dispute with Kant with respect to each one of these problems.

With the publication of *German Philosophy and Politics* (1915), the second phase of Dewey's reaction to Kant began. This book presented one of the most severe criticisms of Kant's moral and political philosophy ever to appear in the English language. Published at the beginning of the World War I and revised during the beginning of America's entry into World War II (1942), the book is likely to mislead us into a belief of its having been a product of the righteous anger against the German culture and outlook. But it certainly is more than that. In its treatment of the problem, it ranges from complete academic detachment like that of L. T. Hobhouse, whose *Metaphysical Theory of the State* (1917) was written under more or less similar circumstances, to scathing criticism of the explicitly chauvinistic statements of Treitschke and Goering. Dewey takes for granted the responsibility of Kant for all that happened in morals and politics from post-Kantian to Nazi Germany. In the revised edition of his book, while Dewey expressed agreement with Karl Mannheim's thesis that mass-democratization results in the release of the irrational,[18] in actuality, in the chapter that he added, he only stretched his own thesis on Kant to be able to explain the rise of Nazi political tribalism and the cult of the leader.

 Epistemological dualism

Dewey, with some justification, treated Kant as a philosopher of immense historical significance. Kant appeared on the scene at a period of tremendous ferment of ideas in European history. No serious thinker could ignore the impressive array of British empiricists. In physics, the repercussions of the ideas of Bacon, Descartes, Galileo, Newton, and others were beginning to be felt. Their ideas were undoing the teachings of the classical thinkers in epistemology in general and the natural sciences in particular. Meanwhile in France, the encyclopedists, Kant's own senior contemporaries, were expressing an unqualified faith in reason and progress. They believed that they had succeeded in discovering the faults and injustices that were inherent in traditional social and political institutions, and that with the help of reason they could reconstruct the society in such a manner as to be able to enjoy liberty and equality. What particular role did Kant play, then, as one of the principal thinkers of his time, in giving direction to the ideas of his time? Dewey's answer to this question is not only different from that of philosophers who belong to a different tradition from his own, but even different from that of George Herbert Mead, a close friend, and a thinker who shared innumerable ideas and attitudes with him.[19]

In his celebrated work, *The Movements of Thought in the Nineteenth Century* (1936), Mead describes Kant as the philosopher of the French Revolution. According to Mead, the rationalism of Kant comes very close to the rationalism of Rousseau. The rationalism which Rousseau popularized and which Mead thought was responsible for the French Revolution also came to be assimilated into the system of ideas of Kant.[20] In order to substantiate this thesis, Mead drew extensive parallels between the self-legislative sovereign individual of Rousseau and the rational individual of Kant, who prescribes laws to nature (experience) as well as to society (conduct).[21] Having identified the rational law-giving individual of Rousseau with that of Kant, it was not difficult for Mead to point out that a similar conception of the individual as rational and law-giving existed at the base of the French Revolution. The conception of a rational and law-giving individual continued to play a vital role in Kant's system of

49

ideas, while in Fichte, Schelling, and Hegel, the emphasis on rationality was transferred from the individual to institutions. Mead therefore called Kant "the philosopher of the Revolution," while he called Fichte, Schelling, and Hegel "philosophers of reaction."

From Dewey's point of view, the exception that Mead makes on behalf of Kant is to be strongly objected to. Instead of viewing Kant in the perspective of the growth of the idea of rational individual, as Mead does, Dewey examines him in the light of the historical influences of his ideas on epistemology in general. Dewey's examination of Kant becomes all the more severe because he regards Kant as the first moral philosopher fully to appreciate the significance of the ideas of the seventeenth-century revolution in science.

It may be recalled that Dewey considered Kant an eclectic, as well as a great original thinker.[22] The genius of an eclectic resides in his ability to recast the diverse elements of thought and the contending claims of different ideas into a system of his own. The central principle of an eclectic system is compromise or accommodation. The compromise which the Kantian epistemology may be said to have attempted was between the ideas of the seventeenth century science, on the one hand, and traditional moral and ethical beliefs on the other. It accommodated their contending claims by making each one of them supreme in its own sphere. Spheres of knowledge were divided in two, and within each, a distinct cognitive process was supposed to operate.

> ... Kant's decisive contribution is the idea of a dual legislation of reason by which are marked off two distinct realms—that of science and that of morals. Each of these two realms has its own final and authoritative constitution: On one hand, there is the world of sense, the world of phenomena in space and time in which science is at home; on the other hand is the supersensible, the noumenal world, the world of moral duty and moral freedom.[23]

Considered in terms of its result, the Kantian epistemology, from Dewey's point of view, had succeeded in continuing the traditional dualism of the "physical" and "mental" subjects at a time when, in natural science, all the ideas inherited from the Greeks were being questioned, and its repercussions were being felt on the various theories of inquiry. At such a moment, Kant, who fully appreciated the philosophical import of the ideas of Bacon, Galileo, and Newton, put a seal, with his learning and authority, on the traditional dualism of "physical" and "mental" subjects. The eclectic genius of Kant had found a place for the ideas of seventeenth century science without giving up the traditional ethical outlook and the technique of its reasoning. This was, then, the nature of Dewey's dispute with Kant as far as the Kantian theory of knowledge in its historical contexts was concerned.

The passage quoted above, though summing up the Kantian epistemological compromise as far as Dewey is concerned, hardly does justice to Kant himself. Dewey's conception of the two realms, phenomena and noumena, as mutually exclusive overlooks the emphasis of Kant on the varying degree of *a priori* element involved in the various objects of knowledge. Kant is indeed responsible for using the terms "phenomena" and "noumena" to indicate the spheres of operation of two different types of cognitive process—one determined by causal necessity, and the other free from it. But the different objects that fall into these classifications were not characterized by Kant as purely experiential and nothing else, or purely *a priori* and nothing else. This was apparently Dewey's own oversimplification of Kantian dualism to square it with the traditional dualism of exclusively physical and exclusively mental subjects.

No justice can be done to Kantian epistemology unless we consider it in the light of a genuine concern with the problem of moral choice and freedom. Dewey was certainly aware of the fact that Kant was driven to expound the dualistic epistemology in the face of an overwhelming emphasis on causal necessity by the seventeenth century physicists, especially Newton.[24] The principle of all-pervading causal necessity is a direct threat to the possibility of moral choice and to the freedom of the will. The problem which Kant raised some two hundred years ago is as alive today as it was in his time, only it has taken a slightly different form. In our time, causal determinism, both physical and psychological, has threatened the possibility not of moral choice so much as of moral responsibility. Our knowledge of causal determination is being employed by the physicalists, historicists, and psychoanalysts in different forms in order to plead for the absence of human responsibility or what Prof. Isaiah Berlin calls the moral "alibi."[25] Professor Berlin himself probably comes very near Kant when he reasserts his faith in the possibility of moral *choice*, in spite of what the determinists and the relativists of all shades have been pleading for.[26] Kantian epistemological dualism therefore represents a problem of far greater importance than can be explained away in the context of history as a typical compromise between two branches of human knowledge. Dewey certainly exaggerated the historical influence of Kantian epistemology. The French positivism and British utilitarianism that dominated the first half of the nineteenth century were in direct contravention to the spirit of Kantian dualism. St. Simon, Comte, Bentham, Mill, Spencer, and others turned to the natural sciences for guidance in their analysis of social phenomena, in spite of the Kantian warning. In his own country, Kant's epistemology did not bring about the Copernican revolution professed by Kant in philosophy. The nineteenth century German philosophical thought did not center around the epistemological problems raised by Kant, but around the philosophy of history, both idealistic (Hegel) and empirical (Marx).

The influence of Kant on subsequent philosophical thought, as Dewey describes it, can hardly be taken seriously. Much of Dewey's case is weakened if we acknowledge that Kantian epistemology reproduced an existing dichotomy in knowledge in a different form. The fact that this dichotomy continued in post-Kantian philosophy does not necesssarily imply that it continued in the Kantian form. There may be some justification in statement that Kant stood in the way of a unified epistemology at a period when attempts in that direction were being made. But the fact that it did not come about does not necessarily imply that it was because of the influence of Kant.

The principle of reason and authority. Dewey's reaction to Kant's rationalism and conception of authority, found in his moral philosophy, exercised considerable influence on his political theory. On the one hand, this reaction appeared to be critical of Kant's conception of reason and authority; on the other hand, it did not totally give up the rationalist position but only restated it.

There are two spheres of operation of Kantian reason: that of *phenomena*, or sense impressions, and that of *noumena*, or morality. Both spheres are concerned with experience; *a priori* reason, however, is needed in both. There are innumerable problems that arise in the sphere of phenomena that cannot be explained empirically— problems of space and time, for example, and the laws of conservation and causation. Of the two spheres, Kantian reason is more at home in the sphere of noumena because there it does not have to work within empirical limitation.[27, 28] Unrestricted by human senses and desires, it acquires a full scope for its operation, and guides the conduct of the agent by prescribing him his duties. The possession of reason on the part of the agent makes his duties self-perceived and self-imposed. However, obedience to the dictates of reason alone does not make an action *moral*. In order to be moral, the action must be performed under the *sense of duty*. Kantian reason therefore tells the agent, not only where and when he must act, but also how he ought to act. Thus Kant attributes to reason something more than what it normally implies. What comes to be added to its normal meaning is the *voice of duty*. This voice of duty is rigorous as well as authoritative.

Kantian reason, therefore, in being more than a mere discriminatory capacity, becomes the target of Dewey's criticism. Dewey attacks Kant on the ground that he substitutes some kind of *principle* of reason in place of reason itself.[29] Furthermore, this principle of reason is not open to investigation, because it is embodied in the moral self, which for Kant is a thing in itself. What Dewey is attacking in Kantian rationalism is its self-evident as well as its authoritative character. It would be beyond the scope of this thesis to undertake a detailed examination of the self-evident nature of Kantian reason emerging from a self-evident conception of the self. We shall therefore concentrate our attention on the authoritative character of Kantian reason and see how Dewey links it up with the post-Kantian conception of political authority.

The authoritativeness of Kantian reason cannot be made directly responsible for the political authoritarianism of Kant's successors. Dewey, therefore, had to argue out the half-logical, half-psychological case that Kant's excessive emphasis on authoritative reason and on the sense of duty created an atmosphere in which obedience to political authority came to be regarded as a moral virtue. He had to argue, furthermore, that Kant himself had no conception of political authority, and that what he had was only an ethics of duty that could be easily extended from obedience to the dictates of one's own reason to obedience to the dictates of politically constituted authority. That is, if any political authority were to combine itself in theory with the reason operating within the individual, obedience to such an authority would not be regarded as obedience to an external or arbitrary authority. In other words, Dewey read into Kant all those arguments that Rousseau had employed in the exposition of the doctrine of general will.

This is precisely what Dewey does in his interpretation of Kant's political philosophy. He neither mentions Rousseau nor his influence on Kant; nevertheless, he reproduces Rousseau's arguments in Kantian terminology. The operation of Kantian moral law is conceived by Dewey in the contexts of Rousseau's general will. Kantian moral law is made to overcome the considerations of expediency and self-interest in the same manner that Rousseau's general will overcomes particular wills. In the same way that Rousseau interpreted the general will as operating both in the individual and in the political authority as sovereign principle, Dewey interpreted the Kantian moral law as operating in the individual as well as in the field of social relationships.

> *The relation between the world of space and time where physical causality reigns and the moral world of freedom and duty is not a symmetrical one. The former cannot intrude into latter. But it is the very nature of moral legislation that it is meant to influence the world of sense; its object is to realize the purposes of free rational action within the sense world. This fact fixes the chief features of Kant's philosophy of Morals and of the State.*[30]

The field of social relationships is taken to be the field of the senses because of the operation of desires and instincts in the field of the senses.

However, Dewey's reading of Rousseau's argument into Kant does not end there. He reproduces in Kant even the anticlimax in Rousseau's attempt to locate the general will. It is commonly believed in political philosophy that Rousseau contradicted his own thesis on popular sovereignty by introducing the Legislator to help the community to locate it general will.[31] Dewey supposes the same position to be arrived at in Kant, where the operation of the moral law in the field of social relationships remains extremely nebulous. The moral law cannot be transformed into the shape of a definite authority that alone can operate in the field of social relationships. Consequently, the entire logical form of the moral law that is supposed to operate in the field of social relationships becomes readily available to the actual law and existing authority. Like Rousseau's legislator, who continues to represent the chief characteristic of the general will, namely the *common good*, actual law and authority take over the functions of the moral law.[32]

Dewey's criticisms of the main characteristics of Kantian rationalism necessitates an analysis on our part regarding Dewey's own position with reference to rationalism in general. Although Dewey strongly opposed the Kantian principle of reason on the ground that it was self-evident and authoritative, he himself never ceased to be a rationalist. This contention can be substantiated on two grounds: first, that Dewey was neither influenced by the Jamesian revolt against reason, nor did he approve of James's definition of "truth," which was the vital basis of Jamesian pragmatism; second, that Dewey restated his own brand of rationalism under the inspiration of the natural sciences. To Dewey's brand of rationalism we propose to give the name of "trial-and-error rationalism." In our analysis of his trial-and-error rationalism, we shall also discover his reaction to Kantian rationalism. We now begin with the James-Dewey relationship.

Dewey's attack on the formal and syllogistic rationalisms in general and that of Kant in particular did not prepare him for an unqualified acceptance of the ideas of James. Although both James and Dewey were engaged in attacking *formal rationalism* in all its shades, their respective attacks, on account of the differences in their temperaments and philosophical sources, acquired different expressions.[33] James, as Dewey himself suggested, was engaged in revising British empiricism,[34] and the two dominant characteristics of James's thought with which he undertook this revision were voluntarism on the one hand and the natural sciences on the other. James was both intellectually and emotionally hostile to rigorous philosophical systems in general interfered with his own attempt pluralistic to let him feel at home with exclusive philosophical systems. Emotionally he was too much of a rebel to submit to the rigorous chain of reasoning of the system-builders. His revolt against philosophical systems in general interfered wih this own attempt at recasting his sporadic ideas and themes into a consistent philosophical framework.

His attack on rationalism was not without the accretions of his own temperament. Nobody can read his lectures on *Pragmatism*, which savagely attacked rational philosophical systems, without becoming aware of the intensely romantic personality that lay behind them. In these lectures, his distrust of rational philosophical systems was extended to distrust of reason itself.

Unlike James, Dewey acquired his basic attitude towards reflective thought from the idealists. His earlier idealist training left behind a deep impression on his mind regarding the value of systematic thinking and logical consistency, and these remained the dominant character of his ideas even when he drifted away from the idealists. Nor did Dewey escape the influence of their attempts at system-building. As an idealist or as a naturalist, or even as a philosopher of science, Dewey's ideas always indicate the presence of a well thought-out system. His familiarity with the high standard of philosophical analysis and of logical consistency of the idealists always made him dissatisfied with the quality of philosophical expression of his own and that of his pragmatist colleagues. Of the chief pragmatists—James, Schiller, and Dewey, Dewey alone remained genuinely concerned with the hostile criticism of the school in philosophy that they were all engaged in developing.[35] By anticipating the criticisms of his own ideas, Dewey invariably introduced far too many qualifications in each one of his statements with the result that his expressions became unduly turgid. Pragmatism as a school in philosophy, however, owes much to John Dewey for having raised its intellectual prestige both at home and abroad.

The idealists not only influenced the quality of Dewey's philosophical endeavor, but they also affected the contents. Dewey's theory of knowledge, which we have examined in Chapter Two, was derived from the idealists, the behaviorists, and the physicists. Hegel's activity of the thought process, which Dewey had once accepted, was not totally given up even when Dewey became a behaviorist. This is because cognitive activity continued to play a far greater part in his theory of knowledge than what could be accommodated within the framework of behaviorism. Earlier we had examined Dewey's inability to identify the cognitive with the behavioral in his theory of knowledge.[36] In his theory of knowledge Dewey was trying to work out a thesis that ideas are hypotheses and that they are deliberately formulated as plans of action. A plan of action precedes action itself. Thus by prescribing to ideas an extremely complicated cognitive function, Dewey made the identity of the cognitive and the behavioral almost impossible. Within his theory of knowledge, ideas come to acquire a unique cognitive function of directing overt activity. But in the function of directing overt activity, ideas are themselves the tools of critical intelligence. Thus Dewey came to prescribe to ideas and to the critical intelligence operating behind them all those functions which the idealists and the rationalists had prescribed to reason. Even in his extreme pragmatic emphasis on consequences, Dewey never renounced the function of critical intelligence of judging the appropriateness of consequences. And in this respect, his emphasis on the role of critical intelligence comes much nearer to the emphasis on reason of the idealists and rationalists.

It must be admitted that the first systematic statement of Dewey's theory of knowledge appeared in *The Quest of Certainty* (1929). Nevertheless, it is not difficult to see that throughout his relationship with James, Dewey did not look happily at the Jamesian brand of pragmatism. His objections to the elements of romanticism and irrationalism in James's philosophy were never openly expressed. He did not publicly deride the Jamesian form of pragmatism as "vulgar pragmatism." On the other hand, his opposition to James expressed itself in his studious avoidance of James's principal ideas. He very carefully drew the attention of his readers to James's *Principles of Psychology* as the only source of James's influence on him.[37] Dewey stated repeatedly that it was the potentially behavioristic psychology of James and not his philosophical ideas that influenced him. In most of his writings on James, Dewey paid tribute to the Jamesian psychology, his doctrine of pluralism, his criticism of schematic unities, his loyalty to facts, his insistence on verification, his genius for understanding the *Zeitgeist*, and so forth, but in none of his writings did Dewey undertake to assess the value of James's contribution to philosophy. He never subjected James to a thoroughgoing philosophical analysis from his own point of view. Dewey's treatment of James as a philosopher always remained an unusual one. While considering James as a philosopher, Dewey invariably pointed out James's highly gifted personality. And while assessing the innumerable gifts of James in terms of the quality of his work, Dewey invariably concentrated on the unrelated topic of the leadership which James gave to the philosophical movement of pragmatism. In such a special treatment of James as a philosopher, Dewey left plenty of scope for his readers to guess about his relationship with James.

The James-Dewey correspondence was spread over a period of eighteen years, out of which only twelve letters have been published, by Prof. Ralph Barton Perry in his two volumes *The Thought and Character of William James* (1935). Most of these letters center around James's interest in Dewey and his colleagues, who later on came to be regarded as the members of "the Chicago School." James was full of praise for the work done by the young Chicago philosophers. Dewey, on behalf of his colleagues, acknowledged their debt to James for his interest in their work and the inspiration given by his *Principles of Psychology*. In 1903, the Chicago philosophers dedicated a group of philosophical essays, published under the title of *Studies in Logical Theory*, to James. James was gratified by the honor done to him. From then on, James was inclined to believe that Dewey, in spite of his idealist past, had come pretty close to him in his philosophical attitude. In his lectures on *Pragmatism*, James mentioned Dewey's name along with Schiller's with a belief that Dewey shared his own basic attitude towards philosophy, although he was gradually becoming aware of the growing difference between them. While reviewing this book for the *Journal of Philosophy* (1908), Dewey openly expressed his disagreement with James on his definition of truth as follows.

> *Since Mr. James has referred to me as saying "truth is what gives satisfaction" (p. 234), I may remark (apart from the fact that I do not think I ever said that truth is what* gives *satisfaction) that I have never identified any satisfaction with the truth of an idea, save that satisfaction which arises when the idea as working hypothesis or tentative method is applied to prior existences in a way as to fulfill what it intends.*[38]

Following his writing of this review, before its publication, Dewey sent an apologetic note to James.

> *I have just finished, for Woodbridge, (one of the two editors of Journal of Philosophy), an account of the pragmatic movement, based on your book* (Pragmatism). *This reminds me that I have not even acknowledged the book. . . . I am culpable, flagrantly so, in the matter of acknowledgements and correspondence generally, but this is one of my worst sins of omission. . . . As it is, I shall have to count on your antecedent knowledge of my appreciation of and indebtedness to all you do.*

> *I have not attempted a review of the book* (Pragmatism), *but rather of the pragmatic movement with reference to what present controversy seems to me to indicate as the points which require more explicit statement and development. Among other things I have become conscious of some points of possible divergence between Schiller, yourself and myself, taken two by two all the way around; and I am not sure that some misunderstandings among our critics might not be cleared away, if our points of respective agreement and possible disagreement were brought out. . . . If there are real differences, and our critics are inclined to make combinations of our respective doctrines which no one of us alone would stand for, this may account for some of the unsatisfactory misunderstandings in the present state of controversy.*[39]

Any inference based on these few published letters cannot be sound. However, the fact remains that, by virtue of their genuine intellectual differences, James and Dewey were not as close to each other as is commonly supposed. Both discarded the unity of philosophical systems in favor of varied and pluralistic experience. Both of them also discarded formal rationalism. But what each of them had to offer instead was fundamentally different. James's alternative to formal rationalism was some sort of unphilosophical subjectivistic utilitarianism,[40] whereas Dewey's alternative to formal rationalism was some form of what we have called "trial-and-error rationalism."

The contention that Dewey renounced formal rationalism, but that his own philosophical point of view continued to be one of trial-and-error rationalism, can be substantiated by bringing together the ideas that are implicit in his theory of experience and theory of knowledge. This contention can also be substantiated by pointing out that trial-and-error rationalism is the basis of the investigatory and the practical aspects of Dewey's political theory.

As we have seen before in Chapter One, that which Dewey calls by the name of "experience" is divisible into primary experience and cognitive experience. The function of cognitive experience is to know and to overcome the obstacles that present themselves in the primary experience.[41] That is to say, the functions of cognitive experience are investigatory as well as manipulative. The cognitive experience undertakes the investigation of the situation in which the obstacle presents itself, and it winds up its operation by suggesting the ways and means of overcoming the obstacles in the primary experience.

For both these purposes, investigatory and manipulative, the cognitive experience employs certain *tools* as well as a certain *procedures*. As we have already seen in Chapter One, the tools employed by cognitive experience are ideas or hypotheses,[42] and the procedure employed by cognitive experience is that of experimentation or trial and error.[43]

The cognitive experience that undertakes its operations under the direction of hypotheses, within the framework of trial-and-error procedure, exhibits two important characteristics of its own. This experience is a conscious or consciously undertaken operation and, second, is capable of intelligent discrimination when alternatives present themselves.

It is a conscious operation, because while investigating and suggesting manipulative measures for the problematic situation, the cognitive experience must bring the problematic situation within the *range* of its own hypotheses. For only those aspects of the problematic situation that the hypotheses succeed in embracing fall within the focus of inquiry. Consequently, in the face of the problematic situation, the entire process of formulating hypotheses becomes a consciously undertaken process. The operations of cognitive experience must include the capacity to discriminate, because crude guesses, half-conscious beliefs, and prejudices tend to present themselves as alternatives to consciously formulated hypotheses. With the help of the discriminatory capacity, the cognitive experience either discards them or assimilates their plausible contents into hypotheses. Discriminatory operations do not end there. They continue to weigh the merits and demerits of different hypotheses while the agent continues to be in an indecisive state. After the final adoption of any particular hypothesis, the discriminatory element undertakes to judge the validity of the claims of a hypothesis, both in investigation and in manipulation.

These two characteristics of cognitive experience, that it is a *consciously* undertaken activity and that it involves a *discriminatory* capacity, make the entire process of cognitive experience a rational process. Its rationality is different from the rationality of a teleological process, which approximates an antecedent goal. Its rationality is also different from one that makes formal consistency the criterion of the rational process. Its rationality is that of trial and error. It recognizes that a situation of deficiency can neither be overcome by a thoughtless action nor by a highly reasoned and yet absolutely certain action, but that it can only be overcome by a conscious and discriminatory process of trial and error.

The chief characteristics of trial-and-error rationalism may be summed up as follows.

(1) Trial-and-error rationalism has its foundations in the belief that experimental and reconstructive intelligence *alone* can help us in investigating and solving a problematic situation that may arise at any particular time and place. It also rests on an assertion that correct investigation and adequate solution are possible only with the help of experimental intelligence.[44]

(2) No certainty can be attached either to the investigatory explanation of a problematic situation or to its manipulative recommendations. Explanations, theories, recommendations, and plans

must be treated as hypotheses to be confirmed. Their existing con-
firmations must not be allowed to disregard any new objection or
exception that is presented against them.[45]

(3) Trial-and-error rationalism eliminates the element of blind-
ness involved in undirected trial-and-error procedure. It does not
leave the process of trial and error to accident or luck. It implies a
clear conception of the consequences wanted, and the procedure of
trial and error therefore is directed towards those ends. It implies,
in other words, a correct understanding of the problematic situation
and the alternatives to it that are desired.[46]

(4) Correct understanding of the problematic situation implies
the recognition of unique factors in it. Trial-and-error rationalism
would, therefore, neither group together the different problematic
situations, nor prescribe a generalized solution, but would treat problematic situations as *specific*, to be solved individually.

Trial-and-error rationalism, then, indicates Dewey's reaction to
the formal and *a priori* rationalism of Kant; but it also indicates
his reaction to the authoritarian element in Kantian reason that he
thought became the basis of post-Kantian political authoritarianism.
Dewey did not feel obliged to substantiate his contention that there
exists a causal relationship between authoritative or absolutistic
philosophy and political absolutism, that the former must inevitably give rise to the latter.[47] To assert this is certainly to overrate
the influence of philosophy beyond academic circles. A more modest
thesis could have been based on the relationship between the expression of national temperaments in speculative philosophy, on
the one hand, and their expression in political habits, on the other.
But such a thesis would have transferred the element of praise or
blame from philosophy to temperament. Bent upon establishing the
causal connection between philosophy and politics, Dewey certainly
would have found this unacceptable. In the next chapter, we shall
point out that the connection between the fundamentals of philosophy and the fundamentals of politics reappears in Dewey's own
political theory, especially when he seems to imply that the trial-
and-error principle is institutionalized both in science and the
philosophy of science, on the one hand, and in the procedure of
democracy, on the other.

◀▬▶ Moral state and economic society

This brings us to the third and the last center of dispute between
Kant and Dewey. Dewey believed that Kant's political writings were

responsible for initiating a division in the German political vocabulary along the lines of *moral state* and *economic society*.[48] Dewey also suggested that the dualism in Kant's political writings was indirectly responsible for the typical German distinction between *Civilization* and *Kultur*.[49] In this section we propose to point out that these allegations of Dewey were far-fetched and that they rest on Dewey's own rendering of Kant's political ideas.

Among other writings of Kant, Dewey regarded "The Idea of a Universal Cosmopolitical History" as the principal statement of the above-mentioned dualisms. In the face of Kant's other political essays, such as "The Principles of Political Rights," "Essay on Perpetual Peace," and so forth, which are more representative of his political views, Dewey's selection of "The Idea of a Universal Cosmopolitical History" becomes significant. It is significant not because it readily supports the two dualisms that Dewey had in mind, but because a careful selection of the passages from this essay helps Dewey to read into Kant's essay the dualism of the inner and the outer. From such a basic dualism it becomes easier for Dewey to deduce the auxiliary dualisms of *moral state* and *economic society* on the one hand and of *Civilization* and *Kultur* on the other.

Kant's essay, "The Idea of a Universal Cosmopolitical History," when considered by itself, does not provide any scope for the interpretation based on the lines of inner and outer dualism. This essay of Kant is an essay on history, its purpose, and the means by which it realizes its purpose. The history is the history of Nature, and what it records is the gradual realization of Nature's purpose. The purpose of Nature is to *bring out* the moral and the rational potentialities of men in the form of "definite practical principles of action,"[50] so that they may be able to guide their conduct when they act individually or in association with others.

Now Nature brings out the moral and the rational potentialities of men by a process of conflict, or antagonism,[51] between the rational and the nonrational elements in men. The crucial question is therefore whether or not the antagonism between the rational and nonrational elements in men, as conceived by Kant, squares with Dewey's formulation of the inner and outer dualism.

Dewey appreciated the role of the negative in Hegel's philosophy of mind and history, but he failed to appreciate the same in Kant. Kant's negative is composed of sensibilities, instincts, and all other nonrational elements. For the realization of the moral and rational potentialities of men, the presence of such a negative is as much necessary to Kant as to Hegel's antithesis for the attainment of the synthesis. In sensibilities and in other nonrational elements in men, Kant sees Nature's own secret design. And this design is:

> . . . that Man shall produce wholly out of himself all that goes beyond the mechanical structure and arrangements of his animal existence, and that he shall participate in no other happiness or perfection but what he has procured for himself, apart from Instinct, by his own Reason.[52]

In order that man may be able to live a life of reason, both individually and in association with others, he must possess a rational faculty that must be both self-developed and mature. His rational faculty acquires these two characteristics by a prolonged process in which man overcomes the nonrational forces which exist within himself. The presence of these forces is essential for the self-development and maturity of man's rational capacity. And for implanting the nonrational forces in men, Nature has her own secret purpose.

> Nature seems to have taken pleasure in exercising her utmost parsimony . . . and to have measured her animal equipments very sparingly. She seems to have exactly fitted them to the most necessitous requirements of the mere beginning of an existence, as if it had been her will that Man, when he had at last struggled up from the greatest crudeness of life to the highest capability and to internal perfection in his habit of thought, and thereby also—so far as it is possible on earth—to happiness, should claim the merit of it as all his own and owe it only to himself. It thus looks as if Nature had laid more upon his rational self-esteem than upon his mere well-being. For in this movement of human life, a great host of toils and troubles wait upon man. It appears, however, that the purpose of nature was not so much that he should have an agreeable life, but that he should carry forward his own self-culture until he made himself worthy of life and well-being.[53]

The conflict between the rational and the nonrational elements in man, far from being a conflict of the inner with the outer, turns out to be one in which the self-development and maturity of the rational element depend on the presence of conflict with the nonrational. The nonrational is therefore not to be condemned at all. On the contrary, the purpose underlying its presence must be understood. Its purpose, as we have seen, is to aid and provide the scope for maturity of human reason. Without it, the human reason would not acquire the stature that is essential for the building up of a rational individual and social life.

At the social level, the conflict between the rational and the nonrational takes the shape of antagonism between the social and the unsocial propensities. By virtue of his being and reason, man is a social animal. But by virtue of his desires and the other nonrational elements in him, he is tempted to behave in an unsocial manner. These two diverse propensities, which Kant described as "unsociable sociability," are then the sources of antagonism as far as man as a member of the society is concerned.

The presence of such an antagonism in man is absolutely essential for the growth of his rational and social potentialities, on the one hand, and for the establishment of a social authority that may be intrinsically related to the needs of his rational social self, on the other. The antagonism between the social and unsocial self within the individual brings to his consciousness the true nature of his being, which is social. He also realizes in this antagonism that it is his social being that must ultimately triumph. The process of antagonism and the consequent attempt to reflect on the nature of one's being strengthens the social and the rational aspects of one's being. The presence of the unsocial, or the negative, fulfills the significant purpose of awakening the consciousness of man and thereby moves him to strengthen the social and rational aspects of his personality. His appreciation of the social and rational aspects of his personality moves him towards the establishment of a social authority that may impose restrictions on the unsocial and nonrational in him. The social authority established with such purpose behind it cannot be external to the personality of the individual. The social authority would be regarded by the individual as the institutionalization of the social and rational aspects of his own personality.

Dewey is, therefore, wide of the mark when he understands Kantian reason as an "inner" faculty perpetually battling against "outer" world of desires and sensibilities and when he conceives the Kantian conception of the state as an authority that imposes moral restrictions on the egoistical and avaricious dealings that take place in the society. Such a dualism of the inner and the outer does not exist in Kant's political writings. Its very formula indicates a total misunderstanding on the part of Dewey as far as the role of the negative in Kantian political philosophy is concerned.

Dewey is right when he says that the use of the terms "society" and "state" in German is different from their use in English.

. . . *in German literature society is a technical term and means something empirical and, so to speak, external; while the State, if not avowedly something mystic and transcendental, is at least a moral entity, the creation of self-conscious reason operating in behalf of the spiritual and ideal interests of its members. Its function is cultural, educative.*[54]

In its usage in English "the state" almost always denotes society in its more organized aspects.

Nevertheless, the beginnings of this difference are to be found not in Kant's political philosophy, as Dewey presumes on the basis of his own interpretation of Kantian "inner" and "outer" dualism, but in Hegel's philosophy. Kant did not even have a clear conception of the state or society, let alone their respective moral and economic connotations. The terms that he used were "civil society", "civil constitution," and so forth. The typical German distinction between state and society appears, as a matter of fact, in Hegel's philosophy of the state.[55] The term that Hegel used for society was "bourgeois society," in order to indicate the economic and industrial activity that takes place within it. According to Hegel, the functions of the state, as opposed to society, were directed towards the maintenance of those conditions in which justice, morality, and common good can be achieved.

Once we admit that Kant's political writings are incapable of being interpreted on the basis of inner and outer dualism, Kant can no longer be held responsible for the typical German distinction between *Civilization* and *Kultur*, which essentially rests on inner and the outer dualism. *Civilization* and *Kultur* in German can be distinguished from each other on the grounds of their respective material and spiritual implications. No such sharp distinction exists in the use of these two terms in English. The term "civilization" denotes, in English, an advanced state, both material and intellectual. Its German use confines this advancement to material and technical aspects only. When Mathew Arnold uses the term "civilization" in order to indicate "the humanization of man in society," his definition certainly implies more than material advancement. It implies the refinement of mind and spirit, a process which is in German described by *Kultur.*[56] Although a similar function of the term "culture" in English can be found, nevertheless its distinction from "civilization" is not so sharply marked off in terms of material and spiritual as it is in its German counterpart.[57]

It cannot be denied that Kant makes a very casual reference to the moral implications of the term "culture" and material implications of the term "civilization,"[58] which for Dewey is of profound significance. Nevertheless, there is nothing strictly "inner" about Kant's emphasis on the moral implications of the term "culture." Morality belongs to the realm of conduct; consequently, culture with its moral significance must guide our conduct in the external world and not merely remain a quality of mind or a quality of attitude.

The very fact that Kant makes such a casual reference to this important distinction between *civilization* and *culture* shows that it was not of his own making and that it was a commonplace in the time in which he lived.[59] If this explanation can be accepted, then an important deduction can be made from it. This deduction is as follows.

The economic and moral implications of the terms "society" and "state," respectively, in the German language, it may be argued, stem directly from the important demarcation that exists between *Civilization* and *Kultur*. Presence of certain words and their meanings sometimes give direction to certain philosophical speculations. Quite often philosophical reflections have been carried out within the framework of the meanings of certain terms. At other times, thinkers have protested against the arbitrary limitations that the accepted meanings of certain terms impose upon their reflections. As the former proposition—reflection being directed by the meaning of the term—is relevant to our purpose, we shall illustrate it. The German term *Recht*, which stands for both "right" and "law," is to a considerable degree reponsible for the organic relationship between them, as found in German political philosophies. There is no German counterpart of the British and French political thought of the seventeenth and eighteenth century that attempted to reconcile the individual with authority. After the breakdown of the ecclesiastical sanctions behind the political authority, the problems of political obligation were discussed both in Britain and in France in terms of the individual and authority. Hobbes, Locke, and Rousseau conducted the political debate of the seventeenth and eighteenth century in a language that was altogether foreign to German political experience, in spite of the fact that the withdrawal of ecclesiastical sanctions behind the political authority equally affected all three countries.

Much cannot be gained by pressing this point of meanings of terms too far, but at the same time the profound significance of the German distinction of the meanings of the terms *Civilization* and *Kultur* cannot be overlooked. As this distinction exists in the German linguistic experience, it was bound to affect different branches of speculation. Marx was not an idealist. It cannot be said of him that he borrowed his ideas on society and the state from Kant or Hegel. His originality in conceiving society and the state in terms of economic activity cannot be doubted. Society according to him was primarily economic and the state an instrument of maintaining the class structure that exists within society. However, when we consider the Marxian concept of freedom we find that Marx himself reproduces the material-spiritual distinction existing between *Civilization* and *Kultur*. Freedom, to Marx, was a freedom from economic necessity. Economic necessity is a necessity from which no one can escape. Hence freedom is not achieved until economic necessities are satisfied. When they are satisfied, our activity and spirit are no longer determined or constrained by external wants. The freedom from economic wants can then be utilized in the pursuit of ideals or self-satisfying, nonexternally determined purposes. Even when Marx visualized the *Kultur* and *Civilization* of a people as determined by the state of production and distribution in the society, he did not escape the influence of the distinction, and it reappeared in his concepts of freedom and necessity.

The division between economic society and moral state that Dewey imagined to be embryonic in Kant's political writings acted as a ferment in his own political philosophy. It was impossible for him to accept this division because behind it lay the dichotomy of Kantian epistemology. Before we examine the political concepts that Dewey formulated on the basis of a nondualistic epistemology, we must disassociate his position from the epistemological as well as the analytical dualists in political philosophy. These two types of dualism in political philosophy may be explained as follows.

There exists in political philosophy an attitude that corresponds to the Kantian theory of knowledge insofar as it regards *a priori* concepts indispensable in the understanding of the whole or a part of empirical experience. Roughly speaking, such an attitude is to be found among the idealists in political philosophy. They believe that problems concerning the nature of political institutions and political values cannot be grasped empirically, and that these problems require the aid of *a priori* concepts or reasoning based on certain *a priori* standards. Hegel, Green, and Bosanquet, for example, regarded the institution of the state as the product of reason. They did not question its origin and development in empirical terms, but only analyzed its character and teleology. All of them connected the institution of the state with either the moral needs of the individual or with the exercise of the individual's reason. They criticized those political thinkers who held that the state is a political order that is born and bred in expediency. In short, both in their analysis and in their reasoning, the idealists in political philosophy employed certain fundamental principles that were either *a priori* or without any substantial empirical reference. Although it cannot be denied that idealists like Hegel and Bosanquet revolted against the epistemological dualism of Kant, nevertheless, in their political philosophies some form of epistemological dualism continued. In this respect, then, the use of certain *a priori* concepts and arguments were indispensable to Kant, as well as the idealists in political philosophy, for the understanding of certain problems. Considering the use of *a priori* principles indispensable in the interpretation of empirical experience may be called "epistemological dualism" in political philosophy.

Analytical dualism in political philosophy may be said to be a recent development, a result of concessions made to the growing empiricism in political theory. The epistemological dualists held the view that it is impossible to grasp the nature of political institutions and political values without the aid of certain *a priori* principles. The analytical dualists, however, seek to point out the element of value of preference operating in empirical investigation on the one hand and the impossibility of using empirical premises to answer questions concerning political value on the other. Charles Beard and G. H. Sabine may be said to be the two representative proponents of analytical dualism in political philosophy. Beard maintains that although we can undertake investigations of a wide range of social and political problems with the help of the empirical techniques, behind the empirical technique itself stand certain intuitively perceived values that we seek to substantiate empirically.[60] Empirical investigation being subservient to such values, it does not and cannot investigate them.

G. H. Sabine, on the other hand, is prepared to concede to the political empiricists much more than Beard. He agrees with the political empiricists that political theory must be subjected to thoroughgoing empirical analysis. However, he presents the political empiricists with the counterquestion about whether their empirical premises are in a position to answer all the questions that we usually ask in political theory. Sabine was, to a considerable extent, a scholar of Hume, and Hume's position that the statements of "ought" cannot be deduced from the statements of "is," or that normative statements cannot be deduced from descriptive statements, repeatedly appear in Sabine's political writings. He holds that political theory cannot overlook questions concerning value and that empirical investigation of political phenomena cannot be the source of value. Consequently, political theory cannot entirely rest on empirical technique.[61]

Dewey's position in relation to the epistemological and analytical dualists in political philosophy can be estimated by bringing together some of the relevant ideas from his theories of knowledge, ethics, and political theory. As we saw in Chapter One, Dewey attributes tertiary qualities to objects for the purposes of developing the theory of common inquiry.[62] As far as Dewey is concerned, the attribution of tertiary qualities brings to an end the part played by subjective perceptions or individual intuition in the understanding of the qualities of an object or a problem. Objects and qualities from this point of view, therefore, become discernable to all. Such a public characterization of the qualities of objects and problems is not without its existential basis. In Dewey's theory of knowledge, problems arise within an existential framework and demand what he calls existential resolutions. In summary, all problems are public as well as existential.

Once the existential basis of problems is recognized, their sub-characterization is not difficult to achieve. Problems may be sub-characterized as economic, cultural, educational, scientific, or political, according to the branch of investigation in which they fall, but no class of problems can strictly be called *moral* problems. This is because problems acquire moral significance, insofar as they have consequences of good and evil, in relation to men. Now such a capacity of good and evil exists in *all* problems. Consequently what may strictly be called "moral problems" become meaningless. What becomes true instead is the moral aspect involved in every problem, an aspect that can only be discovered by examining its consequence of good or evil on the human estate or by making an estimate of the probabilities of such consequences. Nevertheless, the moral aspect of every problem does not interfere with the treatment of a problem as economic, or scientific, or political.

Such independence from the moral characterization of problems enables us to find Dewey's position in political philosophy in relation to the epistemological and analytical dualists. Since political problems, like all other problems, possess an existential and public character, they can be known to all. Although the epistemological dualists would not deny this, what they would not accept is the fact that political problems can be grasped without the use of certain *a priori* concepts. From Deweys' point of view, as we shall see in the next chapter, the role of concepts in the understanding of political phenomena or political problems cannot be denied, but what is to be objected to is their *a priori* character. In Dewey's political theory, the function of political concepts appears to be similar to the function of ideas in his theory of knowledge, that is to say, political concepts in his political theory, like ideas in his theory of knowledge, direct investigations, serve as programs of action, and get themselves tested in the process of investigation and practical manipulation.

As far as Dewey's position in relation to analytical dualism in political philosophy is concerned, the interpretation that political problems are basically existential problems is of considerable significance. Dewey would not deny to Beard the fact that the element of preference is involved in our political analysis. But he would not concede to Beard the independence in our cognitive analysis of the element of preference from the existential situation in which political problems arise. Preference to Dewey becomes meaningless unless it is offered on one's own suggestion for overcoming a particular problematic situation. Under the circumstances, Dewey and Beard do not consider the question of preference within the same frame of reference. Apart from the fact that Dewey's preference, unlike Beard's, is arrived at by a conscious cognitive process, Dewey considers the question of preference only with reference to the specific problem and its solution, not, as Beard does, to the whole of the phenomena. The question of preference can therefore be brought within the empirical and existential framework less inconveniently than it can be in the case of Beard. For Beard, preference is an expression of a fundamental attitude towards social and political order, whereas for Dewey it is merely the expression of what one regards as one's efficacious choice.

Dewey's position in relation to the analytical dualism of Sabine, however, remains vague. Deweyan ethics in the last analysis is an intellectualistic ethics. Having strongly opposed the *a priori* and absolutistic positions in moral philosophy from which the principles of obligation can be deduced, Dewey leaves the individual with nothing but particular situations, on the one hand, and, on the other, critical intelligence to discover what conduct would be appropriate in them. Critical intelligence may be able to point out the deficiency in the situation and the efficacy of a particular act of behavior, but it cannot by itself generate *obligation*. What appears to be intellectually *correct* is not as compelling or obligatory in terms of conduct as what appears to be *right*. Psychological or traditional associations of the latter are not the only sources of its strength. However one defines it, few general principles can be framed on the basis of "right" for the purposes of guiding our conduct. Obligation is then rendered to the principles that are relevant to the conduct and not to any abstract conception of right and wrong. What can be pronounced as intellectually correct remains, in comparison to what can be called morally right, a conception without any intrinsic relation to conduct. Psychologically speaking, it does not generate any feeling of obligation to act.

The absence of the ethics of obligation is therefore responsible for the total absence of the problem of political obligation in Dewey's system of thought. Therefore, when Sabine says that normative statements cannot be deduced from descriptive statements, Dewey has practically no answer. However, it must be pointed out that Dewey does not build his community by tying his citizens to the common principles of political obligation. The bonds of his community lie partly in the community's own consciousness of its wants and aspirations. Free inquiry, communication of the results of research, and education are the foundations of Dewey's community. While the individual is engaged in free inquiry, research, and exchange of ideas, what binds him to his community in his basic realization that he is *part* of the community. Such an intellectual conviction is sufficient, as far as Dewey is concerned, for the individual to be conscious of his civic obligation.

Before we close this section on the manner in which Dewey reacted to the ideas of Kant, three points must be mentioned. First, in Dewey's political theory, the Kantian union of perception and conception plays a very important part. Second, Dewey attempted to formulate political concepts that may be regarded as his alternative suggestions to Kant's alleged dualism of economic society and moral state. Third, Sabine criticized Dewey's antianalytical dualism in political philosophy. As all these topics are closely connected with our interpretation of different aspects of Dewey's political theory, we shall examine them in Chapter Four, which is specially devoted to the task of interpreting Dewey's political theory.

Dewey and Green

Dewey's relationship with Green, unlike his relationship with Kant, is one of initial admiration and subsequent disagreement. Dewey had no kind word to spare for the philosophical achievements of Kant. He opposed all forms of dualism and, for him, Kant was somehow the source of most of them. Nevertheless, Kant seemed to exhaust Dewey's obsession with antidualism. Consequently, while examining the ideas of Green, Dewey could concentrate on problems that were free from the dualism-antidualism controversy. Having been introduced to philosophy at a period when the influence of idealism was at its peak on both sides of the Atlantic, Dewey began with considerable respect and admiration for Green, but this did not last for long. The subsequent change in his own philosophical position made him a critic of the formalistic element in Green's moral philosophy. However, Green's ethical values continued to exercise a good deal of influence on Dewey's own political philosophy, even afterwards, when he had discarded their metaphysical foundations.

What initially attracted Dewey towards Green was the latter's criticism of the British empirical philosophy. Green appeared to Dewey as the counterpart of his own teacher, G. S. Morris, who was also critically examining the British empirical philosophy, although not from the same point of view as Green.

In the year 1889, Dewey published his first paper on Green, which he called by the title of "The Philosophy of Thomas Hill Green."[63] Although the paper's title referred to Green's philosophy, it was restricted to the exposition of Green's thesis on the common spiritual presuppositions of ordinary experience, on the one hand and of moral and religious experience and science on the other.[64] Green's metaphysics, in other words, was regarded by Dewey at this stage to be the biggest contribution of Green to philosophy. Seven years before the publication of this paper, Dewey himself had published his first written work under the title of "The Metaphysical Assumptions of Materialism"[65] in which he had emphatically argued on the inevitable incompleteness of a materialistic philosophy, and on the need of positing more than material substance to be able to answer the question of how the knowledge of matter becomes possible. His first paper on Green, therefore, indicates the continuity of his attitude towards the metaphysical basis of all the theories of knowledge. A very important part of Dewey's subsequent philosophy rests on our correct understanding of his attitude towards Green's thesis of the spiritual presuppositions of science and moral experience. The following analysis indicates the extent of Dewey's appreciation of the metaphysical problems involved in Green's theory of experience and knowledge.

Green's thesis on the spiritual presuppositions of ordinary experience and science, on the one hand, and of moral and religious experience, on the other, rested on his postulate that different spheres of experience have their own *uniqueness,* but in themselves are not *self-sufficient.* Innumerable illustrations can be cited in support of the contention of the uniqueness of different spheres of experience. The field of poetic experience, for instance, can neither be understood nor judged in terms of any other experience. It belongs to a sphere of experience of its own and therefore must be judged in the light of its own intrinsic standards. Similarly, scientific experiences, as well as moral experiences, have their own uniquenesses. A scientific experience, for instance, is a kind of *orderly* experience. It is orderly because it implies the working out of relations and laws that are not visible on the surface.[66] A moral experience is unique because it seeks to discriminate between practical actions as they are and as they ought to be.[67]

Now as far as the incompleteness of these two spheres of experience is concerned, Green's argument may be presented in the following way.

Speaking from the point of view of logic as well as actual fact, scientific and moral experiences imply the presence of human consciousness. These two spheres of experience do not exist by themselves. They are the two parts of the total human consciousness. The human consciousness is a kind of organization brought about by the human self in which different spheres of experience take their proper places. In Green's metaphysics, not only is a sphere of experience dependent on human consciousness, but the human consciousness itself is dependent on what Green calls "the divine consciousness." The human consciousness is for him the reproduction of the divine consciousness. The divine consciousness, through the human consciousness, aims at attaining the *whole* of experience, or "a nature of things," as Green calls it.[68] No matter which sphere of experience we consider, its knowledge implies human as well as divine consciousness. They are, in other words, the extrasuppositions of all the kinds of experience.

This summary of Dewey's appreciation of Green's metaphysics clearly indicates Dewey's familiarity with the problem of presupposition involved in the understanding of different spheres of experience. It also indicates Dewey's awareness of the fact that the knowledge of the presuppositions of any particular sphere of experience enables us to judge its relevance to another sphere of experience. That is to say, if *orderliness* of laws and relations is the presupposition of scientific experience, then orderliness also helps us to judge whether scientific experience is of relevance to moral experience or not. This would certainly necessitate the enumeration of the presuppositions involved in moral experience; nevertheless, orderliness as the enumerated presupposition of scientific experience would facilitate the process of enumerating the presuppositions of moral experience, as it would also help us to judge the relevance of these two spheres of experience to each other.

But surprisingly enough, in subsequent writings in which he displayed a great interest in methodology, Dewey did not return to the question of presuppositions that were involved in his own theory of inquiry. His early training in the logic and epistemology of the idealists, in addition to two of his papers, "The Metaphysical Assumptions of Materialism" (1882), and "The Philosophy of Thomas Hill Green" (1889), leaves no doubt as to his acquaintance with the philosophical problem concerning presuppositions. Why, then, did he totally overlook the question concerning presuppositions of his own theory of inquiry? The answer to this question can only be found in the significant difference that exists between Green's conception of "experience" and Dewey's. Dewey, unlike Green, does not acknowledge the uniqueness of any particular sphere of experience. For him, as we have already seen, every experience is essentially an *existential* experience. Scientific experience, as well as moral experience, can therefore be conceived within the framework of a common existential experience. Likewise, as we have also seen, the experimental theory of inquiry has a universal application. Different existential factors no doubt operate in different problems, but they do not restrict the scope of the application of his experimental theory of enquiry. What they merely demand is a different treatment within the framework of a common inquiry. Thus, by maintaining the unity of experience and universality of particular theory of inquiry, Dewey felt himself exempted from the obligation of going into the philosophical problem of presuppositions.

The omission of the problem of presuppositions did have far-reaching consequences on Dewey's political theory. The lack of examination on his part of the claim of total relevance of the method of science to politics resulted in the inability of his theory of inquiry to ask all the relevant questions in politics. One of the relevant questions in politics that his theory of inquiry did not and could not ask was: What part do value reflections play in influencing and in guiding the organizational activity of politics? By not raising this question, Dewey no doubt remained consistent, because such a claim would have indicated the limitations in the claims of his own theory of inquiry. On the other hand, this resulted in restricting the very empirical data of overt behavior in politics to those activities whose organizational reference could be precisely and empirically stated. It therefore ignored all those activities that are prompted by vague ideals and nebulous beliefs, the activities whose organizational reference is not precisely indicated by their expressed aspirations. Take, for instance, the political activity that is prompted by the ideal of economic equality. Such an activity has no precise organizational goal to indicate; nevertheless, to the extent that such activities in politics are numerous and to the extent that they are excluded, the investigation of political phenomena is impoverished.

Similarly, as far as practical organizational measures are concerned, the manipulative pattern that science offers does not prove to be an adequate model for the problems of manipulation in politics. Even the cooperative conception of authority in science, which Dewey recommends for politics, seems to ignore the differences in the quality of problems that are faced by an authority in science and an authority in politics. A detailed examination of the relevance of the method of science to politics will be undertaken in the next chapter. Meanwhile, suffice it to say that Dewey's inability to return to the problems that he appreciated in Green made him totally oblivious of some of the vital problems that his political theory raised.

The two subsequent papers on Green, "Green's Theory of the Moral Motive" and "Self-Realization as the Moral Ideal," published in 1892 and 1893, respectively, are of some significance from the point of view of Dewey's subsequent political values. They also indicate Dewey's growing suspicion of the element of Kantian formalism in Green's ethics.

The formalistic element in Green centered around his conception of the self, which, from Green's point of view, expressed itself ideally when there was unity in conduct. This for Green became the supreme ethical ideal. Dewey examined this ideal from a practical point of view. Dewey was prepared to admit that there is some kind of longing in the human self to think of itself as one single whole, over and above the diverse activities in which it is engaged. Did Green mean by unity in conduct a psychological unity? The answer was clear from Green's point of view: unity in conduct is more than a mere psychological unity, it is some kind of *practical* ideal. And being an ideal to be realized, it demands adequate social conditions, the adequate social condition being the "social unity" itself. These social conditions are not presented in actuality; consequently, not only unattainable social conditions are demanded, but the ideal is far too remote to act as a guide to conduct. An ideal that fails to guide human conduct on account of its excessive demands begins to exercise a negative influence.[69] Green's ideal of unity in conduct, as Dewey saw it, therefore, is not only a logical abstraction, but would, if accepted, paralyze action instead of guide it.

At the end of this paper, Dewey felt that he had not got down to the root of Green's problem: The abstraction in Green's ideal of unity in conduct stemmed from a still more abstract motion of the self. "Self-Realization as a Moral Ideal" therefore undertook a detailed criticism of Green's conception of the self.

The polarity between Greens' ideal and actual conditions, which exercised a paralyzing influence on human actions, encouraged Dewey to look at the ethical problem from a practical point of view: this problem, he now felt, centered around the attempt of the active human self to realize itself. Ethics, therefore, must not overlook the fact that the self is active and that its realization implies performing overt acts in the midst of concrete situations.

In conceiving of the self as active and realizing itself in the midst of concrete situations, however, Dewey does not establish a concept independent of Kant's and Green's notions of the abstract self. Neither Kant nor Green deny a dynamic character to the self; moreover, neither of the two conceive of the activity of the self *in vacuo*. In order for Dewey to disassociate his conception of the self from theirs, it was necessary for him to point out that their conception of the self was a preconception, existing before it is realized. Dewey therefore conceded, on the one hand, that the conception of the active self does convey a true picture of the self, but that, on the other, its dynamic and overt characteristics would be negated if it were to be regarded as something that exists in advance, for in that case its activity would only amount to "filling up" what already exists.[70] The problem of self-realization, Dewey therefore concluded, is a double problem, for it must not only take into account *how* the self realizes itself, but also *what in actual fact* the self is.

Now it may be argued that there are two ways of inferring the self. One may take into account human activities and point out that they *imply* the presence of a self. The advantage of such an argument is obvious, because the presence of a self now becomes only a matter of inference. That is to say, activity does not emanate from the formal self, but the self is implied by its activity.

The other possibility is of inferring the self from its purposive or intended activities. This would make the self identical with its realization, thereby abandoning the conception of an antecedent self and attempting to make the self a product of those activities that we call by the name of self-realizing activities. For a *present self* is substituted what might be called the conception of a *future self*. Dewey seems to infer the self according to this second argument.

> *The notion which I would suggest as substitute (as against the notion of an antecedent self) is that of the self as always a concrete* specific activity; *and, therefore . . . of the identity of self and realization.*[71]

But a conception of the self that identifies it with its own realizing activities is not without its difficulties, for what is realized in actual practice is so very varied and disjointed that it would be absurd to regard its sum total as constituting the human self.

Dewey, it appears, fails to discriminate between the theoretical and practical considerations involved in the definition of the self and the problem of its realization. Theoretically speaking, it is the self that is realized, and before it can be realized, it must exist: In order to realize my ambition of having an automobile, I must have the desire and the means to have an automobile. The desire and means are no doubt *for* possessing an automobile, but they are not *of* an automobile but of myself. Even if it were to be maintained that only in its realization the self becomes a reality, nevertheless it cannot be denied that something called the self did exist before its realization was undertaken.[72]

Dewey's objection to the conception of an antecedent self is that its realization means the "filling up" of what already exists. But it may be argued that "filling up" is an incorrect analogy. One can have the conception of an antecedent self and yet believe its realization may "bring out" what is implicit in it.

Although Dewey utilized Green's conception of self-realization only in order to arrive at his own conception of the self, his own thesis on self-realization was also embryonic in it. The idea of self-realization is implicit in a conception of the self that is essentially a *prospective self*. The prospective self is the product of purposive or intended activities. Such activities are also carried on through a cultural medium. Dewey's conception of the prospective self therefore invites an analysis both of the purposes of the self as well as of the cultural medium through which they are achieved.

The position that the self has purposes of its own to achieve compelled Dewey to recognize the presence of an *existing* self, and this was recognized by Dewey in his subsequent writings. The next question was how the self comes to acquire its purposes and values. Dewey's answer to this question is to be found in his social psychology. The values and purposes that we possess at any given time are initially furnished by the social milieu in which we live and act, but we do not totally accept what is believed to be socially desirable because our native propensities, arising out of our unique emotional makeup, interact with what is supposed to be socially desirable. What we therefore come to possess, in the end, in the form of our purposes and values, is the product of interaction between what is socially acceptable and what our propensities induce us to achieve. Our values and purposes, being the product of such an interaction, remain in a state of constant change.

Not only the determination but also the realization of our values and purposes is the product of interaction. Our values and purposes are realized through the cultural medium, which may be said to be the product of the interaction and consequent institutionalization of the various activities—economic, social, political, educational, religious, scientific, aesthetic, and so forth—that take place within the society. Their institutionalization indicates the settled ways in which these activities are carried out. Institutionalized activities serve both as means and obstacles in the realization of our purposes and values. Sometimes they succeed in imposing limitations on our values and purposes, and sometimes we succeed in modifying them. Therefore what comes to be realized in the end is the product of interaction between the institutionalized activities of the cultural medium, on the one hand, and our values and purposes, on the other.

Green's ideal of unity in conduct demanding social unity for its realization therefore had its counterpart in Dewey's philosophy, for Dewey, like Green, insisted on the presence of an adequate cultural medium for the realization of the purposes and values of the individual. However, Dewey's conception of the society and the interacting social molecules within it was much too *processive* to allow him to visualize a state of social equilibrium in which would obtain an adequate cultural medium for all times to come. Thus, the search for an adequate cultural medium remained with Dewey a constant intellectual and practical problem.[73]

Earlier Political Writings: Maine, Austin, and Hobbes

The three different papers on political theory that we propose to consider in this section indicate the states through which Dewey's political ideas evolved. They also raise certain important problems around which Dewey's subsequent political ideas were developed.

Dewey's first paper on political theory, namely, "The Ethics of Democracy,"[74] appeared in 1888, the year in which he had also published a book, *Leibniz's New Essays Concerning the Human Understanding*. Leibnizian organicism was therefore likely to affect Dewey's treatment of problems of political philosophy. This paper in fact displayed the pitch of Dewey's affinity with the organicist political philosophy. It attempted to defend democracy from an organicist point of view against Henry Maine's atomistic interpretation of it. The paper also undertook to criticize the quantitative and mechanistic approach to politics.

Dewey's exposition of the organicist political philosophy and criticism of the quantitative and mechanistic method centers around the theme of democracy. Maine had succeeded in deprecating democracy because he took for granted that democracy was a mere *form* of government. Democracy when considered as a mere form of government easily lends itself to a quantitative treatment. From the ideas of Hobbes, Bentham, and Austin on sovereignty, Maine had derived the notion that each society can be divided into *rulers* and *subjects*. To such a division, Maine had applied Aristotle's quantitative method in order to arrrive at the conclusion that although democracy is a government by many, this many is nothing but an amorphous mass, corrupt in its motives and led by self-seeking politicians. Corruption and self-interest are the two main characteristics of the will of the mass that governs a democracy.

Dewey thought that in this treatment of democracy Maine was guilty of a double error. Maine himself was noted for his criticism of the school of social contract from the point of view of history and anthropology. Along with the fiction of the social contract, Maine had rejected looking at society from an atomistic point of view. However, what Maine denied to the contractualists, he permitted himself in his condemnation of democracy, for no better reasons. Maine was therefore not free from inconsistency. Furthermore, Maine did not take enough pains to go beyond Aristotle's quantitative method. Had he taken into consideration Aristotle's philosophy of law, he would have seen the organicist in Aristotle.[75]

Such a criticism of Maine did not leave Dewey altogether satisfied. He began to feel that Maine had not successfully presented the case of an approach in politics—the quantitative and mechanistic—which had widespread appeal; consequently, he decided to critically examine this method himself.

Dewey, we must remember, had written his "Ethics of Democracy" (1888), a year before he had published "The Philosophy of Thomas Hill Green" (1889). His paper on Green, as we have already seen, welcomed Green's emphasis on the uniqueness of different spheres of experience. In his "Ethics of Democracy," we find the roots of Dewey's subsequent agreement with Green's thesis.[76] Here Dewey maintained that the attempt to understand society in terms of atomistic individuals is basically an attempt to apply the quantitative and mechanistic method of physics to politics, also that concepts and methods are intrinsically related to the sphere of experience from which they are abstracted. As each sphere of experience has its own uniqueness, its concepts and methods are of no relevance to any other. Consequently, a nonorganicist political philosophy, by applying the method of physics to politics, displays, therefore, only its own lack of appreciation of the uniqueness of these two spheres of experience.

This was the negative side of his criticism of the mechanistic method. On the positive side, Dewey maintained that only an organicist method is useful in understanding the true nature of society.

Society, as a real whole, is the normal order, and the mass as an aggregate of isolated units is the fiction.[77]

Such a notion of society required a detailed working out of the relation of parts to the real whole and of a common will, through which the parts express themselves in the will of the whole. Not being sufficiently equipped with any original reasoning on the part-whole relationship, Dewey went on repeating over and over again the fact that the individual apart from his membership of the community is inconceivable. The conception of the individual, on account of such a limited description, suffered considerably. The "individual" and the "integral part of the whole" became convertible terms. In all his activities and utterances, the individual is considered to be one aspect or another of the society; even his antisocial and corrupt motives come to be regarded as the expressions of the decadent aspect of the social whole. To such an all-round part-whole relationship, the individual's opinion or vote could not be an exception, consequently, it becomes:

. . . a manifestation of some tendency of the social organism through a member of that organism.[78]

The antithesis between the organicist and the mechanistic approaches to politics that Dewey felt very strongly at this stage was subsequently reconciled in his own political writings. All Dewey's references to the human groupings such as family, society, and state indicate his organicist attitude, from the primary associated living and acting to a kind of communal existence with the highest degree of communication and participation. On the other hand, his mature political ideas speak of the need to consider political problems in nonqualitative terms. Nonqualitative treatment is not essentially a quantitative or mechanistic treatment; nevertheless, for a quantitative treatment what is indispensable is the nonquantitative statement of the problem.

This reconciliation between the organicist and mechanistic attitudes seeems to have been brought about by Dewey's acceptance of the pluralist position. Pluralism did not destroy his organicism, but merely converted it into an organicist attitude with which all the human groupings could be viewed organically. Moreover, within his organicist attitude the conception of part-whole relation was replaced by the conception of *interaction* or *interdependence* of the parts to one another. Consequently, the consideration of parts as parts did not destroy the whole, but, on the contrary, afforded an opportunity for the better understanding of the interaction or inter-dependence of one part to the other.

"The Ethics of Democracy" indicated the presence of an attitude that considered politics as a branch of morals. At this stage Dewey had no conception of political activity as a unique activity that could be considered independently of the moral problems involved. Although he did not go into the details of the relationship between the state and society (or social organism), he certainly was far from regarding the government as mere administrative machinery or a mere *device.*

A government springs from a vast mass of sentiments, many vague, some defined, of instincts, of aspirations, of ideas, of hopes and fears, of purposes. It is their reflex and their incorporation; their projection and outgrowth.[79]

On a similar ground, Dewey sought the ethical justification of democracy. Democracy was regarded by Dewey as the political response to certain moral requirements of human nature. Morality consists in experiencing and realizing what is worth experiencing and realizing all by ourselves. The opportunities for practicing morality are provided by democracy only.[80] To regard democracy as a mere "product of a whole series of accidents,"[81] as Maine did, is merely to display a lack of understanding of the moral foundations of democracy.

In Dewey's *Public and Its Problems,* the attitude emerged that political activity is unique and therefore deserves to be investigated independently as well as in conjunction with other activities. In this work, Dewey was prepared to consider political activity as primarily concerned with the problems of organizing the consequences of coexistence and conjoint activity. Such an attitude towards political activity gave him an altogether different outlook on democracy. He admitted that there is something like political democracy, a device to make the organizational work of the society more efficient.[82] As far as the origin of *political* democracy is concerned, Dewey came very near Maine's view that democracy is "a product of a whole series of accidents." His subsequent view on democracy was as follows:

> *Political democracy has emerged as a kind of net consequence of a vast multitude of responsive adjustments to a vast number of situations, no two of which were alike, but which tended to converge to a common outcome.*

Further, democracy is not,

> ... *the product of democracy, of some inherent nisus, or immanent idea.*[83]

However, political democracy did not exhaust the scope of the *procedure* of democracy. From the operation of the procedure of democracy in the political field, a certain principle of considerable significance to all aspects of human activity emerges: the trial-and-error principle. It can be used for perfecting the procedure of democracy as well as for making other activities more fruitful. But it would be a mistake to regard the procedure of political democracy as the only source of trial-and-error principle. Its real sources are, as we shall see in detail later on, the human search for a dependable form of knowledge and the desirable form of government.

Two other papers on political theory, "Austin's Theory of Sovereignty" (1894)[84] and "The Motivation of Hobbes's Political Philosophy" (1918),[85] are important for their direct bearing on Dewey's mature political ideas. The paper on Austin suggests Dewey's appreciation of the role of concept in illuminating the intricacies of a phenomenon. The paper on Hobbes indicates among other things his admiration for Hobbes's attempt to frame a systematic scheme of concepts and to analyze political phenomena with its help. These two papers manifest, therefore, the two important stages of the evolution of Dewey's political ideas.

Dewey was sympathetic neither towards the premises nor towards the conclusions of Austin's theory of sovereignty. Nevertheless, what he admired in Austin was his use of the concept of *determinateness.* This concept helped Austin to grasp the intricate relationship that exists between the agencies that are legally and morally sovereign, on the one hand, and positive law and moral law, on the other.

Austin's reference to the concept of determinateness is quite explicit in his following definition of the legal sovereignty.

If a determinate *human superior not in a habit of obedience to a like superior receive* habitual *obedience from the bulk of a given society, that determinate superior is sovereign in that society, and the society (including the superior) is a society political and independent.*

The fact that Austin, being a jurist, should have emphasized a precise source of the legal sovereignty was not a matter of surprise to anyone and least of all to Dewey. However, Dewey repeatedly asked himself the question as to why Austin put such great emphasis on determinateness in order to define legal sovereignty, to the point that this emphasis on determinateness drove him beyond the concept of a determinate group of persons to develop the concept of "a determinate human superior." What must have enhanced Dewey's curiosity was the fact that Austin was defining legal sovereignty in the early nineteenth century, when "the King in Parliament" was a fairly satisfactory definition of the legal sovereignty for the jurists in Britain. Was Austin then putting the clock back by making "the determinate human superior" instead of the King in Parliament the source of legal sovereignty? In order to find Austin's answer to this question, Dewey concentrated on Austin's underlying concept of determinateness.

Dewey discovered, on close examination of Austin, that determinateness was not confined to the discrimination between the determinate human superior and the King in Parliament, but that it was also used to discriminate between the positive law and the moral law, between the actual sources of law as opposed to the real sources of law. Positive law enjoys the same degree of precision over the moral law as the determinate human superior over the King in Parliament. Theoretically speaking, Austin was prepared to acknowledge the superiority of moral law, which consists of public opinion, sentiments, beliefs, and so forth, over the positive law. But in matters of actual obedience, Austin showed his preference for positive law on account of its determinateness. Similarly, guided by the considerations of determinateness, Austin again showed his preference for the actual sources of law rather than the real sources of law.

The real sources of law, embracing morality, public conscience, public pressure, customs, traditions, and so forth, are indeed very indeterminate. But the actual sources of law, which may be said to consist of legal agencies, are invariably not as determinate as Austin thinks. The U.S. Congress, the President, and the Supreme Court together enjoy the legal sovereignty in the United States. As actual sources of law such a combination is only relatively determinate, although their combination is indeed more specific than the real sources of law. The U.S. Congress, the President, and the Supreme Court stand in an intricate relationship with the American Constitution. Constitutional law in the United States may not be the actual source of positive law, but it determines the framework within which the three parts operate as the sources of positive law. The actuality of the sources of positive law in the United States is, therefore, difficult to determine on account of the intricate relationship of the three different organs of the government to one another and to the Constitution.

At the end of his analysis, Dewey felt that there was nothing wrong with Austin's technique of approaching the subject but that Austin's concept of *determinateness* was responsible for his inability to make a universal discrimination between the actual and the real sources of law. His concept implied a kind of gap or difference between the two sources that in actual fact does not exist. Consequently from the very start, Austin was handicapped by the presence of a defective conceptual apparatus.

This then was Dewey's earliest exercise in concept-making and concept-testing. It was an exercise that was in part vicarious and in part self-conscious. It was vicarious because Dewey imagined himself to be in Austin's place, watching the intricacies of the problem illuminated by Austin's concept, and it was self-conscious because Dewey was gradually becoming aware of the requirements of an alternative scheme of concepts and hypotheses required for investigating political phenomena. It was in *The Public and Its Problems* that he fulfilled such a requirement.

Dewey's paper, "The Motivation of Hobbes's Political Philosophy" (1918) is of considerable importance to us because of his aim, although he does not actually achieve it. The term "motivation" in the title of his paper is meant to indicate the methodological considerations that lie behind Hobbes's political philosophy, rather than any personal or political motivation, of which Hobbes was accused by a number of thinkers. The paper also indicates Dewey's attitude at this stage: he was now in search of a fresh attitude towards political theory, prompted by the emergence of his own philosophical ideas. His *Studies in Logical Theory* (1903) had defined his attitude towards reflective thought in general and laid the foundation of his naturalistic logic. His *Ethics* (1908) enabled him to make statements concerning right, value, and "moral judgments as judgments of practice" in naturalistic and practical terms. His two important works—*Experience and Nature* (1929), setting forth his naturalistic metaphysics, and *The Quest of Certainty* (1929), setting forth his theory of inquiry, based on theory and practice in the natural sciences—were yet to be published. Nevertheless, his paper on Hobbes, Dewey attempted to formulate an attitude towards political theory that could be easily assimilated within the existing organization of his ideas.

In our search for fresh attitudes, we invariably identify ourselves with the ideas of another thinker. After an initial identification, when we become aware of our differences, in all probability we continue to accept the *problems* that he recognizes. A large number of controversies center around the approaches to problems rather than the problems themselves. Dewey's relation with Hobbes can be understood within the framework of such an explanation. In search of a new attitude towards political theory, Dewey in the beginning identified himself with Hobbes. But soon he discovered that Hobbes's entire political theory rested on a defective psychological foundation. Consequently, his identification with Hobbes came to be restricted to the problems that Hobbes recognized.

From the point of view of Dewey's mature political ideas, Hobbes had more than one attraction. Hobbes had attempted to assimilate other branches of knowledge into his scientific materialism based on "motion." As far as Hobbes's political theory was concerned, such an assimiliation was not difficult to achieve. The psychological foundation on which Hobbes' political theory rests could be easily defined in terms of motion. Thus Hobbes framed the natural laws of human behavior and succeeded in assimilating psychology and politics into the natural sciences of the seventeenth century. The methodological significance of Hobbes's attempt was not unknown to Dewey. He was aware of its defects and its possibilities.

Dewey himself was engaged in an attempt that was similar to Hobbes's. Methodologically speaking, he too was engaged in assimilating morals and politics into a theory of inquiry based on natural sciences. Both Hobbes and Dewey aimed at extending the validity of the natural sciences of their own times to the study of politics. Hobbes extended the laws of motion from natural phenomena to psychological and political phenomena—the behavior of individuals and groups engaged in political activity—thereby achieving a unity. Dewey achieved a unity of framing a theory of knowledge based on experimental natural sciences and by extending its validity to morals and politics. In Hobbes, therefore, Dewey discovered one of his earliest precursors, and his interest in the problem underlying Hobbes's philosophy, that of a comprehensive method, continued.

For the first time in his political writings, he used terms like "scientific method," "empirical method," "historical settings," "science of human nature," "moral and political science," and so forth. Dewey believed that the greatness of Hobbes lay in his attempt to secularize politics and to put it on a scientific basis.[86] But he also felt that Hobbes's attempt loses all its significance unless it is considered in its historical perspective:[87] that the consideration of Hobbes's political theory in historical settings alone can furnish us with his "motivation."

The purpose of considering Hobbes's ideas in their historical settings was essentially to point out the close relation between Hobbes's political theory and the ideas of seventeenth-century science. Quite inadvertently, however, Dewey introduced within his main thesis on historical relativism another thesis that might be called "the relativism of apparently contradictory ideas." Under the spell of his latter thesis, Dewey began to argue that Hobbes was not as antitheological as is commonly supposed:

He is theological in motive and content in the sense that he is deliberately antitheological.[88]

This obscure statement, if we understand it correctly, can only mean that in spite of Hobbes's effort to be antitheological—explaining of human behavior in terms of the laws of nature instead of the fall and the redemption, and justifying political obligation in terms of expediency instead of religious and theological sanctions—his arguments basically remained theological. They had been formulated at a period in history when the controversy between the church and the state still dominated political thinking. Consequently, in spite of his scientific materialism and geometrical and deductivistic rationalism, Hobbes never became a godless person: on the contrary, he exalted reason to the same heights that believers exalt God. Having done this, Hobbes went on to say that reason alone can discover the divine will and design. In his words:

> There is no law of natural reason that can be against the law divine: for God Almighty hath given reason to man to be a light unto him.[89]

Dewey succeeded in establishing his thesis on the relativism of apparently contradictory ideas with the help of Hobbes's text, but he very nearly destroyed his first and principal thesis on historical relativism that claimed to demonstrate the relation between Hobbes's political theory and the seventeenth-century natural sciences. His analysis was deflected because it did not produce the intended results. His original intention was not to establish the point that however contradictory and mutually critical certain ideas are, they are ultimately related to one another at a particular time and place. On the contrary, what he wanted to establish was the relation between the dominant ideas in mathematics and physics in Hobbes's time on the one hand and his political theory on the other. Instead of that, Dewey considered the ideas of Hobbes in their historical settings only in order to discover what he did not want the ideas to reveal. Dewey proved Hobbes to be theological, *in spirit* if not in utterance, while he wished to prove him a thinker who worked out in detail the ideas of science in psychology and in political theory.

Although Dewey's principal thesis on the discovery of the connection between the seventeeenth century developments in science and mathematics and the political theory of Hobbes remained unattempted and unsubstantiated, he took the conclusions of this thesis for granted. Hobbes was declared by him to be "scientific" in political theory because he:

> . . . deduces the need, the purpose, and the limits of sovereign power from his rationalistic, or utilitarian, premises . . .[90]

But in what relation the method of Hobbes—postulating certain rationalistic or utilitarian axioms and deducing general conclusions from them—stood with reference to his own time was not argued out, in spite of the fact that Dewey's paper claimed to consider Hobbes in his historical settings.[91]

From the standpoint of Dewey's political philosophy, Hobbes was not only a scientific political theorist, but the first of his kind. He was the Galileo of political theory in the age of Galileo. Hobbes was, in fact, one of the first few modern thinkers at whose hands political reflection took place outside the framework of medieval theology and the aesthetic rationalism of the Greeks. Like Galileo, who viewed physical phenomena quantitatively, Hobbes stated his investigation of political phenomena in purely *political* terms. Again like Galileo, who did a great service to physical science by emancipating it from the aesthetic qualities of the Greek physical science, Hobbes rescued politics from theology and gave a realistic empirical turn to ethics by founding it on psychological utilitarianism. From his own point of view, therefore, Hobbes's contribution to political theory deserved much greater attention than Dewey actually paid.

The search for a new attitude in political theory on the part of Dewey, which began with considerable sympathy and admiration for the ideas of Hobbes, did not go far enough. Before he could completely and correctly analyze the unity of scientific method in Hobbes's ideas, his interest in him began to fade. He began to distrust Hobbes's psychology. Although his paper on Hobbes ended with a note that a better psychological foundation would remove all the defects of Hobbes's political theory,[92] in actual fact Hobbes's entire attempt began to appear to him as pseudoscientific. In his last major work on political philosophy, namely *Freedom and Culture* (1939), Dewey went as far as regarding Hobbes's scientific political theory as a tautology. This is because while the political theory of Hobbes rested on his deductions from psychology, Dewey felt that his psychology itself was based on the pattern of his politics.[93]

On the Threshold of a Scientific Political Theory

The difference in Dewey's attitude towards political theory, as revealed in his *Ethics of Democracy* (1888), and in his paper, "Austin's Theory of Sovereignty" (1894), in spite of a gap of only six years, is considerable. Considered in terms of their respective attitudes towards political activity, the works belong to radically different traditions in political philosophy. In the former, political activity is not treated as something unique, but merely as a branch of moral activity. This was largely due to the fact that Dewey in this work did not consider the government and the governed in terms of the unique relationship that he later called "the political relationship."

In order to have a distinct conception of the political relationship, we must first of all admit the uniqueness of political activity, as distinct from moral or economic or industrial activity, on the ground that it is an activity undertaken in order to regulate and control the affairs of society. Although such an activity does have moral and economic implications, it remains distinctly political, because its primary function is to organize and regulate different needs and problems of society. Political activity is largely carried on within governmental institutions and on their periphery. It is by virtue of this that the relationship between the citizen and government becomes political.

In his first paper, Dewey, in his anxiety to defend democracy against the tirades of Maine, as we have already seen, declared democracy to be an essential condition of morality and government and an instrument that registers and executes the moral will of individuals. What was therefore overlooked was the fact that government is composed of men whose business it is to govern, responsibly or otherwise. Responsibility may or may not be a quality of the government. Only a clear distinction between morals and politics and a clear conception of their interrelation can reveal the essentially political character of a government, with or without moral implications.

The above-mentioned, essentially *political* nature of government seems to be implicit in Dewey's paper on Austin. Our analysis of Dewey's treatment of Austin has centered around Austin's use of the concept of *determinateness*. The change in Dewey's attitude towards government as essentially *political* is not hard to find. We have already seen that Dewey was not prepared to admit Austin's clear-cut distinction between the real and actual sources of law. Behind Dewey's rejection of Austin's point of view lies Dewey's desire to secure the responsibility and subordinate legal sovereignty to the real sources of law—namely, morality, public opinion, custom, beliefs, and economic need. Since legal sovereignty is always located in the various organs of the government, what Dewey was trying to secure in his refusal to admit the distinction between actual and real sources of law was the responsibility of the government to the citizen. Dewey's point of view was essentially ethical, but what was tacitly implied in it was the possibility of a government that may be purely *political* and hence irresponsible. All that Dewey wanted was *political* government to be morally responsible. This was, therefore, a substantial advance as far as Dewey's attitude towards the nature of political activity was concerned. It probably expressed Dewey's anxiety that political activity could become an amoral activity and that it is our task to make it moral.

By the time Dewey published his paper, "The Motivation in Hobbes's Political Philosophy" (1918), the conception of political activity as unique and of the political relationship as different from other forms of social and economic relationships was deeply entrenched in his mind. Dewey admired Hobbes for his attempt to analyze political relationships in nontheological terms, and moreover, for his attempt to analyze political relationships with the help of axiomatic laws of motion, which Dewey readily called "scientific." Although Hobbes's psychological axioms were unacceptable to Dewey, he certainly felt that a rationalist technique like Hobbes's based on empirical foundation had tremendous possibilities in the interpretation of political phenomena. But the development of rational techniques imposed two basic demands on Dewey. First was the formulation of concepts that can be related to particular political relationships. This meant that Dewey had to reject accepted concepts in politics such as "the state," "the individual," and so forth, because in their claims to universality they had become abstract and therefore irrelevant to specific situations; what Dewey needed were concepts that could guide the investigation of specific situations. Second was the need to treat these as hypotheses to be modified or confirmed by the empirical phenomena they illuminate.

In his ambitious series of lectures, *Reconstruction in Philosophy* (1921), Dewey accomplished the task of pointing out the futility of universal concepts like "the state" and "the individual," in the interpretation of specific political relationships. The immediate effect of such criticism on his own political attitude was not the substitution of consciously formulated concepts in place of universal concepts for the interpretation of specific political relationships, but the acceptance of some kind of crude political empiricism.

Dewey criticized universal ideas on the ground that they invariably shift our attention from specific situations to their own inner logic. The concept of the state as a universal concept, for example, shifts our attention from the complexity of surrounding phenomena to the question of the state's own meaning and character. Each universal concept may succeed in telling us about some general aspect of a particular political situation,[94] but after that we are more likely to know more about the concept itself than about the specific situation for which its assistance was sought.

91

In his reaction to the use of universal concepts, Dewey swung to the other extreme, namely, a crude form of political empiricism that was highly particularistic and in which the role of concepts was not properly emphasized. He remained far too eager to get down to the phenomena that underlie universal concepts to point out the cooperative relationship between empirical data and concepts.

Empirical political phenomena *can* be approached, Dewey's argument now implied, without the aid of any concept. The first thing to do is to release empirical political phenomena from the logical grips of universal concepts such as "the state," "the individual," and so forth. Empirical political phenomena would then at once present us with certain genuine problems that await our attention. Political theory would thereby become empirical as well as functional.

What Dewey ascertained by getting down to the empirical political phenomena that exist behind universal concepts was the fact of the infinite plurality of human associations and some general criterion of judging the quality of these associations. The term "society" now became with Dewey the principal term for indicating the plurality of human associations.

Society . . . is many associations not a single organization.

He goes on to say:

Society means *association; coming together in joint intercourse and action for the better realization of any form of experience which is augmented and confirmed by being shared.*[95]

The term "society" represented for Dewey the entire fact of association or, better still, the coming together of human beings. But in this explanation, Dewey himself could not help going from the particular to the universal. For, although the term "society" was used only in order to indicate the manifold associations that are found in actual experience, what inadvertently came to be emphasized was the fact of the *association* that is inherent in all associations. It would be beyond the scope of this volume to point out in detail the various universalistic commitments of the various nominalistic positions in Dewey. But what we must take into account is the fact that Dewey's crude political empiricism brought him back to the place from which he had started. Instead of looking at empirical phenomena through the traditional universal concepts, Dewey now started looking at them through his own universal concepts. One indisputable fact that emerges is that we cannot approach phenomena without the help of concepts. To maintain the opposite is only to be unaware of preconceptions, beliefs, and prejudices that take the place of concepts. In *The Public and Its Problems*, therefore, Dewey once again revived his emphasis on the use of concepts. In the place of universal concepts, he suggested the substitution of conceptions with the help of which generic discrimination of the peculiarities of political phenomena may be possible.

The shift in Dewey's attention from comprehensive universal concepts to empirical political phenomena consisting of manifold associations helped him to acquire some sort of functional attitude to political theory. According to Dewey, associations exist for the sake of the different activities that their members pursue. The purpose of different associations ought to be the equitable distribution of the fruits of activities of their members. Over and above the distribution of concrete benefits resulting from the activities of its members, each association ought to encourage the communication of mutual experience and participation in its work. As the greatest bulk of work in every society is done within the various associations, the only function of the state is to supervise and coordinate the work that they do. The task of political theory is therefore to enlighten and direct the supervisory and coordinatory functions of the state.

Although Dewey succeeded in formulating some sort of empirical and functional political theory, the purpose of which was to enlighten and guide the work of the state, in terms of his attempt to formulate a scientific political theory this remained a retrograde step. It was retrogression from the position that he had reached while expounding his own ideas on Austin and Hobbes. In his attempt to understand their points of view, Dewey had acquainted himself with the possibility of understanding the complexities of political phenomena with the help of consciously formulated concepts and their deductions. A scheme of concepts and their deductions must face its own test of empirical confirmation. It is understandable, therefore, that Dewey should have placed a greater emphasis on the empirical aspect of investigation in his *Reconstruction in Philosophy*. But in so doing he totally ignored the part played by concepts themselves in the investigation of empirical phenomena.

93

4

DEWEY'S MATURE
POLITICAL THEORY

THIS CHAPTER IS AN ATTEMPT to interpret some of
the mature philosophical and political ideas of Dewey. This interpretation implies that Dewey had some interesting ideas to express on
political theory, and that they can be treated as epistemological,
functional, and manipulative aspects of his political theory. It also
attempts to point out that due recognition has not been given to
Dewey's ideas on political theory.

The chapter is divided into four sections. The first section deals
with the analysis and criticism of some of the views expressed in
Dewey's principal work on political theory, namely, *The Public and
Its Problems*. The next three sections deal separately with the
epistemological, analytical, and manipulative aspects of his political
theory.

The Public and Its Problems (1927) may be regarded as the
first systematic statement of Dewey's views on political theory. His
two other major works—one on epistemology, called *The Quest for
Certainty* (1929), and the other on naturalistic metaphysics, called
Experience and Nature (1929)—were published two years later. *The
Public and Its Problems* belonged to a period when the problems
concerning the knowledge of natural, social, and human phenomena
were uppermost in his mind. As a book on political theory, therefore,
it raised some basic problems concerning political analysis. We
shall proceed to examine to what extent the reviewers of *The Public
and Its Problems* regarded it as a work on the problems of political
analysis.

The Public and Its Problems was reviewed by Prof. Harold Laski for the *Saturday Review of Literature*.[1] He maintained that Dewey had merely rectified the defects of Walter Lippmann's thesis in *Public Opinion* (1922). It is true that both Lippmann and Dewey were certainly engaged in the understanding of the true nature of the public, which, according to Lippmann, had become some sort of a "phantom" public, in order to make possible the pursuit of what might be called "enlightened politics." Nevertheless, their respective methodological equipment and the problems that they proposed to examine were entirely different. The central thesis of Lippmann's *Public Opinion* is that discriminating and courageous public opinion alone make the pursuit of enlightened politics possible. Equipped with an inductive methodology, Lippmann went through an enormous mass of factual data in order to conclude that what stands in the way of discriminating and courageous public opinion is the presence of what he calls "the pseudo-environment;"[2] in other words, he claimed that our intellectual attitudes and moral preconceptions substitute a conception of the environment different from what, in fact, exists. Dewey, on the other hand, did not restrict his investigations to the discovery of those factors that interfere with the pursuit of enlightened politics. He went deeper into the very problem of understanding the environment of politics. This in turn directed his attention to the problems of formulating an elaborate scheme of hypotheses and of testing them empirically as well as functionally. In ignoring this aspect of *The Public and Its Problems*, Professor Laski did not do full justice to Dewey's attempts at political analysis. But, at the same time, Professor Laski also confessed the difficulties involved in grasping Dewey's ideas in general and those contained in *The Public and Its Problems* in particular.

Like everything (Dewey) writes, (The Public and Its Problems) *is extraordinarily suggestive; also, like everything of his I am fortunate enough to know, it is quite extraordinarily difficult.*[3]

Prof. William Benett Munro reviewed *The Public and Its Problems* for *The Yale Review*.[4] He enthusiastically welcomed it, calling it a "... stimulating, fresh, and cogent" piece of work. He maintained that Dewey had done "much suggestive and forceful writing, but none better than this."[5] Nevertheless, in his review his main emphasis fell on aspects incidental to the principal theme of the book, from the chapter "The Problem of Method." This chapter is one of the most violent attacks on the traditional approach to political phenomena from the individual or social point of view. It was, in fact, the continuation of the line of argument already developed in *Reconstruction in Philosophy*, an attempt to approach empirical political phenomena without the interference of the universal concepts.[6] The principal thesis of the book, however, makes use of a highly complicated scheme of concepts, deductions, and problems of testability, and the chapter on the problem of method may be considered nothing but a negative qualification. By exaggerating the importance of this chapter, Professor Munro missed the principal thesis, that is, the conceptual scheme of which the book was an illustration.

In spite of the fact that Professor Munro was considerably impressed by the chapter on method, it is doubtful if Dewey succeeded measurably in converting Professor Munro to his own method of political investigation. In the same year (1928), Professor Munro delivered his presidential address to The American Political Science Congress, under the title of "Physics and Politics—An Old Analogy Revised." This paper is superficially reminiscent of the movement in political analysis with which Dewey himself was associated. In it, Professor Munro reproduced one of the key phrases from Dewey's chapter on method, "the continuous redistribution of social integrations,"[7] without acknowledging it. Dewey and, after him, Munro used the phrase to indicate the need to take into consideration some of the stable aspects of every changing human association. Professor Munro made an extremely naive attempt to adapt the method of physics to politics, without making sufficient reservations:

> . . . *The science and the art of government still rest upon what may be called the atomic theory of politics—upon the postulate that all able-bodied citizens are of equal weight, volume, and value; endowed with various absolute and unalienable rights; vested with equally absolute duties.*[8]

As the natural philosophy this contention rests on has moved to the position of divisible atom, the analogy in politics ought to be similarly readjusted.[9] Instead of an atomistic individual, what we should have now is what Munro calls "the hydrogen citizen."[10]

Needless to say, such an attempt to make politics "scientific," displays a correct understanding neither of the problems to be investigated in politics nor of the methodological significance of science to the procedure of political analysis. It merely rests on a kind of enthusiasm that makes even serious attempts in that direction appear naive. A careful examination of the chapter by which Professor Munro claimed to have been inspired would have been a salutary warning to him against his attempt to reduce politics to the level of deterministic physics. Dewey very clearly asserts that:

> The assimilation of human science to physical science, represents . . . only another form of absolutistic logic, a kind of physical absolutism.[11]

Prof. W. E. Hocking reviewed *The Public and Its Problems* for the *Journal of Philosophy*.[12] Unlike Laski and Munro, Professor Hocking succeeded in seeing a consistent attempt at a "general theory of political order" in this book. Being a political scientist, Hocking did not take long to find out that Dewey had a sound theoretical premise to his general theory of political order.[13] This premise, according to Hocking, consisted of two interrelated arguments: first, that human beings live and act in different associations, and second, that their existence and activity, on account of their effects on the general well-being, imply the need for a regulatory political organization. Hocking found Dewey's premise, consisting of these two arguments, to be reminiscent of Locke:

> Its discovery concerns resemble those of Locke's body politic, namely, the effective regulation of social incidents by officers rather than by each man for himself, and the normal subordination of these officers to that definable purpose.[14]

However, there were two significant differences between Dewey and Locke. First, Dewey's body politic, unlike Locke's, was a product, not of contract, but of mutual recognition of the need to regulate common consequences. Secondly, Dewey had no conception of the atomistic individual. Unlike Locke, he always thought of the individual in terms of his membership in one form of association or another.

Although Hocking did not express his disapproval at the virtual disappearance of the state in Dewey's political theory, as a near-idealist, he was probably by no means happy about Dewey's mentioning the organization of the state in the same breath as the organization of other associations. Not only did he associate the state with the generic "family," but he also deprived its activities of their primary moral significance. He considered associations—

social, economic, educational, cultural, scientific, and so forth—to be the main centers of activity. In spite of the fact that these associations undertake specialized activities, their activities are not without a moral reference. This moral reference is to be found in the fact that they all have the *mutual benefit* of their members as their main purpose.

The moral reference of the activities of the state is far too *indirect* in Dewey's political philosophy not to escape the attention of a near-idealist like Hocking. It is *indirect* because associations remain not only the main centers of human activity, but also the main centers of the consciousness of good and evil. As we have seen before, the problem of good and evil in Dewey's ethics is a problem that concerns the situation of deficiency and the efficacy of particular measures to overcome it. The problem of good and evil is therefore a practical problem connected with actual situations of deficiency and the actual undertaking of human activities to overcome them. As these activities take place primarily in various associations, various associations become the centers of consciousness of good and evil.

It may be asked: If the state is treated as one of many associations, why then is the moral quality of its activity distinguished from the moral qualities of the activities of the other associations? The answer may be given as follows: The state, as an association, is not the center of primary activities, as is a textile mill, a football club, or a church. These exist for the sake of activities of their *own*, as the state does not. The state, on the other hand, exists for the sake of regulating the activities of associations that pursue primary activities. Its activities are essentially of an organizational nature. The contrasting primary and organizational natures of these activities of the various associations and the state, respectively, make the difference in the moral quality of their respective activities. The organizational nature of the activities of the state are by their very nature impersonal and indirect. No mutual give and take is involved in its activities; instead, we have in the state two groups of people, the rulers and the ruled, bound together in a political relationship, whose purpose is to ensure that the rulers exercise the power that is authorized by the ruled. Now, the rulers and the ruled do not have a *common source* of their notions of good and evil. The rulers' notions of good and evil center around the enacted laws. The citizens, or the ruled, continue to reflect on the primary activities and their consequences. The impersonality inherent in all political relationships affects the moral quality of the activities of the state.

Although the activities of the state are not primarily moral nevertheless, it cannot be denied that its organizational activities that undertake to regulate the working of numerous associations have their own consequences of good and evil. The measures of the state either enhance or interfere with the activities of those associations over which it enjoys supervisory and regulatory authority. In this sense, then, the activities of the state are indirectly moral.

Hocking did not enter into such an analysis of Dewey's notions. He probably was much too aware of his differences with Dewey. Consequently, he merely described *The Public and Its Problems* as an attempt to frame a "general theory of political order"[15] and left it at that.

In spite of the fact that Hocking was the only reviewer of *The Public and Its Problems* who succeeded in seeing a consistent theory of political order, he too overlooked its implicit attempt to lay down a verifiable method of political investigation. Indeed, apart from its reviewers, *The Public and Its Problems* received very little attention at the hands of a generation of political scientists in America who claimed to be inspired by John Dewey's writings.[16] It was not without any sound reason that Dewey, whose prodigious output spanned a period of seventy years, himself declared ". . . probably the best balanced of my writings is *The Public and Its Problems*. . . ."[17]

This book, in spite of its obscurity and unreadability, deserves much greater attention than it has so far received. It is a unique experiment in political analysis by a thinker who himself was not primarily a political theorist. Consequently, the book has its flaws of disproportion and exaggeration. As an experiment in political analysis, however, it has many valuable suggestions to offer. In the remainder of this chapter we propose to point out the three different aspects of Dewey's political theory—epistemological, analytical, and manipulative—that are revealed in *The Public and Its Problems*.

The Epistemological Aspect of Dewey's Political Theory

With the help of the term "political epistemology," we propose to establish a connection between certain epistemological problems and the problem of investigation of political phenomena in Dewey's political theory. The use of the term "political epistemology" calls for some explanation. Roughly speaking, "epistemology" stands for all those investigations that attempt to tell how knowledge is pos-

Here, the term "knowledge" implies the knowledge of the entire human experience rather than any particular part of it. In using the term "political epistemology," therefore, we are no doubt restricting the scope of epistemological investigation to a *part* of human experience—namely, the political experience. Nevertheless, in this unconventional use of "epistemology," we shall not depart from the fundamental problems of epistemological investigation.

All epistemological investigations, among other fundamental problems, concern themselves with the respective functions of sense impressions and ideas in our knowledge of reality or understanding of human experience. Different functions have been given to sense impressions and ideas by epistemologists such as Plato, Locke, Kant, and Dewey. Plato gave primary importance to ideas, Locke gave primary importance to sense impressions, whereas Kant and Dewey emphasized the cooperative character of sense impressions and ideas in the process of knowledge.

If by the term "political epistemology" we mean *the explanations that concern the part played by political facts and political ideas in the understanding of political phenomena*, then, in all probability, we do not make any improper use of the term "epistemology." However, it must be admitted that our analogy between sense impressions and ideas, on the one hand, and political facts and political ideas, on the other, does not claim any similarity between the quality of impact of existential phenomena, which are the source of experience in general, and political phenomena, which are the source of political experience. Political phenomena do not possess what may be said to be the primariness of the existential phenomena. This is because, in the temporal order, political activity is always preceded by some other form of activity, such as social activity, economic activity, religious activity, and so forth. Political activity, as a matter of fact, comes into existence in order to regulate and organize the results of all those activities that precede it. It cannot be denied that institutionalized political activity is bound to affect the primary social, economic, and religious activities; nevertheless, it can be argued that the *general experience* of a community is always prior to its *political experience*, and that the general experience is utilized by political activity in its task of organization and control. The quality of political experience, as compared to the quality of general experience, is not a primary quality. This distinction, however truistic it may sound, must be recognized for the justification of the use of the term "political epistemology."

There is a sense in which Kant's epistemological dictum, "Perception without conception is blind, and conception without perception in empty," throws enormous light on the problem of understanding political phenomena. Not only are the primary sense impressions chaotic and incomprehensible without the aid of ideas, but so, also, are the facts of political experience. It is not without any basic need that political concepts and theories have been formulated from time to time for the interpretation of political phenomena. Political activity, in spite of the fact that it is confined to the task of organization and control of the conditions that affect common well-being, is by no means simple and directly comprehensible. In its totality and in its varied pursuits, and also because of the manifold motives that are associated with it, political activity is as devoid of a consistent meaning as the Kantian sense impressions. Considered in its totality, political activity is confounding, not only because it is engaged in various pursuits, but also because it perpetually changes its methods and objects of pursuit within the framework of its general task of organization and control. This incomprehensible mass of political activity necessitates the use of political ideas and concepts, for these alone are able to reveal its meaning and purpose.

The political concepts that have been employed in the interpretation of political phenomena have been numerous as well as varied. Conspicuous among them are concepts such as justice, social contract, general will, "the greatest good of the greatest number," the classless society, and the welfare state. However, political activity did not come into existence *after* the formulation of any one of these concepts. Rudimentary political activity of the oldest of human communities existed long before any of the political concepts were employed to understand it.

Plato was the first thinker to make a conscious use of political concepts in the understanding of political phenomena of the Greek city-states. The cycles of political change in the Greek city-states turned reflection in the direction of a political structure that was changeless. The political structures of the Greek city-states kept on changing because they did not perform their functions properly. In order to grasp the proper functions of a city-state, Plato made use of the concept of "justice," and, with the help of this concept, he reached the conclusion that the discharge of the proper functions of a city-state depends on the discharge of their duties by the individuals who constitute it.

The other significant concept used in the interpretation of political phenomena was the concept of "social contract." The fiction of the social contract was regarded by the contractualists as the principal causal factor in the origin and growth of political phenomena. The interpretations that such contractualists as Hobbes, Locke, and Rousseau gave to the nature and purpose of political activity was based on their respective conceptions of what the social contract embodied. It was the use of this concept that made possible the reinvestigation of political phenomena after the breakdown of what may be roughly described as the medieval political theory.

The concept of general will (Rousseau) is one of the most ingenious concepts devised in the history of political theory. Its purpose was to explain as well as reconcile the three widely divergent demands of the late eighteenth-century political conditions. The nation-state, having won its historic battle against the church and the nobility, demanded absolute juristic and political sovereignty, but such a demand came into direct conflict with the growing conception of individual freedom. The conception of individual freedom grew first of all in the religious field, as a result of the Reformation slogan "the right to private conscience." Its extension into the political and economic fields was brought about by the teachings of Locke, especially in his emphasis on the natural rights to life, liberty, and property. A third demand came from the need to subordinate the laws of the state to the laws of reason and morality. There was a growing dissatisfaction with the divergent interpretations of natural law to which the laws of the state were supposed to be subordinate. Moreover, in Rousseau there was a reaction against the belief that reason is the source of morality. Rousseau himself felt that morality was rooted much deeper in the human personality than in the sophisticated reason.

These three divergent demands of the late eighteenth-century political conditions were reconciled in Rousseau's general will as follows: The general will, being the expression of the right element in the wills of all individuals, leaves individuals in complete freedom as long as their thought and action are guided by it. Freedom in opposition to the right element of which the general will is an expression is inconceivable. The general will, hence, is both morally right and politically sovereign. Rousseau's concept of the general will, we may conclude, enabled him to perceive some degree of underlying harmony in the apparently conflicting political demands of the late eighteenth century.

102

There are concepts, such as "the greatest good of the greatest number," the classless society, and the welfare state, that do not seek to reinterpret political phenomena so much as to reconstruct the political forms in which political activity happens to be organized. In each of these concepts, certain psychological, economic, and moral references are involved. However, the chief value of these concepts lies in the fact that in the light of them we can discover the inadequacies in the social and political arrangements of the existing society. Unlike concepts devised in order to understand or investigate political phenomena, these are supposed to guide the process of reconstruction. Their value as reconstructive concepts is lost unless they are converted into precise practical propositions.

These, then, are a few of the many political concepts employed in order either to understand, reinvestigate, or reconstruct political phenomena. Later on we shall examine the importance of all these functions of political concepts in Dewey's own political philosophy.

In order to clarify the analogy between the cooperative use of conceptions and perceptions in epistemology in general, on the one hand, and in political epistemology, on the other, let us anticipate the following criticism: the contention that, as opposed to epistemology in general, the political epistemology is an *ex post facto* epistemology. By this we mean that our effort to know the nature of political phenomena with the help of political concepts implies that the facts of politics are *already* there, waiting to be known with the help of concepts. It implies that in political epistemology our effort to make use of concepts is a *conscious* effort undertaken with a view to make an incomprehensible situation comprehensible. As opposed to this, the Kantian dictum that "perception without conception is blind, and conception without perception is empty," to which political epistemology is supposed to represent a political counterpart, implies that the coordination of sense impressions and ideas is not consciously brought about for the sake of knowledge, but that in the process of knowledge, sense impressions and ideas are inseparably coordinated. As far as Kant is concerned, his conceptual categories are not deliberately employed, and the sense impressions, whenever they become comprehensible, inevitably pass through the categories.

The *conscious* use of political concepts in the various illustrations that we have given cannot be denied. The concepts of justice, social contract, general will, and so forth, are indeed both consciously formulated and consciously employed. This, however, does not imply that whenever concepts are not consciously employed we stand face to face with the sensory data of political phenomena. As a matter of fact, what we invariably possess when consciously formulated concepts are absent are vague notions, prejudices, and predilections that express themselves in the form of our opinions. Every now and then we come across statements such as: "Politics is a game of power," "Democracy means self-government," "Socialism means equality," and so forth, phrases that provide a kind of attitude or conceptuality for looking at political phenomena. But being inherently limited, involving either bias or untestable contentions, they merely succeed in giving a distorted picture of the phenomena. Hence, it is not altogether correct to say that while the knowledge of objects and events of ordinary experience, sense impressions, and ideas are inseparably coordinated, their coordination in the knowledge of political phenomena is artificially brought about. What can be said with justification is that political phenomena, being more complicated, call for a greater degree of consciousness in formulating and in testing of their concepts than is required, for instance, in knowing the arts of gardening, rowing, or cooking. But even in our knowledge of these arts, we are increasingly substituting consciously formulated ideas for those that have been accidentally acquired. Political epistemology cannot be contrasted with epistemology, in general, with conscious formulation of concepts as their differentia; the part played by consciously formulated concepts differs only in degree.

With Kant, the conceptual categories involved in the interpretation of sense impressions enjoy an *a priori* status; similarly, in political theory an axiomatic status has been claimed for many concepts. The concepts of justice, sovereignty, natural rights, self-determination, and so forth, have been regarded at one time or another as self-evident concepts. However, the main emphasis of political epistemology falls on the need for *consciously* formulated political concepts that must be neither *a priori* nor universal.

This brings us to the end of our exposition of the case for a political epistemology. We shall now examine Dewey's political writings, among them *The Public and Its Problems*, to see whether they shed any light on the problems associated with political epistemology.

▶◀ The conceptual framework for political investigation

The contention that Dewey's political writings deal with the problems that can be associated with political epistemology, or the theory of political knowledge, can be substantiated on the following grounds: that in Dewey's view, the knowledge of political phenomena is not possible without the help of political concepts or a political theory (here considered as a set of interrelated political concepts); that he believed causal, *a priori*, and universal concepts and theories to be incapable of explaining the peculiarities of political phenomena; and that Dewey himself attempted to frame certain concepts that helped to some extent in the generic discrimination of the problems of political phenomena.

However, before we undertake to make an analysis of these arguments, it is necessary for us to place them in the perspective of certain crucial problems that have arisen in political theory. This will enable us to appreciate the strength of these arguments in relation to problems of political theory. We shall therefore state, in brief, what these crucial problems are. We will then go on to examine the suggestions that emerge from the three principal ideas of Dewey's political theory.

The Public and Its Problems (1927) was published in a period when a reaction against political theory was taking place in American political science. This reaction[18] to political theory expressed itself in the form of an overwhelming emphasis on empirical research into administrative problems, on the one hand, and overt behavior in politics, such as public opinion, voting, and so forth, on the other. The political theorists who did not share this reaction did little or nothing to combat the wave of unqualified empiricism that had overtaken American political science.

During the interwar years in America, an enormous number of projects concerning problems of administration, voting, decision-making, and so forth, both at the state and national levels, were undertaken and their results were published. During this period in America, the prestige of political theory, even as an academic discipline, was at its lowest. This was largely due to the fact that, as opposed to the piecemeal but precise projects of empirical research, the political theorists could not adequately define the central purpose of their own study. Generations of students, impressed by the statistically summarized results of empirical research, began to feel that political theory either was too much committed to the past, in constructing *a posteriori* theoretical patterns on the basis of the changes that had already occurred in the society, or that political theory was too preoccupied with the future, and the realization of remote and impossible ideals. In addition to this, there was also a widespread feeling that political theory as a branch of knowledge did not discharge its function of shedding light on the ever-present problems of political reorganization.

Apart from these weaknesses, which were brought to the surface by the growth of empirical research in political science, the basic reason for a general indifference towards political theory can be found in the inability of political theory to define its own province. Political theory is as old as Western moral and philosophical thought. The classical political theory was not as limited in its scope and ambition as political theory has come to be in our own time. For all practical purposes, political theory is regarded now as a statement concerning the arts and ideals of political control, which are intimately connected with economic, moral, and juristic problems. When we desire to know how political theory is connected with these problems, we study economics, jurisprudence, and moral philosophy. We do not expect political theory to tell us in detail about the relations of its problems with the problems of other disciplines.

As opposed to this, the Greeks had a far more comprehensive notion of political theory, encompassing theory of morals, law, economics, and education. The point that we are trying to emphasize here would be missed if we were to contend that the evolution of human knowledge has been in the direction of a greater degree of specialization and that if classical political theory included morals, law, economics, and education, its claims were no different in that respect from the equally comprehensive claims of other branches of classical knowledge. Greek political theory was comprehensive, not because it came to be formulated in the prespecialized age, but because of the tasks that Greek political science, to which Aristotle gave the appropriate name of "the master science," prescribed to itself. With the Greeks, political theory was concerned with the securing of all those conditions that the medieval thinkers would have called by the name of "salvation," excepting that it was to be of this earth. Take Plato's *Republic:* its purpose was not restricted to the exposition of an administrative machinery that could look after the various organizational problems of the society, a purpose that would have satisfied the students of political theory in our time. It set forth a set of closely interconnected theories of morality, education, and economics that could be put into practice within the framework of its politics.

The greatest single difference between our own attitude towards political theory and that of the Greeks is to be found in the fact that, unlike the Greeks, we are more or less inclined to regard politics as an *external matter*. Although we do not often admit it, we do in fact regard political theory as a statement of general principles involved in the organization and regulation of problems that affect common well-being. We no longer expect political theory to go into the causes of the factors that affect our general well-being. We expect subjects like economics, moral philosophy, psychology, and education to deal with causes.

Although the central purpose of political theory, as suggested above, is to make a general statement concerning the principles involved in the organization and regulation of the problems of common concern, in actual fact it suffers from a considerable degree of imprecision. Before we can make any statement concerning the general principles involved in the task of organization and control of the problems of common concern, we must be able to investigate the phenomena with the help of our tentative concepts and theories. The boundaries of what may strictly be called *political phenomena* are still not clearly drawn. The earlier association of political theory with other disciplines has left behind its own legacy. We are still not prepared to admit that in spite of a close relationship with morality, law, economics, and so forth, political theory must independently be able to investigate the problems that strictly fall into its own province. Political theory has gradually acquired its independence from jurisprudence and economics, but its attempt to be independent of ethics is considered to be an advocacy of amoral politics.

Against such a fear of amoral politics, it may be argued that no branch of human knowledge can ultimately get rid of the problem of good and evil or its relation with morality. Every branch of specialized knowledge, in the last analysis, is concerned with the problem of good and evil as related to its own specific problems presented for our discrimination and judgment. The ultimate choice in making judgments rests with us only. Meanwhile, we ought to allow each branch of knowledge to shed light on the problems unique to it. In order to know what is politically good and what is politically evil, we must allow political theory to make a statement of its problems and principles, *in its own terms.* Its inability to do so has considerably impaired its prestige as a branch of knowledge.

◄══════► *The need for political concepts or political theory*

Dewey emphasized the need for political theory or political concepts in the investigation of political phenomena on two grounds: first, on the ground that the technique of political investigation based on "political facts" and nothing else is a false technique; second, on the ground that political facts and concepts are not as mutually exclusive as is commonly supposed, and that political facts imply the presence of political concepts and *vice versa:*

> *The moral . . . to drop all doctrines . . . overboard . . . is simple and attractive. But it is not possible to employ it. . . . The different theories . . . do not grow up externally to the facts which they aim to interpret; they are amplifications of selected factors among those facts.*[19]

To give up all political doctrines would certainly help us to get rid of an enormous number of controversies that have grown up around them, but the strength of such a suggestion rests on the strength of the alternative implied in it. The alternative implied in this suggestion is that of collecting "political facts" independently of political concepts or theories. Now, on further analysis, such an alternative seems to rest on a complete misunderstanding of the respective natures of political facts on the one hand and political concepts and theories on the other. This is because when the search for political facts is presented as an alternative method of political investigation in place of political theory, some sort of self-sufficiency in their respective claims and hence a rivalry between them is necessarily established. The failure to grasp the true natures of political facts and theories is also responsible for our inability to realize their appropriate places in political investigation.

Political facts, like any other facts, can neither be ascertained without the help of certain operative concepts and theories, nor can they be made to speak when collected without the help of concepts and theories. Both in the collection and in the articulation of facts, the part played by political concepts and political theories cannot be denied. This is because the collection of political facts cannot be undertaken by an investigator unless he knows *what* he is looking for and *where* he is going to find it. Now *where* to look for something is essentially a consequence of *"what* to look for." It means that the aspect of a phenomenon that interests one cannot be approached unless one is clear about what one is looking for.

The question of what to look for is different with different investigators. Every investigator has his conscious or unconscious beliefs and crude or sophisticated guesses. These beliefs and guesses present themselves as competing propositions while he is undecided about what to look for. After he finally succeeds in formulating a proposition for himself, he looks for the substantiation of his proposition with the help of facts. What is therefore normally called "the process of collecting facts" is nothing but the conscious or unconscious substantiation, modification, or rejection of the proposition that he has in mind.

It is within such propositions that our vague or precise acquaintance with concepts and theories relevant to our propositions find their expression. The more thought-out and sophisticated our propositions, the greater is their assimilation of the dialectic of the relevant concepts and theories. The dialectic of concepts and theories then enables the discovery of the latest meanings and relations of facts. In this respect, therefore, the collection of facts A, B, C would consist not merely in putting one beside the other, but in making explicit the innumerable relationships that exist among them.

A similar conclusion can be reached regarding the correlativity of facts and concepts or theories, even when we start from concepts or theories and see whether or not they include some sort of facts. Most political theories express their theses by presenting selected aspects of a selected group of facts, that is to say, they do possess *some* factual basis in support of their contentions. Their theses continue to enjoy the support of facts as long as the arbitrary selections of facts is not questioned. Consequently, for all political theories some sort of factual basis exists. What may or may not exist is a factual basis which can be regarded as satisfactory.

Political facts and political concepts or theories, to summarize, are neither self-sufficient in themselves nor can they become the exclusive basis of political investigation. To oppose them as alternative methods is only to overlook their intrinsic correlativity.

◄━━━━━ *The inability of casual, a priori, and universal concepts to explain the peculiarities of political phenomena*

Concepts for causal analysis. In the investigation of political phenomena, the temptation to use concepts that allow causal explanation is always very great. The temptation exists because causal explanations give the impression of getting down to the root of the problem. We may speak of specific causal explanation and general causal explanation, and there is an important distinction between them. Specific causal explanation takes for granted that there exists an efficient cause that directly gives rise to the problems under investigation. By a process of discrimination and isolation, we can determine the exact nature and operative position of the efficient cause. The emphasis of specific causal explanation falls on *precision*, among other things. As opposed to this a general causal explanation puts much less emphasis on the precise nature of causes and on the extent of their efficiency and presents instead a set of plausible and hypothetical causes. It fully appreciates the complexities of various phenomena and therefore remains satisfied with some kind of imprecise explanation.

The history of political theory is full of attempts at both varieties of causal explanation. Specific causal explanations have been advanced with the help of concepts such as social instinct (Aristotle), private gain (Machiavelli), fear (Hobbes), moral decadence (Rousseau), pleasure (Bentham), power (Nietzsche), and surplus value (Marx). These were regarded by their respective users as the sole causal forces of problems confronted in political phenomena. As opposed to this, political theorists of the post-Marxian period such as Graham Wallas and Laski, benefitting by Marx's economic sociology and the reactions that it produced in psychology and cultural anthropology, have advanced the concept of what Professor Laski appropriately termed "the plurality of social causation." The guiding motives of human activity are regarded by them to be many, interacting differently in different individuals at different times and places. General causal explanations also consider the sum total of interacting motives of men in some kind of interactive relationship with the physical and social environment.

The distinction between specific and general causal explanations, however truistic it may sound, must be carefully noted, for in any political investigation the part played by causal analysis cannot be done away with. The notoriety earned by specific causal explanations in the various monistic political theories may urge us to give up all attempts at causal analysis. We must, therefore, guard against identifying specific causal explanation with general causal explanation.

Political phenomena are a superstructure upon highly complicated existential phenomena—physical, biological, psychological, and cultural. The political problems that we observe are directly or indirectly connected with existential phenomena. What, therefore, can be the justification of specific causal explanations?

As far as Dewey is concerned, his acceptance of the general causal explanation is pretty clear in his writings subsequent to *The Public and Its Problems*. He wrote in his *Logic: The Theory of Inquiry* (1939) as follows:

> . . . *instead of a state of rigid alternatives of which one must be accepted and the other rejected, a plurality of hypotheses is positively welcome. For the plurality of alternatives is the effective means of rendering inquiry more extensive . . . and more flexible, more capable of taking cognizance of all the facts that are discovered.*[20]

Earlier, in *The Public and Its Problems*, he criticized specific causal explanations on the ground, first, that they are limited, and second, that they mistake an effect for a cause.

Specific causal explanations impose their own limitations on the scope of our investigation. Concepts such as social instinct, private gain, surplus value, fear, power, and so forth, that claim to explain political phenomena necessarily exclude human motives: conflict, sympathy, altruism, and voluntary cooperation for mutual benefit. Each of the previous concepts is a jealous and an exclusive concept, excluding not only its exact opposite but even motives that differ from it in degree. Consequently, each one cause, taken independently of the others, will explain only a fraction of the reality of the political phenomena. Even the most comprehensive among them, namely social instinct, was found by Dewey to be unsatisfactory in explaining political phenomena:

> *Appeal to a gregarious instinct to account for social arrangements is the outstanding example of the lazy fallacy. Men do not run together and join in a larger mass as do drops of quicksilver, and if they did* the result would not be a state nor any model of human association.[21]

Social instinct, therefore, may tell us at the most that human beings by virtue of instinct are found in the company of one another. But this cannot be taken as a *causal* explanation for the growth of a political society, for it is far too limited.

Dewey's second criticism of specific causal explanations, that they mistake effects for causes, arises out of his own conception of the environment and the determining influence that it exercises on human personality in general. From his point of view, specific causal explanations, by attributing causal properties to human motives, overlook the fact that human motives are themselves determined by the environment. The following are the four stages through which Dewey's conception of the environment and the determining influence that it exercises on human personality developed.

(1) Dewey was in his psychology an anti-individualist long before he became a behaviorist. In one of his earliest papers on psychology, namely, "Psychology and Philosophical Method" (1899), he had set before himself the task of criticizing the notions of "consciousness" and "individual" as found in the rationalist psychology of the late nineteenth century. At this stage, Dewey did not have the conception of the environment that was to dominate his subsequent social psychology and social philosophy. Consequently, he clung half-consciously to the Hegelian point of view that the universal expresses itself in and through the particulars:

> Modern life involves the deification of the here and the now; of the specific, the particular, the unique, that which happens once and has no measure of value save such as it brings with itself. Such deification is monstrous fetishism, unless the deity be there; unless the universal lives, moves and has its being in experience as individualized.[22]

Nevertheless, his view of consciousness and the individual did imply a vague conception of the environment. Psychology would have meaning for philosophy, these views suggested, only when it treats consciousness as a symbol of a natural and social existence; a psychology that does not treat consciousness or the states of consciousness as *mediatory* between the individual and his natural and social surroundings is defective. Furthermore, the states of consciousness neither exist *by* themselves nor *for* themselves.[23] As far as the conception of the self-sufficient individual in rational psychology was concerned, Dewey maintained that it did not belong to psychology proper and that it was transferred from economics and politics.[24] However, he did not attempt to criticize the conception of the self-sufficient individual in economics and in politics because this required an adequate conception of the environment that he did not develop until *Human Nature and Conduct* (1922).

(2) *Human Nature and Conduct* may be regarded as Dewey's first systematic statement of the influence of environment on human

behavior. The principal thesis of the book is that the human organism lives and grows in an environment. In order to carry out its activities in its environment, it is required to develop some kind of psychophysical mechanism. Therefore, human behavior cannot be explained independently of the psychophysical mechanism, nor can the psychophysical mechanism itself be understood independently of the environment that necessitates its development.

The environment with which the human organism transacts its business is physical as well as social. The psychophysical mechanism through which its business is transacted is composed of habits, impulses, and intelligence. Habits, besides, are the matrix of this psychophysical mechanism. They mould impulses and invariably lay down the line for intelligence to follow.

In Dewey's psychology, the term "habit" has a special meaning. He considers habits to be responses as well as devices. They are responses to the demands of our environment, both physical and social, and they are devices because with their help we can act in the environment.

> ... Habits are arts. They involve skill of sensory and motor organs, cunning or craft, and objective materials. They assimilate objective energies, and eventuate in command of environment. They require order, discipline, and manifest technique. They have a beginning, middle and end. Each stage marks progress in dealing with materials and tools, ... in converting material to active use.[25]

Although each individual forms his habits for himself, the actual formation of habits is not an isolated process. On the contrary, it is a process that is essentially carried out through the medium of society. Each society has its own institutions, customs, conventions, practices, and so forth, and it expects the individual to conform to it in his formation of habits. He is required, in short, to reproduce in the form of his habits the psychophysical pattern of behavior that his physical environment demands and of which the social medium approves.

The relationship between habit and the other two elements in the psychophysical mechanism, namely, impulses and intelligence, is worth nothing. The environment, physical as well as social, is not "all of one piece."[26] There are innumerable conflicting factors in it, and they make conflicting demands on the individual. All conflicts induce reflection. The continued need to reflect results in a capacity to reflect that we call by the name of "intelligence." Intelligence thus born, remains critical of habits that, on account of their cease-less repetition, have sunk to a physiological level. Whenever our intelligence is critical of our habits, it seeks to reorganize the impulses that normally flow through the grooves of our habits. In so doing, it comes in direct conflict with our habits. Its success in redirecting our habits becomes the basis of our individuality.

Dewey's ambivalence about the relationship between habits and intelligence, which runs throughout *Human Nature and Conduct*, must be carefully noted. On the one hand, enormous emphasis is placed on the environment, and hence on habits. On the other hand, human individuality is rescued by bringing into play intelligence and its ability to reorganize impulses and redirect habits. This ambivalence is most seriously felt in the relationship that is supposed to exist between habits and intelligence. On the one hand, habits are supposed to be grooves not only of impulses but also of intelligence. On the other, intelligence is granted an independent position of its own from which it is supposed to redirect habits.

This ambivalence continues even in Dewey's *Freedom and Culture* (1939). In this work, the notion of environment, as opposed to that in his *Human Nature and Conduct*, is far more sophisticated. In place of an overwhelmingly physical and institutionally bound social environment, Dewey substitutes the term "culture" in order to indicate an amalgam of physical, biological, economic, political, religious, aesthetic, moral, scientific, and educational factors. They interact with one another and also with what is called human nature in its "native makeup."[27] In this connection, the term "interaction" is used with considerable emphasis to indicate the native activity of human personality that does not totally submit to the determining influences of the environmental factors. In this sense, it was a definite improvement upon the highly deterministic tone of *Human Nature and Conduct*, where the psychophysical mechanism was supposed to be determined by the environment and intelligence had a dubious role to play. Nevertheless, even in *Freedom and Culture* the old ambivalence continued in a new form. On the one hand, culture was considered to be exercising a determining influence on the desires and attitudes of men. On the other hand the knowledge of this determination was sought for the purposes of greater freedom in choice and action.

These ambiguities notwithstanding, Dewey's emphasis on the environment and its determining influence played a very important part in his philosophy of education. In view of the direct influence of the environment in shaping human behavior and personality, Dewey maintained that the presentation of the environment to children must be well thought out. The purpose of the school is to provide all that is best in society. Consequently, he came to regard the school as a kind of "special environment."[28] As every child is essentially a citizen in the making, the school must provide an environment of a social community in miniature.[29] The importance of the environment was also emphasized in Dewey's philosophy of education in *becoming by doing*. He maintained that school children can be prepared for their future responsibilities of citizenship only when they are made to *act* as citizens—engaged in various professions, and living together in cooperation and helpfulness at their own level. Only the "selected environment" inculcates the sense of belonging to a community and of discharging the obligations that it imposes.

(3) In *The Public and Its Problems*, Dewey added some qualifications to his contention that the environment determines human behavior and personality. These were that human wants, the means by which they are satisfied, and the standards of their satisfaction are determined by the conditions that exist in the environment.[30] Such qualifications were necessary for the development of his subsequent thesis that the "ruling motive" at any given time is determined by the conditions of the environment.

Dewey's conception of human wants, the means by which they are satisfied, and the standards of their satisfaction, as determined by the material and social conditions of the environment, was the basis of his criticism of the classical economists. The classical economists had attempted to prove that the interference of the state in economic activities of the society was both unnecessary and harmful. They had argued that if the interference of the state were to be brought to an end, the natural law of wants and their satisfaction would create a fruitful and harmonious equilibrium. Underneath such an argument lay the conception of a self-sufficient and self-determined individual. Such a conception of the individual arose from a belief that the individual has his natural wants and has the natural ability or resourcefulness to satisfy them. Dewey, on his part, argued that the entire reasoning of the classical economists was based on a fallacious conception of the term "natural." Natural wants, in the sense of organic wants, are food, sex, and

115

shelter, and one's natural ability to satisfy them means a precarious and chance-ridden satisfaction of these wants, similar to their satisfaction in primitive man in the hunting stage. Human wants as expressed by individuals, Dewey argued, are in fact the products of the social *milieu* in which they live and act. Moreover, the satisfaction of these wants depends upon the technique of production that a society possesses at a particular time. Even the standards for judging the manner of their satisfaction depend upon the customs and mores that are reflected in the social consciousness at any given time.

The Public and Its Problems succeeded in pointing out the dependence of human wants and their satisfaction on the conditions that exist in the environment. Nevertheless, it did not point out how the conditions of the environment at different periods of history brought into prominence different specific causal explanations, necessarily concentrated on a single motive chosen by social and political theorists at different times. *The Public and Its Problems* did not go beyond his assertion that certain motives are deliberately attributed to human nature by political theorists in order to undertake a specific causal analysis of political phenomena.

> *To explain the origin of the state by saying that man is a political animal is to travel in a verbal circle. It is like attributing religion to a religious instinct, the family to marital and parental affection, and language to a natural endowment which impels men to speech. Such theories merely reduplicate in a so-called causal force the effects to be accounted for.*[31]

In short, *The Public and Its Problems* did not explain why the selection of a particular motive is an effect, not a cause.

(4) The answer to this question was attempted by Dewey in *Freedom and Culture*. Here he pointed out how different motives have been made to appear predominant at different times by the conditions existing in the environment.

> *It is significant that human nature was taken to be strongly moved by an inherent love of freedom at the time when there was a struggle for representative government; that the motive of self-interest appeared when conditions in England enlarged the role of money, because of new methods of industrial production; that the growth of organized philanthropic activities brought sympathy*

*into the psychological picture, and that events today are readily
converted with love of power as the mainspring of human action.*[32]

These ruling motives of freedom, self-interest, sympathy, and
power were brought into prominence by different forces operating
in the environment at different times. They were the *effects* of the
forces in the environment and not their *causes*, as specific causal
explanations mistook them to be. The ruling psychological motives
that become the nuclei of specific causal explanations themselves
require a general causal analysis.

Undertaking any criticism today of specific causal explanations,
as they appear in historical political theories, is like flogging a dead
horse. The contemporary social sciences have come under the influence of the current findings of sociology and anthropology. Consequently, no *single* psychological motive or socioeconomic factor
can be emphasized as the sole causal force behind social and political
phenomena. However, it must be admitted that in contemporary
political theories the concept of power continues to play an important part.[33] Nevertheless, power is being treated as a characteristic
mark of political phenomena rather than their generative cause.
Power as a characteristic is also used in order to discriminate political phenomena from phenomena of other types.

Now let us examine an important problem that arises if general
causal explanation as a technique of investigation is accepted. The
technique of general causal explanation must be able to give a satisfactory answer to the following question: Does the general causal
explanation allow investigations to be conducted in specialized
branches of knowledge along the lines of specific causal explanations,
the results of which may be correlated at the end? Or does it emphasize the fact that since every problem is a product of interaction of
innumerable causal factors, one causal factor must not be considered
independently of the other? The entire spirit of general causal explanation would be negated if the first position were accepted, for
this would only mean that specific causal explanations that are
found unsatisfactory in broader fields are suitable for specialized
fields of inquiry. Nevertheless, the second position, which appears
to be in keeping with the spirit of general causal explanation, is not
very easy to accept, because no investigator enjoys knowledge ade-

quate to investigate the interaction of *all* causal factors in a problem. This would therefore mean that investigators with different specializations will have to work together in order to investigate every problem. Each specialist has his own emphasis on the causal efficacy of the factor belonging to his own field of interest. In other words, general causal explanations are impossible to undertake unless a team of specialists engaged in an investigation learn to work together in the spirit of understanding and compromise.

The greatest difficulty that the technique of general causal explanation creates is that it makes political theory totally dependent upon general sociology and anthropology; for political theory, as we maintained earlier, must first of all define the boundaries of the phenomena that it seeks to investigate. Dependence upon sociology and anthropology would indeed make the problem of definition of the boundaries of political phenomena very difficult, but this would certainly enable political theorists to appreciate the interdependence of their concerns and those of other social scientists.

A priori concepts. Before undertaking any investigation, in defining his boundaries, the investigator usually begins by making a general statement concerning the problems in which he is interested.

For Dewey, the problems of his political inquiry were clearly indicated. He was not interested in the nature and origin of the state. On the contrary, his interest was confined mainly to the understanding of the political organization of society in the light of its observable functions. This no doubt demarcated the scope of his inquiry. Nevertheless, it did not remove the obstacle that stood in the way of such an inquiry. This obstacle was the nature of existing conceptions about political phenomena in which the *a priori* concept of the state played a vital part. Consequently, Dewey undertook to criticize the *a priori* character of the concept of the state. The following arguments may be stated in support of Dewey's criticism.

The concept of the state has been regarded by historical political theorists as a concept that represents the whole of political phenomena.[34] The analysis of this concept has been invariably regarded as a discourse on the problems of political phenomena. Consequently, various political theorists have never analyzed political phenomena firsthand, but have instead from time to time analyzed the nature of the state.

Various generations of political thinkers have approached the problem of the meaning of the concept of the state in the light of their own historical circumstances. Consequently, only the *form* of this concept has remained unchanged, not the characteristics attributed to it. Since the form of the concept survived, it was felt by every generation of political thinkers that this form had a standard meaning that ought to be discovered. Mr. T. D. Weldon, in his controversial book *The Vocabulary of Politics* (1953), pointed this out as an established convention of all historical political speculation.[35]

The *a priori* character of the concept of the state does not reside in its supposed characteristics. These are the products of historical circumstances. The *a priori* character of the concept of the state resides instead in its claim to represent the whole of political phenomena. It is meaningless to dispute this *a priori* character on the ground that the province of the state is not coextensive with that of political phenomena, for the state as a formal concept can be stretched to embrace and represent, for the sake of argument, whatever may be supposed to lie outside its province.

However, the *a priori* character of the concept of the state can be challenged on the following four grounds. First, the state, as a formal concept, fails to indicate what precisely it stands for. Second, even if the state were to be regarded as identical to the sum total of its characteristics, it is impossible to agree on these characteristics. Any agreement on its characteristics would require a satisfactory degree of empirical confirmation, and this cannot be undertaken on account of the vastness and generalities of the characteristics of the state. Third, the state, as defined by Garner for the sake of widest possible agreement with respect to population, territory, government, and sovereignty, is so very general that with the help of this definition we cannot discriminate between the quality of one political organization and another. Finally, political phenomena are highly individualized phenomena because of the operation of different cultural factors in different societies. In order to distinguish the similarities and differences between different political societies, we must have concepts that can be tried and modified over and over again. Such a function can be performed by a concept only when it gives up its *a priori* character.

Nothing is gained by political theory in retaining the concept of the state, which in terms of its logical character is an *a priori* assumption and in terms of its empirical reference is confusing. On the other hand political theory has much to lose and suffer on account of this concept. This is because the concept of the state always gives the impression of indispensability. We wonder, therefore, that so much historical political speculation has taken place around this concept. This impression of indispensability also seems to have prevented attempts to consider the state as a necessary conceptual fiction in law and in politics. Consequently, all political inquiry has had to take the concept of the state seriously and has had to spend considerable time in getting across its various historical definitions.

The so-called characteristics of the state that are invariably considered to be intrinsic are in fact the products of the reflection of various political thinkers on the forces of their own societies. Consequently, no adequate procedure has been followed in finding out what the permanent characteristics of the state are. As historical characteristics are directly attributed to the state, the logical authority of the concept of the state is used in order to support the claims of its characteristics. Consequently, not only does the concept of the state remain as an *a priori* concept, but its characteristics do as well. None of these characteristics are submitted to any empirical test, with the result that they are neither modified nor given up. The students of political theory are thus offered a wide variety of choice among the historically accumulated characteristics of the state. This invariably results in the neglect of the study of actual political activities of a society:

> *The moment we utter the words "the State" a score of intellectual ghosts rise to obscure our vision. Without our intention and without our notice, the notion of "the State" draws us imperceptibly into a consideration of the logical relationship of various ideas to one another, and away from the facts of human activity.*[36]

In summary, the presence of the *a priori* concept of the state, unless it is declared a fiction, is not likely to encourage the formulation of other concepts that may be felt necesssary for political inquiry.

Universal concepts. The needs of political investigation, according to Dewey, cannot be satisfied by the use of universal concepts. The state as a universal concept, although applicable to all the political organizations that have population, territory, government, and sovereignty—if we accept Garner's definition—does not assist us in discriminating one type of political organization from another. Such a function can only be performed by *generic concepts* consciously designed for this purpose.

The need for generic concepts is implicit in the individualized character of the instances and the occurrences of existential phenomena.

History is full of ingratitude. All existences . . . have qualities of their own and assert independent life. There is something of King Lear's daughters in all offspring.[37]

Instances and occurrences are neither identical nor repetitive.[38] No matter how very similar they appear, they cannot be adequately represented by universal concepts. Nevertheless, more or less similar instances and occurrences can be grouped so that the similarities and differences that exist among them may be determined. To do this, we need *discriminatory*, not *representative*, concepts. This discriminatory function is performed by generic concepts.

In the investigation of political phenomena the need for generic concepts appears to be all the greater, because political organizations, although universally present, cannot be specifically indicated with the help of universal concepts. The term "the state" cannot signify anything other than the four attributes that, according to Garner, are universally present in all political organizations. For every further qualification of political organization, we have to use an additional universal term and still remain a long way from grasping unique differences that can exist between different political organizations. To say, "Britain is a democratic state," "Russia is a totalitarian state," "Israel is a theocratic state," and so forth, is to add one more universal qualification each time. At the same time, "democracy," "totalitarianism," and "theocracy" do not tell us anything about the peculiarities of the actual states, because these qualifications can be applied to Sweden, Bulgaria, and Pakistan in the same manner. All subsidiary qualifications of a principal universal concept like "the state" are likely to be universal in their reference and hence indicate nothing in particular.

Universal qualifications, like universal concepts, are not *meant* to assist the groupings of more or less similar instances for the sake of their relative differentiation. However, they do have the function of pointing out, on the other hand, that none of the universal concepts or their qualifications can be a starting point for further inquiry.

They (universal concepts and their qualifications) are general answers supposed to have a universal meaning that covers and dominates all particulars. Hence they do not assist inquiry. They close it. They are not instrumentalities to be employed and tested in clarifying concrete social difficulties. They are ready-made principles to be imposed upon particulars in order to determine their nature. They tell us about the *state, when we want to know about* some *state.*[39]

◥◣▬▬◢ *Concepts for generic discrimination of the peculiarities of political phenomena*

In this section we shall examine the concepts that Dewey formulated in order to discriminate the peculiarities of political phenomena. But before we undertake the examination of these concepts, their various presuppositions and discriminating capacities, we shall briefly point out what Dewey regarded to be the scope and limits of political phenomena.

Scope and limits of political phenomena. Political phenomena may be said to be coextensive with the area in which political activities are undertaken. Political activities are carried out within the various institutions of government and on their periphery. The purpose of political activity is to acquire the support of various organized and unorganized forces of society that may be said to be instrumental in effecting, modifying, or revoking fractional or total arrangements of society. The pursuit of political activity is, in other words, a pursuit of means to effective power. Political phenomena may therefore be said to include all those activities that are carried on in order to sustain, alter, or repeal the arrangements of society through conventional or unconventional means.

Now the conception of political phenomena that Dewey had in mind—to which he himself did not adhere—was narrower and hence more easily definable than one that we have mentioned above. It was narrower because it restricted itself only to the *institutionalized* aspects of political activity and took into consideration only the established political institutions which rest on *settled* political habits. Such a conception of political phenomena sprang from Dewey's views on social psychology. According to Dewey, as we have already noted, human habits are human responses to the demands of the physical and social environment. Political institutions, being a part of the environment, also create appropriate political habits in order to ensure their existence and activity.[40]

Settled political habits necessarily exclude certain activities having political implications—those activities that are undertaken in order either to alter the course of settled political habits or to by-pass them in their effort to control organized power. Such activities are political in their implications because they compete with the settled political habits in acquiring the support of precisely those forces that are instrumental to the maintenance and transformation of the arrangements of society. The scope of political activity, in other words, is not coextensive with settled political habits. Only in a politically mature as well as politically stable society are settled political habits the expressions of the bulk of political activities. But there too, the scope of political phenomena cannot be restricted to the settled ways of sustaining and transforming the arrangements of those societies.

The contention that the scope of political phenomena is wider than the settled political habits of any particular society can be sub-stantiated as follows: Within the frame of reference of Dewey's so-cial psychology, the settled political habits are nothing but the psychophysical counterparts of the established political institutions. Political institutions, like any other social institutions, live and act through our habits, that is to say, for every institutional datum in politics, we must have a corresponding behavioral datum. Now it is not difficult to point out that such an identification is misleading, for there are innumerable institutional forms that have no behav-ioral counterparts, and vice versa. Many institutional forms or de-mands fail to mould our habits and consequently are either openly resisted or connived at in the hope that they will be modified in future. Prohibition of liquor in America in 1920 was one such insti-tutional demand. On the other hand, there are many well-established activities and attitudes for which no institutional counterparts exist. This can be found in the demand to alter the electoral law in Switzer-land that debars women from voting. Activities and practices that call for new institutional forms are in fact outgrowths of settled political habits, and hence for them no corresponding institutional forms exist. The demand of women in Switzerland to be enfranchised is the outgrowth of the settled political habit of manhood suffrage. Consequently, what lies outside the scope of settled political habits is not devoid of political significance.

If we consider political phenomena as coextensive with the settled political habits of any particular society, then political in-vestigation would be debarred from all those activities that are undertaken in order to modify our *settled* political habits, such as the activities of political parties, the press, trade unions, and the unions of vested interests. These activities lie in a twilight zone that exists between the primary economic, social, religious, and recreational activities, on the one hand, and the settled political habits that give rise to settled ways of dealing with them, on the other. If political phenomena were to be considered as coextensive with settled political habits, such limitation would prevent political investigation of those situations where demands for regulation and control of the results of primary activity constantly give rise to one form of political activity or another.

As we said before, Dewey himself did not stick to a conception of political phenomena that made political phenomena coextensive with settled political habits. He extended his analysis to all those associated activities that give rise to some form of political concern or another. Political concern is the product of what, in unfamiliar terms, he calls "indirect and enduring consequences of associated activity." This, in other words, means that activities affecting others who are not directly involved or affecting the general well-being give rise to some kind of political concern. Political concern eventually brings into existence regulatory or organizational measures. For Dewey, therefore, every stage of activcity, from political concern right up to the actual enactment of regulatory measures, acquired some form of political significance; hence the scope of political investigation was for him not confined to the settled political habits or the settled ways of enacting regulatory measures. It extended, instead, to all public activities that mobilize public opinion, in part or in whole, to bring into existence regulatory measures.

To repeat, for Dewey the scope of political phenomena extended to all areas where primary activities call for regulatory measures on account of their effects on general well-being. That is to say, it included all those organizational or regulatory measures that are undertaken to safeguard general well-being. By also including in his political investigation activities that express themselves as demands for the extension or curtailment of the regulatory limits of state authority, Dewey came to regard the scope of political phenomena as coextensive with potential as well as actual organizations.

"Organization," however, is a very comprehensive term. It calls for a criterion that may enable us to discriminate political organizations from nonpolitical ones. For these purposes Dewey introduces an extremely dubious criterion, namely, that a political organization is one that is run with the help of special "officials." Now such a criterion does not help us to discriminate political organizations from nonpolitical ones: all organizations employ "officials" of some sort to look after them. Dewey therefore requalified the discriminatory criterion. He now maintained that in political organizations, officials carry out their work through the various administrative agencies of the government.[41]

By virtue of this requalification, not the officials but the administrative agencies through which they act came to be the discriminatory criterion. This no doubt made the discrimination of political organizations from nonpolitical ones an extremely simple and straightforward process; nevertheless, it redefined the scope of political phenomena and therefore reimposed certain limitations on political investigation. On account of the requalification of his discriminatory criterion, the scope of political phenomena came to be restricted to those activities that are carried on by the government within its various organs. No attempt was made by Dewey to remove the element of incongruity in his attitude towards political phenomena. On the one hand, he continued to regard the scope of political phenomena as coextensive with actual and potential organizations. On the other, he maintained that the activities in political organizations are conducted by special officials through the agencies of the government.

Dewey, it appears, remained oblivious of the incongruity in his attitude towards the scope of political phenomena. He paid considerable attention to those activities that demand alterations in the existing arrangements of society, and he even felt that the real problem of the public is how constantly to reorganize itself in the face of obsolete and obdurate political forms which tend to perpetuate themselves.[42] On the other hand, his belief that the presence of officials and administrative agencies make phenomena political continues beyond *The Public and Its Problems*. In the year that followed the publication of *The Public and Its Problems*, Dewey reviewed *The Origin of the State* by R. H. Lowie for the Columbia Law Review (1928). In this book Lowie was attempting to refute Oppenheimer's thesis that the state comes into existence as a result of the exploitation of the conquered by the conqueror—that the conqueror takes with him some form of political organization and imposes it on the conquered. Lowie maintained that all communities—including the most primitive—have some form of rudimentary political organization of their own. Simultaneously, he was attempting empirically to confirm Thurnwald's thesis that:

Our modern state . . . is no more than one of many abstract possibilities (in political organization) and has varied in time.[43]

To confirm this, Lowie was trying to find in primitive communities what he called the "psychological equivalents"[44] of the governmental machineries in the civilized communities. Now as far as Dewey is concerned, he felt that Lowie had convincingly demonstrated that:

. . . unless we arbitrarily define the state in terms of modern political entities, the evidence goes to show the historic function and structure so that we are entitled to speak of the state in connection with primitive societies.[45]

The point relevant to our analysis of Dewey's conception of the scope of political phenomena is that in the primitive communities there was only one organization, which performed political and economic as well as religious functions. The scope of investigation of the historical political phenomena is therefore well extended in recognizing the political aspects of the organization of primitive communities. However, the notion of one *single* political organization that finds it counterpart in modern political phenomena would certainly restrict the scope of our investigation.

Concepts for generic discriminations. Each society has a political arrangement peculiar to itself, springing from its own composition. Dewey's thesis in this conception is that with the help of three of his concepts—consequences, perceptions, and organization—we can consider every political arrangement in relation to its own social composition and thereby be able to discriminate the peculiarities of one political arrangement from another. The concept "consequences" is used by Dewey to indicate the results of associated living and acting. The concept of "perception" is used to indicate people's awareness of these consequences. "Organization" is used to suggest that a people affected by the consequences of their associated living and acting attempt to bring about a regulatory control over those consequences with the help of an organization. Before we go on to examine the extent to which Dewey's claims may be regarded as satisfactory, we must note some of the presuppositions that are involved in these concepts. We must also examine two other

126

relevant problems: whether the use of collective nouns such as "state," "society," and so forth, in the plural assures their empirical reference, and the psychological implications of the term "public."

These topics are dealt with in the following order: the presuppositions of Dewey's concepts; the fallacy of empirical plurals; the psychological implications of the use of the term "public;" and generic discriminations.

Consequences, perception, and organization—the three concepts used by Dewey to discriminate the peculiarities of the political arrangements in different societies—presuppose the fact of *associated living*. The fact of associated living is with Dewey both universal[46] and axiomatic.[47] He never allows himself to ask why human beings come together. What he asks instead is: How do human beings come to be in the peculiar social and political relationships in which we find them in our experience? Unlike the contractualists, he does not reduce his individuals to self-sufficient units and then attribute to them certain motives for entering into the civil society. He takes for granted the fact that human beings live and act together. He does not allow the fact of associated living and acting to explain away the peculiar social and political relationships in which human beings are found in our experience. The peculiar social and political relationships in which different political arrangements of different societies bind their individuals are treated by Dewey as problems to be analyzed and understood with the help of his concepts.

The second presupposition of Dewey's concepts is the presence of some form of organization in the fact of associated living. This can be pointed out in terms of the nature of the analysis that is supposed to be undertaken with their help.

When we closely examine the nature of the operation of each one of these concepts, we find that they are designed to undertake some form of *retrospective analysis*. That is to say, with their help, we can trace existing political arrangements back to the fact of associated living. As far as Dewey is concerned, such a retrospective analysis is indispensable, because the peculiarities of different political arrangements can only be understood against the background of the different social compositions that give rise to them. Unless we make explicit the organization inherent in the fact of associated living (Dewey's second presupposition), his three concepts are incapable of undertaking retrospective analysis.

These three concepts, considered independently of the second presupposition, make Dewey's political analysis similar to that of the contractualists. This can be illustrated as follows.

Associated living and acting produce innumerable consequences. These consequences can be separated into direct consequences, which affect people who are directly involved in an activity, and indirect consequences, which affect people who are not directly involved. Indirect consequences are those that affect the general well-being and give rise to some kind of common concern. When the implications of indirect consequences are fully recognized or perceived by the people, they demand certain regulatory measures. With the help of those measures, indirect consequences are regulated or organized in the interest of general well-being. As a result of a continued demand for regulatory measures, which are required from time to time, some form of political organization is permanently established in order to meet such demands.

Now this illustration of the origin and growth of political organization is not very different from those offered by the contractualists, especially Locke, to explain the origin of the state. While Dewey had no desire to go into the problem of the origin of political organizations, he wanted to discriminate the pecularities of one political arrangement from another as found in actual experience. Moreover, while reviewing R. N. Lowie's *The Origin of the State,* Dewey had agreed to Lowie's contention that in the earliest human communities rudimentary organizations performing political functions can be found. However, unless the second presupposition, implying the presence of some kind of organization in the basic fact of associated living, is made explicit, any investigation to be undertaken with the help of Dewey's three concepts would be directed towards the question of the origin of political organizations rather than the detection of their differences. Dewey, it appears, remained unaware of his second presupposition; this lack of awareness did not deflect his discriminatory analysis. It merely made his statement of these three concepts appear less logical than they could otherwise have been.

Earlier we examined Dewey's criticism of the use of universal concepts such as "the state," "society," and so forth. His criticism of them was largely based on the ground that when we want to know about some state or society *in particular,* universal concepts tell us something about "the state" and "society" in the abstract. Now in order to assure that a collective noun like "society" refers to a society that actually exists, Dewey, like other thinkers, prefers to use it in the plural.[48] Our contention in this connection is that using collective nouns in the plural does not help us to make empirically testable statements, that for such a purpose some additional qualifications become necessary.

The practice of using collective nouns in the plural is fairly widespread among those political thinkers who believe that every piece of empirical reference strengthens their reasoning. It is with such purpose in view that they prefer to use the term "states" instead of "state" and "societies" instead of "society." What is tacitly implied in their use of collective nouns in plural is that they are self-evidently empirical, but a statement that makes use of collective nouns in the plural is as much open to doubt and requires as much additional qualification as does the collective noun in the singular. This can be illustrated as follows.

In the following statements, empirical reference is commonly absent: "Society looks after its young as well as its old" and "Societies look after their young as well as their old," "Society is primarily concerned with law and order" and "Societies are primarily concerned with law and order," "Society possesses the means for peaceful change" and "Societies possess the means for peaceful change."

It may be argued that the above-mentioned statements in the singular do not aim at pointing out any *particular* society, and that the statements in the plural only point out what is true as a general rule. That is to say that societies do, as a general rule, look after their young as well as their old, maintain law and order, and possess the means for peaceful change. Nevertheless, innumerable instances can be cited to challenge the generality of statements in the plural or to point out that the functions mentioned above are not performed by various societies.

It may, therefore, be pointed out that the statements in the plural are not by themselves indicative of their empirical reference but need certain extra qualifications that may be—as far as statements in politics are concerned—regional, political, or numerical. With the help of these qualifications, we can restrict the generality of statements in the plural to more or less definite groups of instances:

"Societies in *Western Europe* do not prohibit drinking."
"*Totalitarian* societies investigate the background of candidates before they are nominated."
"*Five* societies are capable of thermonuclear warfare."
All such statements in the plural with added qualifications denote more or less definite instances. Such qualifications are thus obviously indispensable for statements in the plural to have empirical reference.

Statements in the plural, we may therefore conclude, have nothing inherently empirical about them. What the plural number secures is only the multiplicity of singular instances. Multiplicity of singular instances does not by virtue of number make a statement empirical.

Dewey remained under the misconception of the self-evident empiricalness of statements in the plural about "states," "publics," "societies," and so forth. The detection of fallacy of empirical plurals was important for Dewey's purpose because he sought to discriminate·the peculiarities in the political arrangements of different societies, and such a discriminatory analysis cannot be undertaken unless it is preceded by statements that bring together different political societies in appropriate groups.

The term that Dewey has used in order to indicate a society with a political organization of its own is "public." "Public" therefore might appear to be Dewey's substitute for the term "state" for a politically and legally organized society. Although Dewey himself uses the term "public" as a substitute for the term "state," he means in actual fact much more than that. The use of the term "public" by Dewey, indicates not only a society with a political organization of its own but also a society that gradually becomes aware of the problem of its well-being and devises ways and means to solve those problems. We shall attempt to analyze here the notion of well-being that Dewey associates with the term "public."

The term "public" figures very prominently in two of the major works of Walter Lippmann, *Public Opinion* (1922) and *The Phantom Public* (1930). Although Dewey acknowledged his debt to both these works, his notion of the term "public" remains totally different from that of Lippmann, for whom "public" meant a group of people, who by positive law or persuasion seek to control the behavior of its members as well as its rulers. The separation between the rulers and the ruled—or, to use Lippmann's terms, "agents" and "bystanders"—being well marked in his political philosophy, the public's control of its rulers was supposed to be indirect.[49] Lippmann was intensely aware of the extraordinary complexities of social and political phenomena, on the one hand, and the limitations of the average individual, on the other. Realistically speaking, he maintained, a society is "a complex of social relations;"[50] consequently, it is a mere illusion to claim to know it fully.

Modern society is not visible to anybody, nor intelligible continuously and as a whole. One section is visible to another section, one series of acts is intelligible to this group and another to that.[51]

The democratic form of government, however, takes for granted that the average individual is an omnicompetent sovereign individual who is capable of making intelligent decisions on public matters. "My sympathies are with him," says Lippmann, "for I believe that he has been saddled with an impossible task and that he is asked to practice an unattainable ideal."[52] The ability to take interest in public affairs is restricted to a small group of people who are engaged in public life, and hence it is not true to say that "the whole people takes part in public affairs."[53] What is true is that the small fraction of the public that is vigilant and articulate succeeds in indirectly influencing the people who enjoy the power.

Dewey did not share Lippmann's pessimism over the limitations of the individual in participating in public affairs. Being primarily an educationalist, Dewey carried with himself an unshakeable faith in the potentialites of human beings to overcome their physical as well as social problems. Such a faith helped Dewey to fight back the feeling of despair that runs through Lippmann's works. Although Dewey was far from being an academic recluse, his acquaintance with *actual* problems of public life, compared with that of a political analyst like Lippmann, was not firsthand. Consequently, it was easier for him than it was for Lippmann to preserve his faith in the ability of the average individual to participate in public life.

For Dewey, only a part of the total participation of which the average individual was capable was in public life. Earlier we had noted that Dewey's philosophy of education puts an enormous emphasis on *becoming by doing*. He meant, in other words, that we develop our personality only when we *express* and *act*. Our expressions and overt behavior are reactions to external stimuli, physical as well as intellectual. As we always live and act in association with others, our expression and overt behavior must find its place in the expressions and overt behaviors of the community. The problem of participation therefore is not restricted to participation in public affairs.

Dewey acknowledged the presence of innumerable obstacles to the individual's participation in public life. He agreed with Lippmann that public affairs are far more complicated and impersonal today than ever before. Nevertheless Dewey felt the problem of participation of the average individual was not as unsurmountable. While Lippmann in his despair entitled his book *The Phantom Public*, Dewey went in search of ways and means of making individuals conscious of being integral parts of the public. The contrast between Lippmann's title and *The Public and Its Problems* is extremely significant.

Apart from these differences, Dewey's use of the term "public" deserves independent consideration. He included in "public" some of the psychological associations that the term is capable of arousing. When "public" is mentioned, not only do we visualize a group of people, but we visualize a group *to whom something is done*. This is because the term is used more often to denote certain organized welfare schemes (or the need to have welfare schemes) rather than to denote an assembly of people. In using this term, we therefore arouse associations similar to "public service," "public utility," "public benefit," "public welfare," "in the interest of the public," "against the interest of the public," and so forth. Similarly, Dewey takes for granted that the public consists of people who are organized to some extent and who seek to extend or modify their existing organization *in the interest of general well-being*. The following statement indicates the presence of the sentiments of general well-being in the act of extending or modifying the existing organization of the public.

> . . . *public is organized and made effective by means of representatives who as guardians of custom, as legislators, as executives, judges, etc., care for its especial interests by methods intended to regulate the conjoint actions of individuals and groups.*[54]

This use of the term "public" reintroduces moral considerations into political activity and political organization. This might seem to contradict his earlier advocacy of the formulation of political problems strictly in their own terms. But such a contradiction is more apparent than real. No set of problems is without moral significance. A set of problems—whether physical, biological, scientific, or political—acquires moral significance *only* when human beings consider it in terms of its capacity for good and evil effect on the human estate. That is to say, these problems can first of all be investigated and stated in their own terms. This will then facilitate our discriminatory judgment concerning how they effect our general well-being, and to what extent. All kinds of problems acquire a moral dimension when we consider them in terms of their effects of good and evil. However, before any moral consideration can be brought into the field, the problem must be investigated and state in its own terms. Moral considerations ought to follow rather than precede any cognitive or investigatory process. To be able to choose and act, we must first of all know and be able to discriminate. The moral implications of well-being involved in Dewey's use of the term "public" do not contradict or prevent the formulation of political problems in strictly political terms. On the other hand, the formulation of political problems in their own terms helps him to acquire a clearer notion of this well-being.

Dewey's presupposition of associated living, which we have noted before, does not explain away the various peculiarities in the political arrangements of different societies. These differences, which we have noted before, spring directly from the geographical, economic, religious, and psychological compositions of different societies. In order properly to appreciate genuine differences in various political arrangements or political organizations, we must consider them in the context of the respective social forces that give rise to them. Dewey's claim in this connection is that with the help of his political concepts—namely, consequences, perception, and organization—we can do this, and thereby understand the peculiarities of one political arrangement or organization and discriminate it from another.

Before we go on to analyze and criticize this particular claim, it is necessary to point out that we shall not treat his concept of the public as a hypothesis to be confirmed. In *The Public and Its Problems*, Dewey gives the impression that the public, as a hypothesis, can be tested with the help of what may be regarded as the external marks or characteristics of political organizations that we find in our experience. Now Dewey himself did not assert anything definite when he used the concept "public" to make its confirmation possible. On the one hand, he gave the impression that discriminatory investigation cannot be undertaken unless we call a society with a political organization of its own by the term "public" rather than "state." This is because he believes that the term "public" invites further investigation into its nature and the extent of its organization, whereas "state" does not. We will recall, that Dewey made a similar distinction between "data" and "objects." Earlier[55] we noted that, according to Dewey, Galileo succeeded in treating objects as data in physical science. "Data" indicates material for further use or further investigation, whereas "objects" gives the impression of finality. Data are something on which we build, a kind of first rung in the ladder. However, if the use of the term "public" opens up, as it were, all the doors to investigation, the same does not and cannot assert anything definite in the form of a hypothesis to be confirmed.

Now Dewey believed that the political character of every public could be discriminated as well as stated with the help of his three concepts: namely, consequences, perception, and organization. He saw the public as a group of people who are politically organized or seeking to extend and modify their existing organization for the purposes of general well-being. Some kind of general assertion concerning the capacity of his concepts to help us in our discriminatory analysis is implied, but such an assertion does not in any way make his concept of public a hypothesis to be confirmed. The problem of confirmation applies only to his claim that these concepts are able to discriminate the peculiarities of different political organizations.

We shall therefore restrict our attention to the claim about his concepts. We shall examine our ability to discriminate the peculiarities of different political organizations with their help. We shall conduct this test in the light of the three external marks or characteristics mentioned above, plus a fourth, the *assimilative* tendency of political organizations.

In order to test the discriminatory capacity of his concepts, Dewey first of all pointed out that political organizations differ from one another both in kind as well as in degree of organization.[56] Such differences arise on account of the peculiar social composition that lies behind every political organization. The test of the discriminatory capacity of his concepts lies in their ability to intelligibly point this out.

Differences in *kind* of political organization arise as a result of the different primary activities that different societies pursue. Primary activities pursued by agricultural societies would be different from the primary activities of industrial societies. The primary activities of one agricultural society would be different from those in another agricultural society. This is true because every society, agricultural or industrial, is the product of unique geographical, economic, climatic, racial, and intellectual factors. These factors affect the quality of the primary activities of every society. They are therefore responsible for bringing about differences in *consequences* of the primary activities of different societies. Since political organization of every society is a response to the demand for regulation and control of its consequences, the differences in kind of political organization arise as a result of the differences of various societies that they regulate and control.

The difference in the degree or the extent to which a society is politically organized depends upon the consciousness or perception of a society of the various consequences, on the one hand, and the presence of adequate means to bring about regulatory measures, on the other. In different societies, the consciousness of consequences of primary activities and the adequate means to regulate them exist in differing degrees. Together they are therefore responsible for the difference in the degree of political organization of various societies.

In this respect then, the concepts of consequences, perception, and organization help us to see the difference between one political organization and another. However, the *actual* differences require further investigation. Once we acknowledge the fact that political organizations differ from one another because of their intrinsic relationship with various societies, we enter into a wider field of investigation in which we can examine specific political organizations against the background of the specific societies that they seek to regulate and control. A vast field of investigation is opened—into the political apparatus possessed by different societies, the part played by political parties, public opinion, press, means of mass communication, and so forth, in those societies, and into the extent to which the political apparatus of different societies respond to those means of arousing social consciousness.

Whatever discriminations in the peculiarities of political phenomena we can make with the help of Dewey's concepts are therefore extremely general. Nevertheless, the merit of Dewey's concepts lies not in their ability actually to discriminate but in their theoretical acknowledgment that political organizations have peculiarities of their own and that it is our business to investigate them.

The second characteristic with the help of which Dewey tests the discriminatory capacity of his concepts is as follows: In every political society, the regulation and control of *consequences* of primary activities increases or decreases roughly in proportion to society's own estimate of good and evil that results from those consequences.[57] To illustrate the discriminatory capacity of his concepts, Dewey uses justice, religious freedom, and intellectual freedom. The increase or decrease in political control of these three has varied in proportion to what different societies regarded their *consequences* to be.

Historically speaking, the administration of justice passed from relatively private hands to the political organization of society. It was gradually realized that the consequences of administration of justice are vitally important for the general well-being of the society. Consequently, in course of time the administration of justice came completely under the control of the political organization of society. Society's attitude towards religious and intellectual freedom has been diametrically opposite. Different societies have realized in different degrees that the consequences of religious and intellectual freedom are ultimately beneficial to the various shades of opinions and beliefs that are to be found in such societies. And in different societies, the relaxation of political control of religious and intellectual matters has been in proportion to the appreciation that these societies have of the consequences of religious and intellectual freedom.

Such a discriminatory analysis appears to be confined to the relation between perception or appreciation of consequences and their consequent political control or relaxation of control. In fact, it is capable of more than that, for Dewey's concepts are adequate enough for the purposes of investigation of the historical expansion or contraction of the authority of different political organizations, which in turn enables us to grasp the character of existing political organizations as they have evolved .

The third characteristic of political organizations used by Dewey to test the discriminatory capacity of his concepts is as follows: Every politically organized society tends to protect children, dependents, and weaker parties in every transaction. In other words, its protection of the weak extends beyond what is normally provided in equality before the law.[58]

Now every society differs from others in the extent of its protection of the weak, minors, and dependent persons. With the help of his concepts, Dewey can state the extent of protective legislation that exists in different societies. The difference in the protective legislations of different societies, however, is an empirical one. Each society has definite legal enactments by way of protective legislation, and their effects on the weak, minors, and dependent persons are not difficult to determine. The merit of Dewey's concepts lies in their ability to combine an empirical differentiation with what is more difficult—a determination of the kind of public consciousness that had put forward each demand for protective legislation.

The fourth characteristic that Dewey uses to test the discriminatory capacity of his concepts is as follows: Political organizations have a tendency to assimilate into their own framework what may be described as well-established behaviors and practices.[59] However, Dewey was mistaken in regarding this as a characteristic of political organizations, for two reasons. First, a well-established manner of behavior or practice, in order to be assimilated into the framework of political organization, must be one on which the general well-being of the society depends. Not all well-established practices are in the interest of society. No political organization would assimilate into its own framework, and thereby legalize, the well-established practices of black market, corruption, or nepotism. Secondly, a well-established practice that is regarded as being in the interest of society would not require any judicial aid because it is, *ex hypothesi*, already well-established. It requires judicial support only when its frequency is dubious, in which case it cannot be regarded as well-established.

The true characteristic of political organizations is not that they assimilate into their framework all the well-established behaviors and practices, but that they assimilate only those on which the general well-being depends, for political organizations cannot risk the danger of lapses in these behaviors and practices; consequently their performance is made obligatory.

Now Dewey's concepts certainly enable him to discriminate the extent to which different societies regard certain manners of behavior and practices as indispensable for their well-being and the extent to which they succeed in making their performance of these behaviors obligatory, as well as the extent to which they enable him to make these discriminations separately.

▰▰▰ *Difficulties in Dewey's concepts*

These are, then, a few of the characteristics of political organizations with the help of which we have tested the discriminatory capacity of Dewey's concepts. Our main purpose has been to find out whether Dewey is correct in his claim that different political organizations have peculiarities of their own, and that we need concepts to discriminate them in our investigation. Needless to say, what we have tried to do here is only to test Dewey's concepts, not to undertake actual discriminatory investigation with their help.

It must be admitted, however, that although Dewey's concepts do enable us to make a few intelligible discriminations, the actual test of their own discriminatory capacity is very limited. Their success in making intelligible discrimination and in encouraging further investigations of the four characteristics of political organizations than we have considered does not guarantee their success in discriminating other characteristics of political organizations that we may seek to deal with. However, it must also be admitted that the temper of his political philosophy being essentially experimental, Dewey would not have any objections to replacing or modifying any one of these discriminatory concepts if they were to be found unsatisfactory.

Nevertheless, Dewey's concepts present a few genuine difficulties when we consider them in the light of what they imply. First of all, Dewey's concepts essentially view political activity as working in the direction of some kind of *organization*. This means that the entire discriminatory analysis that can be undertaken with the help of his concepts is essentially confined to those activities directly or indirectly connected with the problem of organization.

Now in any satisfactory definition of political activity, one cannot help emphasizing the fact that it implies an organizational reference. Political activity is certainly brought into existence for the purposes of regulating and controlling the consequences of primary activities, and any attempt at regulation and control essentially implies some form of organization or other. In any discourse on political activity, therefore, a reference to organization cannot be objected to at all.

On the other hand, what can be objected to is a view that insists on analyzing and discriminating the peculiarities of different political organizations in terms of *organization* only. Such is the impression that one gets from Dewey's concepts. His concepts do not do enough justice to those factors whose contribution cannot be observed in terms of organization, such factors as national temperament, moral beliefs, and historical traditions. To be able to determine the extent to which the former factors together with the latter are responsible for giving any political organization a character and peculiarity of its own, a set of concepts should be able to discriminate them.

While Dewey's concepts helped him to bring out the peculiarities of political organizations against a background of economic, geographical, and technical factors, they did not help him to discriminate the peculiarities of political organizations against a background of national temperaments, moral beliefs, and historical traditions. Every political organization unmistakably bears the marks of the temperament, beliefs, and traditions of a people whose problems it undertakes to look after. These may or may not find an expression in the formal political organization of the society in which they exist. Nevertheless, they are no less responsible in giving character and peculiarity to that political organization. Dewey's discriminatory analysis, therefore, remains incomplete.

A second difficulty with Dewey's concepts, apart from their discriminatory capacity, is that when they are considered together, they do not give an altogether reliable picture of the way in which political activity comes into existence. Consequences, perception, and organization—the three different stages in the constitution or the reconstitution of a political organization—give the impression of falling into a kind of sequential order such as in which consequences produce perception, and perception is responsible for bringing into existence some sort of regulatory organization. Such an impression is certainly misleading, for the regulatory organization of consequences may or may not take place as a result of the consciousness or perception of the society. The existing organization may itself take the initiative in bringing about the regulatory control of the new consequences. Or the existing political organization may make a provision in advance to meet the contingency of unforseeable consequences, such provision as is often made in the laws of society. At other times, the existing political organization may deflect consequences in such a manner that they may not be perceived by the society. All these illustrations are not at all hypothetical. They do show that the sequential order of consequences, perception, and organization is capable of giving an incorrect impression.

A third difficulty is that consequences and organization, when considered together, give the impression that the regulatory control or organization of consequences is *the* remedy of all the possible consequences. Examples can be given, however, in which neither the extension nor the curtailment of the existing organization is capable of giving a satisfactory solution. The tendency of newspapers to concentrate in fewer and fewer hands is a case in point. Neither the growth of unobstructed newspaper syndicates nor the nationalization of the press would solve the difficulty that the press in a democratic society is exposed to.

Finally, any attempt at generic discrimination tends to arrange the data for the purposes of comparison. Roughly similar entities are brought together and common terms devised in order that their relative differences can be enumerated. These are precisely the conditions which must be fulfilled in order to pass comparative judgments. Dewey abruptly stops in his analysis precisely at the point where the results of his discriminatory analysis furnish the possibility of comparative judgments. He did not favor comparative judgments.[60] He merely wanted to reach a stage in the understanding of political phenomena that might be a guide to enlightened action in politics.

The Analytical Aspect of Dewey's Political Theory

Unlike the epistemological aspect of Dewey's political theory, which concentrates on the problems of understanding the peculiarities of political phenomena, the analytical aspect deals with the questions concerning the analysis and resolution of specific problems in politics. However, in spite of the fact that the epistemological aspect and the analytical aspect differ from each other both in the range of their interest and the nature of their problems, the latter takes for granted the results of the former. The analysis and resolution of specific problems in politics depend upon the previous knowledge of the peculiarities of that particular political organization to which the specific problems under investigation belong. Consequently, while moving from the epistemological aspect to the analytical aspect of Dewey's political theory, we do not encounter any abrupt change in his ideas on political investigation.

As we have said before, the analytical aspect of Dewey's political theory deals with the questions concerning analysis and resolution of specific problems in politics. In this section we propose to examine Dewey's ideas under the following three headings: investigatory hypotheses and policy hypotheses; factual, casual, and evaluative analysis; and democracy as a necessary condition of formulating and testing social hypotheses.

Investigatory hypotheses and policy hypotheses

A political theory that lays great stress on causal analysis of specific problems with a view to resolving them must be able to distinguish between investigatory hypotheses and policy hypotheses. Their confusion or identification creates serious difficulties in the resolution of specific problems.

The fact that a concept, theory, or assertion that is used in investigation ought to be in the form of a hypothesis to be confirmed whenever challenged hardly needs any justification. Reality is complex. Different people think about it or approach it differently. Every specific problem, being a fraction of reality, carries with it all the complexities of reality. Any concept or theory or assertion that claims to direct our investigatory operations of a specific problem can be nothing but a hypothesis. This is because we ourselves might find it unsatisfactory in the face of an actual investigation and try to replace it, or others might wish to challenge it. In this case we would have to demonstrate its confirmation publicly. In either case, the character of the concept, theory, or assertion used for the purposes of investigation essentially remains hypothetical.

On the other hand, measures to be put into practice after necessary investigation should also be treated as hypotheses. No matter how thorough our investigation of a problem may be, in the actual implementation of a preplanned measure certain modifications invariably become indispensable. It might, of course, be argued that what a preplanned measure requires is *flexibility* rather than hypothetical character. But the answer to such an objection is as follows. When a preplanned measure is treated as an hypothesis, flexibility is actually implied. But something more than that is also implied: that it is going to be confirmed by its own results. First it is theoretically confirmed in terms of an estimate of the practical results of its introduction. Budgetary policy, for example, rests on some such theoretical confirmation. Such a confirmation, which is essentially practical, is far from satisfactory; nevertheless, in the absence of the results of its practical introduction conclusively pointing out its merits or demerits, the psychological implications of treating a practical measure as an hypothesis to be confirmed are certainly significant. Treating practical measures as hypotheses enables us to avoid feelings of certainty or cocksureness that invariably prevent us from taking into consideration the unpleasant aspects of our estimates. It also helps us to be less dogmatic about the assertions implied in a measure for the simple reason that the test of the measure is transferred from its internal rationality or consistency to its results.

Investigatory hypotheses and policy hypotheses, although having different spheres of operation, can be confused, especially in those investigations that immediately precede the adoption of practical measures. We shall illustrate this contention with the help of two examples. The first is the example of a fictitious Royal Commission's Report on the condition of old-age pensioners. The second example is that of the Marxist law of dialectical materialism, in which these two hypotheses are actually confused.

A Royal Commission, in order to report on the condition of old-age pensioners, first of all investigates the ability of the average pensioner to afford necessary items like food, rent, clothing, and other miscellaneous items. In order to determine the ability or inability of the average pensioner to afford these necessary items, the Commission would be guided by its own hypothesis on the absolute minimum or the "poverty line." With the "poverty line" as the tentatively fixed standard, the Commission would sort out pensioners unable to spend what it regards to be an adequate amount on the necessary items. The Commission then investigates the causes of their inability to spend an adequate amount on necessary items. Among such causes, the Commission may find that certain pensioners make too much use of tobacco or go to films and theatres far more than they can afford. It may find others, who on account of their background, spend too much on clothing. There may be still others who are used to their expensive suburban homes and gardens and consequently are unable to move to less expensive dwellings. In all these instances the Commission might feel that the pensioners who fall below the "poverty-line" do not conform to the budget it has in mind for them. However, by the time the Commission completes its investigations, certain facts are revealed that show whether or not its own absolute minimum is adequate, thereby confirming or rejecting the Commission's *investigatory hypothesis.*

The Commission then goes on to make necessary recommendations, which might be to raise the absolute minimum for the old-age pensioners by a few shillings. This recommendation might be guided by an estimate of a probable rise in the cost of living. Whatever the recommendations, the Commission remains aware of the fact that only the results of the implementation of its recommendation, or *policy hypothesis,* can confirm whether or not the amount is satisfactory. The Commission demands future investigation of the results of its recommendation.

Although from a practical point of view the difference between the Commission's investigatory hypothesis and its policy hypothesis is that of a few shillings only, in theory this difference is extremely significant. In theory, these two hypotheses enjoy two different kinds of confirmation; consequently, the feeling of certainty that can be attached to one is radically different from the feeling of certainty that can be attached to the other. Investigatory hypotheses have more reliable data to confirm them than policy hypotheses. It is therefore a mistake to attach the same degree of certainty to policy hypotheses that is attached to investigatory hypotheses. Let us now examine a second illustration in which these hypotheses are identified and the feeling of certainty is transferred from one to the other.

The identification of investigatory hypotheses with policy hypotheses invariably results in the formulation of general laws of behavior, both past as well as future, of certain social and economic movements. In such an identification, a kind of belief is implied that we can precisely determine the causal factors of these movements and can predict the particular course that they would follow.

The law of dialectical materialism that Marx confirmed with the help of his phenomenal knowledge of social and economic history may be considered his investigatory hypothesis. The purpose of this law, the extent to which it could be tested with the help of historical data, was investigatory. It served as an instrument of making social and economic history intelligible. At the same time, the logic of change or the rhythm of social and economic evolution, as implied by the law of dialectical materialism, could be confirmed, as far as Marx was concerned, with the help of the available social and economic data. In that respect, therefore, Marx's investigatory hypothesis was not without its confirmation.

However, Marx was so very confident of his analysis of social and economic history and his formulation of the law of dialectical materialism that he visualized its inevitable operation in the future, and thus it became for him, as translated into our terminology, some kind of an inevitable policy hypothesis. There was no question of choosing such a policy hypothesis. All that one could do was to cooperate and facilitate the course of its operation. Moreover, as far as Marx was concerned, its future operation did not require any confirmation. For him the fact that the law had operated in the past was a sufficient guarantee that it would also operate in the future. The fact that such a law would have to operate amid an unknown number of unknown spatiotemporal variables did not alter the feeling of certainty that he attached to its operation in future. In plain language this meant that "what will happen" can be deduced from "what has happened." What Marx did, stated in our terminology, was to identify the investigatory hypothesis with the policy hypothesis in his law of dialectical materialism. Thus he transferred to the latter the feeling of certainty attached to the former. The members of the Royal Commission, in our previous illustration, would have shared Marx's error had they attached the same feeling of certainty to their recommended raise in the old-age pension that they did to their investigatory hypothesis after completing their investigations, and had they not asked for a periodic investigation of the conditions of old-age pensioners.

Dewey is very emphatic about the hypothetical character of both the concepts or theories or assertions used for the purposes of investigation, on the one hand, and the measures to be implemented, on the other. His theory of ideas, as well as his criticism of the use of *a priori* concepts in politics, well emphasizes the hypothetical character of his own investigatory hypotheses. His position with respect to the hypothetical is well expressed in the following, that

. . . policies and proposals for social action be treated as working

hypotheses, not as programs to be rigidly adhered to and executed. They will be experimental in the sense that they will be entertained subject to constant and well-equipped observation of the consequences they entail when acted upon, and subject to ready and flexible revision in the light of observed consequences.[61]

Dewey was a great advocate of planning, and nowhere else is there a greater need to emphasize the hypothetical character of the measures to be introduced as in planning. He therefore made a clear distinction between what he called "a planned society" and "a continuously planning society." The former indicates a blueprint to be adhered to and executed, whereas the latter takes into consideration the consequences of implementing every item in the plan. A "continuously planning society," in other words, constantly ascertains as well as confirms the rightness or wrongness of a planned measure in the light of its results and reactions of individuals to it.[62]

Dewey did not make any conscious discrimination between investigatory hypotheses and policy hypotheses; nevertheless, in his case this did not affect the quality of his causal analysis. He regarded natural and social phenomena as composed of both terminable and interminable processes having rigid sequential orders as well as contingencies within themselves. Such a mixture of opposites directly ruled out the possibility of analyzing the phenomena as a *whole*, as was the case with Marx; the scope of causal analysis was essentially restricted to *specific* problems and processes. Dewey's interest in the histories of these phenomena was well qualified in advance, because within the framework of his theory of knowledge only those objects and events that present themselves in the form of "obstacles" receive cognitive attention, and the principal consideration is either to secure something or to prevent something.[63] In the manipulative aspect of Dewey's political theory, we shall analyze the philosophical basis provided for *specific problems* and the demands that they make on our own engineering efforts. Suffice to say here that his lack of discrimination between investigatory and policy hypotheses did not lead him to use causal analysis to formulate general laws of the behavior of movements, as Marx had done.

◄▬▬▬► *Factual, causal, and evaluative analysis*

Having noted the difference between the investigatory and the policy hypotheses in politics, we shall now go on to examine Dewey's

145

views on the relation between the investigatory hypothesis and the various types of analysis applied to any particular problem. In any investigation, the end-in-view of an investigator is to confirm his hypothesis with the help of relevant data obtained and the help of factual analysis, causal analysis, and evaluative analysis. Such analyses cannot be undertaken without the help of the investigator's hypothesis. In order fully to appreciate Dewey's ideas about the relation of hypothesis to factual, causal, and evaluative analysis, we shall first examine his ideas in the light of Prof. G. H. Sabine's criticism in his paper, "What Is Political Theory" (1939).[64]

This paper was a sequel to an earlier paper, "The Pragmatic Approach to Politics" (1930).[65] In this paper, writers like Thorstein Veblen, W. C. Mitchell, W. W. Cook, and Harman Oliphant are criticized for not resisting the ferment in the fields of economics and law caused by "pragmatism in action." The subsequent paper, "What Is Political Theory," was devoted to an examination of the ferment in political theory caused by the pragmatic viewpoint.

Sabine attacked Dewey for attempting to bring the correlativity of fact and value into political theory. Sabine thought that to do this was to revive, in a new form, the relationship that existed between "causal exploration and an immanent ethical criticism" in Hegelian logic, and "causal and moral necessity" in Marxian dialectical materialism.[66]

In his attack, Sabine stated his own theoretical premises far more clearly than he stated Dewey's. A political theory, Sabine maintained, includes "either expressly or by implication, a judgment both about what is likely and a judgment about what is desirable."[67] He maintained that "there is no such thing as disinterested political theory" and that every political theory implies a definite element of policy.[68] Sabine used the term "policy" in a very broad sense, to mean both "an estimate of probabilities and an estimate of value."[69] In other words, a political theory includes statements concerning facts that are relevant to their chances of coming into existence and relevant also to the purpose of the theory. For the sake of making such statements, some sort of factual and causal analysis is undertaken. In addition to this, a political theory also includes statements explaining how and why certain things ought to take place, and must be evaluated through analysis. According to Sabine, three kinds of analysis are involved in the statement of political theory—factual, causal, and evaluative.

Sabine believed that these three kinds of analysis have three essentially different functions to perform. Nevertheless, he was prepared to concede the fact that factual and causal analysis *can* be jointly undertaken, because statements concerning relevant facts essentially have to be made in terms of the probabilities of their coming into existence. Evaluative analysis, as opposed to factual and causal analysis, undertakes a totally different kind of function; consequently the essential difference cannot be done away with.

From such a premise, Sabine attacked Dewey for having considered factual-causal and evaluative elements jointly in every "act of thought," both in his philosophy in general and in political theory in particular.[70,71] For Sabine, these two elements were different from each other in quality and would not be considered together or treated alike.[72]

In order to indicate the relationship existing between the different types of analysis in what Dewey regards as a cognitive act, Sabine had used Dewey's own phrase "acts of thought." However, he overlooked the important qualification in Dewey's conception of the cognitive act, namely, that these three types of analysis can be discriminated only *within the process of reflective inquiry.*

To return to a direct discussion of Dewey's philosophy, correct understanding of Dewey's position rests on the ability to grasp the significance of this qualification. It is a kind of logico-psychological qualification. In Dewey's philosophy, the factual-causal and evaluative analyses are "logical forms" of some sort that arise and are employed within the psychological process of inquiry. They are therefore relevant to the inquiry in which they take place.[73]

Once Dewey had chained down the "logical forms" of various analyses to the psychological process of inquiry in which they arise, his next step was to chain down the psychological process of inquiry itself to a particular hypothesis and the problems of its confirmation, or to what may be said to be an investigator's end-in-view. But the latter position—namely, the intrinsic relationship between the inquirer's end-in-view and the psychological process of his inquiry— was implicit in Dewey's conception of inquiry in general. Earlier we noted that, according to Dewey, the career of an inquiry begins with a doubt or a conflict or a tension and ends with its resolution. One does not have to go, therefore, in search of the goal of one's inquiry. The psychological process of one's inquiry, on the other hand, is preceded by one's appreciation or knowledge of a problem. Consequently for Dewey the three kinds of analysis were intrinsically connected, because each one of them was to be undertaken with the same end-in-view, namely, confirmation of the inquirer's hypothesis.

Two distinct parts of political theory—namely, the descriptive and the normative—are capable of independent statement. This fact interfered with Sabine's analysis of Dewey's political theory. Sabine expressed his disapproval at the semblance of unity in the descriptive and the normative parts of Dewey's political theory because he felt that Dewey had arbitrarily unified them, irrespective of the genuine differences in their natures and functions. What Sabine overlooked, however, was that the descriptive and normative were both joined, in Dewey's political theory, with the inquirer's end-in-view. From Dewey's point of view, Sabine had cut loose the descriptive and the valuational parts from what was common to both of them and consequently believed that their interrelation was arbitrary, because he failed to see what connected them.

Dewey's position concerning the relationship between the three different kinds of analysis and the investigator's end-in-view may be illustrated as follows.

The investigatory hypothesis is an assertion of an investigator about the problematic situation. The end-in-view confirms his assertion or hypothesis with the help of relevant data. For the sake of our illustration, apathy in voting in Britain may be regarded as the problematic situation. The assertion or hypothesis may be stated: *The apathy in voting in Britain today is due to lack of faith in the ability of politics to change the society.* The investigator then proceeds to confirm his hypothesis by obtaining the answers of a representative cross-section of the people on questions relating to interest in politics. He also subjects his hypothesis to the views of leading writers and public men who take interest in the problems of voting. The entire range of activity engaged in by the investigator, from the formulation of this hypothesis right up to its satisfactory confirmation becomes his end-in-view.

Factual-causal and evaluative analysis essentially become the procedural tools of the investigator's end-in-view. In the above example, factual-causal analysis of the data is undertaken in order to establish the hypothesis that people in Britain suffer from a lack of faith in politics to change society. The hypothesis itself acts as a guiding factor in sifting, discriminating, and establishing causal connections between itself and its confirmatory data.

148

Such a hypothesis is not devoid of normative, or valuational, significance. Thus the evaluative analysis is made an internal part of factual-causal analysis. The valuational significance of the hypothesis and the consequent evaluative dimension in the factual-causal analysis may be explained as follows.

The fact that *politics* itself is singled out among other factors as responsible for apathy in voting is significant. One can certainly catalogue a host of other reasons for apathy in voting. Some of them are lack of leisure, lack of civic sense in appreciating voting as a civil obligation, need to vote for a party and its program rather than the individual, inability to identify oneself with one of the two contending parties, and so forth. All these factors can be—and are—responsible to a greater or lesser degree for apathy in voting. The fact that the investigator has selected "lack of faith in the ability of politics to change the society" reveals his own emphasis and preference for one factor over others.

Although this does not commit the investigator to a position, it does indicate the investigator's preference for a condition in which people would either have greater faith in politics or would resort to some other means in order to change the society. Between these two latter alternatives, the investigator's position is not clearly defined. However, it is clearly defined in respect to the existing "lack of faith in politics," that is to say, his position indicates a kind of antipathy towards the continued existence of a set of conditions. The investigator, in this particular instance, does not have to commit himself to a position that "the lack of faith in politics" is a good or a bad thing. Such judgments are not demanded by the nature of the problem that he is investigating, namely, apathy in voting. Within the framework of inquiry of his problem, there is, as a matter of fact, no other possible expression of preference than what is implied by his hypothesis. To summarize, the process of evaluation or evaluative analysis takes place through the agency of the hypothesis and its function of directing the factual-causal analysis.[74]

At the bottom of the dispute between Sabine and Dewey seems to be dissimilar views on what in fact a political theory ought to indicate. Sabine seems to speak of the valuation factor having in mind a theory that refers to the entire political phenomenon, for he believed that a political theory, being a product of a social milieu, essentially expresses the aspirations and technique of controlling that milieu.[75] Political theory was therefore a comprehensive attitude towards the arrangements and ideals of a society. It is with such a conception that he insisted on the distinction between descriptive and normative statements in political theory. For Dewey, no such comprehensive theorization about the entire political phenomenon was meaningful. We previously noted that his attempt to formulate a conceptual tool of inquiry was inspired by the need to discriminate the peculiarities of different political organizations. It was his belief that this was the first step towards the solution of specific problems. Consequently, political theory as a *Weltanschauung* of a political thinker towards the world of politics, as suggested by Sabine's conception, is significantly absent in Dewey. Dewey seemed to revolt against the idea of treating the world of politics as one single whole, as he also revolted along with William James against the conception which treats the physical world or reality as a "block universe."[76] The epistemological aspect of his political theory indicates, in fact, his attempt to formulate a methodological basis for observing and recording the diversities and pluralities that exist in the world of politics. As opposed to this, Dewey's conception of the world of politics was highly pluralistic; consequently, political theory, from his point of view, could not undertake to indicate a comprehensive attitude towards the world of politics.

Sabine's and Dewey's differing conceptions of what a political theory is made all the difference in their respective conceptions of the relationship between factual, causal, and evaluative analysis. Sabine conceived political theory as a comprehensive attitude towards the world of politics; consequently, he could clearly visualize a strict division between the world of politics as it is and as it ought to be. Against the background of such a division, factual-causal and evaluative analysis came to acquire two strictly different functions. From his standpoint, therefore, Dewey's attempt to visualize these analyses in terms of their intrinsic relationships was an error of the first order. We have seen that no such comprehensive attitude embracing all the different political organizations is involved in Dewey's political theory. From the very start his political nominalism restricted the statement of his political theory to the possibility of discriminating one political organization from another. Such a theoretical exercise was not undertaken for its own sake, but for Dewey was only a preliminary to the analysis and resolution of specific problems that we confront in our experience. In the actual analysis and resolution of specific problems of a society, different investigators choose different problems for their investigation. Each investigator indicates his attitude towards the problem with the help of his hypothesis. His hypothesis then expresses a specific attitude rather than an attitude towards the world of politics in general. His hypothesis places his factual-causal and evaluative analyses in intrinsic relationship with each other. These three types of analysis form integral parts of his effort to analyze the problem under the direction of his hypothesis.

Sabine and Dewey, to summarize, did not have a common frame of reference, and this was largely responsible for their prescribing different functions to the three types of analysis.

◄═══► *Democracy as an essential condition of formulating and testing special hypotheses*

In our exposition of the analytical aspect of Dewey's political theory, we have so far examined the light shed by his ideas on hypothesis and analysis in political investigation. In this section we shall deal with the central belief of his political philosophy, that only democracy can provide the scope for investigating our hypotheses and experimenting with them, both at the individual and at the social level. His thesis, which emerges out of this belief, is that democracy, like science, has institutionalized the procedure of trial and error. Science, however, has perfected trial and error and has built up an entire superstructure on the basis of this procedure. In that respect, science is far ahead of democracy. Politics in general (and democracy in particular), consequently, have much to learn from science. It is this particular thesis of Dewey that we shall expound and criticize in this section.

Behind the existing institutionalization of the trial-and-error procedure, both in science and in democracy, there lies the long and checkered history of the human search for the dependable form of knowledge and the desirable form of government. There are two significant phases through which this search has evolved. They are the authoritative phase and the experimental phase.

The authoritative phase in knowledge, as well as in government, is noted for the use of religious and rational dogmas,[77] which, historically speaking, have been used as authorities in the process of reasoning both in science and in politics. The Greeks freely used rational dogmas in expounding their science and politics. Plato's transcendent idealism was his rational dogma. He used it as his

151

authority in order to declare the objects of the physical world to be inferior copies of the archetypes. He also used it in order to support his contention that rule by philosophers is the best form of government, because they alone can grasp the transcendent nature of reality. In the case of Aristotle, his theory of "ends" served as his rational authority. With the help of this theory, he determined the processes of the physical world, the forms of thought, and the superiority of one form of government over another. Although Plato and Aristotle carefully reasoned out these problems, they did not subject their rational authorities to as adequate examination. During the middle ages, religious texts, accepted on faith, were freely used as authorities for the purposes of either justifying or refuting the arguments concerning the physical world and government—for example, the justifications of the divine right of kings and the theory of the earth as the center of the universe.

With Bacon and Galileo in science and with Locke and the Utilitarians in politics begins the experimental phase in the human search for the dependable form of knowledge and the desirable form of government. It would be quite improper to suggest that science and politics have retained their experimental character ever since. Departures from the experimental attitude, as far as reasoning in politics is concerned, have been the rule rather than the exception. Concerning science, although there have been no significant reverses in its experimental attitude, it certainly has taken centuries to develop and perfect its technique of experimentation.

The experimental phase in science consists of gradual renunciation of all forms of dogmatic and *a priori* authorities previously used in the process of its reasoning. It is a phase in which science embodies the rationale of trial-and-error procedure into a method of testing the claims of various hypotheses and theories. The human search for a reliable method of testing the claims to efficacy and plausibility of various concepts and theories.

The rationale of trial-and-error procedure is fully embodied in the method of science. Science accepts a theory only after subjecting it to its own tests and also acknowledges only a statistical, not an absolute, confirmation. In so doing, it not only subjects a theory to trial but acknowledges that its own testing procedure is itself on trial.

Science consists of a body of hypotheses that are confirmed or confirmable in different degrees. For those hypotheses that are confirmed today, science admits a possibility of their refutation to-

morrow. Certain of its hypotheses have partial or defective confirmation. Nevertheless, it provisionally retains these hypotheses
because of their ability to answer parts of certain questions. Moreover, the practice of statistical confirmation is about the greatest
safeguard that it has against defective hypotheses and theories. By
an endless procedure of formulating and testing hypotheses and
also by repeatedly testing the correctness of its own methods of
testing, science has evolved the most dependable form of knowledge
that human beings have known so far. Behind its method lies its
conviction that there is no other more reliable method possible
than the method of trial and error. All that we can do with what we
regard as an intellectually correct and practically sound hypothesis
is to subject it to a process of intelligent trial and careful detection
of its errors.

The search for a desirable form of government cannot be strictly
divided into an authoritative phase and an experimental phase.
This is because, unlike science, politics is mainly concerned with
organized authority, and the thinkers who have either justified it
or denounced it have drawn their support mainly from religious
and rational dogmas. With the gradual development of the technique of trial and error, science totally gave up reasoning based on
religious or rational dogmas: the trial-and-error procedure, as a
technique for obtaining the most dependable form of knowledge,
is in fact an *alternative* that science offers in the place of reasoning
based on dogmas and authorities. In politics, however, the search for
the desirable form of government embodying an experimental attitude has not been of this nature. The desirable form of government embodying experimental attitude is democracy, and the justification of democracy itself is not devoid of reasoning based on
dogmas and authorities. Mr. T. D. Weldon shocked the readers of his
Vocabulary of Politics by arguing that our traditional conception
of democracy rests on as deep a metaphysical foundation as fascism
or communism. According to him, two of its basic metaphysical
elements are the Newtonian atom and the Kantian moral self.[78] To
this, one can certainly add the third important metaphysical element, namely Rousseau's omnicompetent sovereign individual. The
experimental phase, therefore, is not as easily distinguishable from
the authoritative phase in politics as it is in science.

The experimental attitude, as a matter of fact, has been far
more limited in political reasoning or thinking than in practical

politics. Locke was the first thinker to maintain that all governments are on trial with respect to protecting the life, liberty, and property of their citizens. He therefore justified the replacement of one government by another if it did not succeed in protecting these natural rights. However, Locke strictly confined his experimental attitude to governments and their ability to protect the natural rights of citizens. He did not allow himself to question the rational dogma of natural rights on which his reasoning was based. Bentham maintained that political and judicial measures ought to be examined in the light of their consequences on the happiness of individuals. Like Locke, he was not prepared to question the dogmatic basis of his reasoning, namely, the assumption that all men desire pleasure and shun pain.

In the field of practical politics, however, the growth of responsible governments based on adult franchise has succeeded in embodying the experimental attitude to a far greater extent than has been detected or acknowledged so far by political theories. Broadly speaking, a people who are governed by a periodically elected legislature and executive are in a position to scrutinize the election program of various parties, their past records, and their ability to implement what they promise. On the other hand, a political party also learns about the validity of its ideology by being able to put it into practice. The British Labor Party's program (1945) for the nationalization of key industries of Britain is a case in point. The nationalization of the railways and the mines produced certain expected as well as certain unexpected results. It was in fact a very great and a very valuable experiment, and the Labor Party, the people of Britain, and the world as a whole have much to learn from its results. The Conservative Party, reluctant to continue the heavy tax-structure bequeathed to it by the Labor Party in the 1952 election, similarly learned by going into office that the network of welfare schemes that had become an integral part of British society could not be maintained unless the level of taxation continued to be the same. Day in and day out, governments, political parties, the press, and private individuals undertake innumerable investigations, polls, sample surveys, and so forth, in order to discover and to communicate the result of various policies that are put into practice. In all these efforts, some sort of experimental attitude is implicit. Individuals, political parties, and governments learn more about what they profess or believe by a process of trial and error. But trial-and-error procedure is not a self-sufficient procedure. It must be accompanied by free inquiry about whatever is tried and by unobstructed publicity about its findings.

The political order that provides a scope for subjecting our ideas and policies to a procedure of trial and error is democracy. In a democracy both the rulers as well as the ruled learn more about the validity and efficacy of their ideas and policies by experimenting on the basis of them. Democracy is the most desirable form of government also because it is the only form of government that allows us to learn by our successes and failures.

Dewey's views on the institutionalization of the trial-and-error procedure, both in democracy and in science, are quite evident from the following passage.

It is difficult to see how any a priori or any systematic absolutism is to get a footing among us, at least beyond narrow and professional circles. Psychologists talk about learning by trial and error or success. Our social organization commits us to this philosophy of life. Our working principle is to try, to find out by trying, and to measure the worth of ideas and theories tried by the success with which they meet the test of application in practice. Concrete consequences rather than a priori rules supply our guiding principles.[79]

Dewey was certainly aware of the fact that although democracy, like science, has assimilated into its framework the procedure of trial and error, the extent to which this procedure has been allowed to operate is extremely limited.

I would not claim that any existing democracy has ever made complete or adequate use of scientific method in deciding upon its policies. But freedom of inquiry, toleration of diverse views, freedom of communication, the distribution of what is found out to every individual as the ultimate intellectual consumer are involved in the democratic as in the scientific method.[80]

From Dewey's point of view, the procedure of trial and error in democracy is restricted to what may be called *retrospective analysis*, that is to say, it is confined to the investigation of the results of those measures already introduced. The trial-and-error procedure, however, involves not only the investigation of measures that are already introduced, but also the deliberate introduction of practical measures in the light of the estimate of their probable consequences.

In other words, the rationale of trial-and-error procedure implies positive action as much as it implies retrospective analysis in which results are traced back to the various measures introduced. The reason that Dewey discovers for such a limited application of the trial-and-error procedure in democracy is the widespread belief that knowledge is an individual possession and that only individuals in their capacity as individuals can make use of it. It is the presence of such a belief, Dewey imagines, that is responsible for the lack of positive social measures based on social knowledge.[81] Now let us examine to what extent Dewey's explanation concerning the limited application of trial-and-error procedure is sound.

As we have implied above, Dewey is not correct when he argues that the trial-and-error procedure in a democracy is restricted only to retrospective analysis or to the investigation of results of measures that have already been introduced. Every democratic society periodically introduces a large bulk of positive measures based on the investigation of the results of its previous policies. Even in the laissez-faire democracy of the United States, against which Dewey's criticisms in his *Liberalism and Social Action* (1935) were directed, positive measures were not altogether lacking. The period of the New Deal is notable in American history for its extensive legislation on currency and employment. Such legislation, however, did not satisfy Dewey because he favored comprehensive as well as radical social measures.[82] Comprehensive measures, however, are in fact in direct contravention to the spirit of trial-and-error procedure, which implies cautious, well-thought-out, and manageable experiments so that the harm done by any errors may not be irremedial. Trial-and-error procedure is a conscious and a rational process presupposing knowledge of the problem and well-thought-out proposals to remedy them.

Dewey would not dispute the fact that our knowledge of the social phenomenon that constantly present us with innumerable specific problems is extremely limited. Moreover, specific problems are neither understood nor solved once and for all. What they require, as we shall see in the manipulative aspect of Dewey's political theory, is some sort of constant engineering effort on our part. Consequently, Dewey's advocacy of positive measures is invariably carried to the extent where these measures come in direct conflict with his laboriously argued out philosophy of trial and error.

In his criticism of the belief that knowledge is an individual possession, Dewey tends to ignore the part played by individuals in

156

enriching it or in applying it in practice. Nobody would deny that behind the discovery of penicillin or the formulation of statistical methods or the invention of electronic machines there exists a series of endless human efforts of which these discoveries are the fruits. Einstein and Freud made the two greatest contributions to human learning in the twentieth century. It was Einstein who said that he probably owed more to his predecessors for what he had contributed than is commonly believed. Similarly, when Freud was pronounced the "discoverer of the unconscious" on the occasion of his seventieth birthday, he is supposed to have said: "The poets and philosophers before me discovered the unconscious . . . . what I have discovered was the scientific method by which the unconscious can be studied."[83]

Nevertheless, what cannot be denied is the fact that a *unique* angle of vision was present in Einstein's examination of the exceptions to the Newtonian laws of nature and in Freud's examination of the determining influences that the unconscious exercises over the conscious. Their contributions were the products of their ability to develop what they uniquely perceived.

The role of the individual in the application of accumulated knowledge in such a manner cannot be denied. Knowledge is a product of social endeavor, but it is *individuals* who put it to fruitful purposes—individuals differing in insight, aptitude, and resourcefulness. Application of social knowledge at their hands consequently yields differing results. It cannot be argued, therefore, on the grounds of mere logic that since knowledge is social, its application and fruits ought to be social too. Such an argument overlooks the fact that knowledge is applicable only through the agency of individuals who differ in their capacities. Such application creates, as a matter of fact, a political problem of the first order. It is a problem far more complicated than one in which natural inequalities among individuals are eliminated by acknowledging their equality before law. No such equalization solves the problem: The society cannot afford to take away the initiative of the skilled and the gifted. At the same time it cannot let them amass the fortunes that their superior abilities create. The political solution has two aspects. On the one hand, it must aim at eliminating the unhealthy extremes of riches and poverty. On the other, it must leave a substantial pecuniary reward to the skilled and the gifted along with a due social recognition of their achievements. Such a solution, although it appears to be very simple, is in fact extremely complicated and it calls for continuous readjustment of innumerable social and economic factors. Consequently, it must be treated as a continuously recurring problem, which can be further broken up into innumerable specific problems, rather than as "solved," as Dewey claims to have solved it, in the realm of logic.

The fundamental similarity of trial-and-error procedure as found in science and in democracy misleads Dewey into believing that what holds good in science is equally relevant to politics. Such a belief appears to be the basis of his attempt at prescribing the nature of authority in science as a model for authority in politics.

The thesis that the operation of cooperative intelligence as displayed in science is a working model of the union of freedom and authority does not slight the fact that the method has operated up to the present in a limited and relatively technical area. On the contrary, it emphasizes that fact. If the method of intelligence had been employed in any large field in the comprehensive and basic area of the relations of human beings to one another in social life and institutions, there would be no present need for our argument. The contrast between the restricted scope of its use and the possible range of its application to human relations—political, economic and moral—is outstanding enough to be depressing. It is this very contrast that serves to define the great problem that lies before us.[84]

Authority in science, composed of a body of postulates and hypotheses, rests on the cooperation of men of science. It does not curb their freedom of enquiry, initiative, and variation, and it assimilates into its framework whatever they satisfactorily prove or disprove. Scientific activity cannot be carried on without an utmost degree of cooperation. If men of science were to fail to communicate to one another the results of their findings or to openly express their doubt or acceptance of such findings, science as an organized body of knowledge ceases to have any meaning. The importance of this cooperation and the freedom to refute accepted explanations or to contribute results of specialized inquiries cannot be overemphasized. Authority in science, in other words, is a cooperative authority.

There is a considerable degree of similarity between authority in science and authority in politics when they are compared in terms of *cooperation*. Both in science and in politics,[85] the function of authority is to organize the results of various activities pursued in their respective fields. Authority in both fields aims at providing a maximum degree of individual initiative and variation. Authority in both fields is maintained with the explicit purpose of narrowing down the area of conflict and of widening the area of cooperation and freedom. In both fields, the actual functioning of authority rests on the cooperation of those upon whom the authority is exercised. Science has its own body of postulates and hypotheses. Similarly, political organizations have their own sets of rules and regulations. Both science and politics are open to public scrutiny and criticism. Science, however, displays a much greater degree of willingness to give up what is proved to be unsatisfactory in its accepted body of postulates and hypotheses than does politics. Nevertheless, this does not indicate any lack of cooperation between authority and people upon whom the authority is exercised. It only indicates a greater degree of concern and caution on the part of political authority in the face of rash, ill-considered changes suggested by the people.

However, authority in science and authority in politics, when compared in terms of their actual institutionalization, reveal very marked dissimilarities. Politics being a field of authority proper, the institutionalized expression of its authority is very different from the institutionalized expression of authority in science. Authority in science appears to be academic or intellectual in comparison with authority in politics, which exists in order continuously to implement a complicated system of laws and regulations, a function to which science has no counterpart. As compared with this system of laws and regulations, which requires the presence of an organized authority to enforce it, the postulates and hypotheses of science are spontaneously accepted by scientists. Moreover, since they are purely of an intellectual nature, the nonacceptance of these postulates and hypothesis or the disbelief in any part of them would not threaten the stability of society so much as would exceptions to the laws and regulations of the state. Being directly connected with the protection of general well-being, the importance of stable authority is in fact much greater in politics than it is in science. Men of science are able to carry out their work and communicate to one another the results of their findings only when political authority provides them with the security of law and order. It would indeed be improper to suggest, especially in our time, that authority in science is of no consequence to the life of the body politic. Nevertheless, the fact remains that the adequate functioning of political authority is the basic condition for the pursuit of all other kinds of activities, including scientific activity.

Since political authority is of primary importance to the lives and well-being of individuals, its institutional form is far more rigid than the form of authority in science. Engaged in a vital task, political authority cannot undergo rapid transformations as can a body of scientific doctrines. The political authority can never completely foresee how far its institutional transformations may affect the lives and well-being of the people who are governed by it, a concern not directly associated with changes in scientific doctrines. Consequently, political authority moves and acts with caution and circumspection.

The relevance of science to politics, as far as the problem of authority is concerned, is therefore limited to the relationship that authority in science maintains with individual freedom. Admittedly, science points out the fruitfulness of having a cooperative authority like its own, which provides an unlimited scope for individual initiative and variation. Nevertheless, we must not overlook the fact that this ideal cooperative authority exists in an extremely narrow intellectual field where human desires, sentiments, interests, and prejudices have been reduced to their absolute minimum. No such condition exists in the field of politics; consequently the authority in science cannot become a model for authority in politics.

The Manipulative Aspect of Dewey's Political Theory

Finally, we come to the analysis and examination of those ideas of Dewey that throw light on the possibility of manipulating specific problems in politics. Manipulative efforts are essentially human responses and devices to meet the demands made by specific problems of their environment. Consequently, we must consider these efforts against the background of what are regarded by Dewey as the main characteristics of specific problems. Those characteristics that emerge from his philosophy in general are that specific problems are unique as well as dynamic. We shall therefore analyze and illustrate his ideas on the problems of manipulation against the background of these two characteristics. After discussing characteristics of specific problems and the scope of manipulating them, we will consider Dewey's political theory as a theory of art of control. The section concludes with a criticism of the manipulative aspect of Dewey's political theory.

▰▰▰ *Characteristics of specific problems and the scope of manipulating them*

The specific problems that arouse political concern and call for some sort of organizational manipulation share with objects and events of existential phenomena two of their basic qualities, namely, uniqueness and a processive character. Specific problems are unique as well as dynamic because they are the products of interactions of objects and events that are themselves unique and dynamic, that Dewey calls by the name of "existences" and that are, in his words, "something more than products," that have "qualities of their own and assert independent life."[86]

According to this statement, objects and events cannot be explained completely in terms of *causal antecedents*. That is to say, an object or event has something more in it than all its conceivable causal antecedents put together. According to this argument, two razor blades, similar in their causal antecedents in the sense that they are of the same make and metallic composition and are made by the same procedure, will not give equal satisfaction or service to the same user. The quality that characterizes each of these blades is brought to the surface demonstrably when both of them are subjected to practical use. A scientist in that field is able to give a technical and perhaps more convincing reason as to why such razor blades differ in their quality, and hence in their respective sharpness. In this sense, existences, however similar, remain in fact unique and differ from what they apparently resemble.

Dewey's emphasis on the uniqueness of objects and events is evident in his philosophy of science, where he attacked the widespread belief that the laws of science are the laws of uniform behavior of certain bodies.

From Dewey's point of view, the uniqueness of existences does not prevent the formulation of propositions or statements about them or even of laws of their behavior. Such statements can be made in terms of constants and variables. That is to say, although in relation to one another existences are variable, an attempt can be made to formulate propositions concerning the part of their relation to one another that is constant, and through such relational propositions to state the constant factor in the behavior of different existences. Mathematics enjoys enormous scope in matters of relational propositions. Its equations are its relational propositions. With reference to certain equations, the mathematical problems that fall within the framework of those equations are constants, but with reference to one another they are variables and possess their independent existences.[87]

Something similar to this, although on a much smaller scale, is attempted in the laws and propositions of science. Those laws and propositions of science that indicate the behavior of different bodies do not claim to state anything concerning their behavior as such: what they indicate is only the relationships existing between certain propositions themselves and the behavior of different bodies, therefore, only a limited aspect of this behavior of different bodies. To illustrate, let us take X as the proposition of the behavior of certain aspects of bodies P,Q,R. The proposition X does not tell us anything about the behavior of P,Q,R as such, but tells us something about the behavior of P in relation to X, of Q in relation to X, and of R in relation to X. The behavior of P,Q,R independently of X may have nothing in common among themselves. What makes the common aspect in their behavior explicit is proposition X. X in this instance is a relational proposition that grasps and states the "invariant relation" existing between P, Q, and R.

The proposition X that refers to a common or invariant aspect of P, Q and R is therefore not a proposition concerning their uniform behavior.

The term "uniform behavior" for what is supposed to underlie the laws and propositions of science is often used to indicate the *entirety of behaviors* of different bodies, on the one hand, and an *indefinite number* of bodies, on the other. Dewey's opposition to the former meaning expresses itself in his emphasis on the basic uniqueness of different bodies and a highly qualified similarity (similarity only with reference to a relational proposition) in their behaviors. His opposition to the latter meaning manifests itself in his belief that the laws and propositions of science can only be statistically formulated,[88] that is to say, a proposition or law, as far as the behavior of a group of bodies is concerned, is strictly numerical and is therefore limited only to those bodies whose behaviors individually confirm the contention that is implicit in the proposition or law. When we examine closely the constantly interacting forces or processes that underlie every specific problem, we

162

find that they are in fact a series of sequential orders of differing contingencies and differing composition, which provide the means as well as the scope for our manipulative efforts. The rigidity or flexibility of a sequential order is in proportion to the element of contingency in it. The proportion of contingency in a sequential order indicates the extent to which human beings can intervene and manipulate it. Nothing can be done to alter the rigid sequence in which night follows day. Nevertheless, much can be done to alter the sequences that produce the particular size of a grain or the particular color of a flower. In the former, as opposed to the latter, the sequential order is impregnably rigid.

In considering the differing rigidities and contingencies in the sequential orders of different processes, we might believe that the sequential order that is immutable and provides no scope for our intervention is of no use to our manipulative measures. This is not true, because causal analysis of rigidly sequential processes can make possible some kind of foresight and prediction. When we try to analyze the part played by every process interacting to produce the specific problem, we can be reasonably certain of the part played by processes with rigidly sequential orders. Besides, manipulation is as much a matter of *adjustment* as it is of reconstruction or redirection. In the face of a weather forecast for a heavy rain, carrying of an umbrella or a mackintosh is in principle as much an act of manipulation as is the manufacture of a complicated refrigerating gadget for the purposes of protecting food. Nothing can be directly done against rain or heat. Nevertheless, we can devise ways and means of protecting ourselves and the means on which we subsist.

Our knowledge of the unique and dynamic character of specific problems opens before us the possibility of manipulation. Such knowledge helps us to direct our manipulative efforts towards the actualities of the problem as well as towards its sources. Every business cycle in its own time is a unique phenomenon. It is a product of the unique interaction of production, the credit system, the price mechanism, export, import, the tariff, the employment policy, and other factors. Nevertheless, as an event that recurs periodically, a business cycle is also a specific dynamic problem. In spite of the fact that each business cycle is a unique phenomenon in its own time, we can certainly discover certain common elements between two or more business cycles and the interactive factors responsible. Such common elements can be discovered among the various factors that we have listed and their interaction with one another. An elaborate study of their genesis can be undertaken so as to enable us to detect the embryonic stages of future business cycles and prevent their recurrence.

By and large, our knowledge of existential phenomena is restricted to the perimeters of specific problems that we confront. Our cognitive contact with existential phenomena is essentially brought about by the presence of specific problems. Through our effort to observe and analyze these problems we catch a glimpse of a fraction of sequential orders, contingencies, processes, and uniquenesses that underlie existential phenomena. Consequently, there is no way of discovering "laws" of existential phenomena into which all their sequential orders, contingencies, processes, and uniquenesses would fall. The absurdity of any attempt to do this would be apparent once we recognized the variety that characterizes existential phenomena.

It is therefore fallacious to suppose that an attempt to solve specific problems ought to be preceded by a complete knowledge of the existential phenomena in which they occur, as there is no such thing. What normally precedes the manipulation of a specific problem is some sort of *workable* knowledge that claims to have grasped the uniqueness of that problem and the efficient interacting forces that have produced it. Our claim of workable knowledge of the problem is tested when we undertake manipulative measures on the basis of this knowledge. When it successfully undergoes its manipulative test, workable knowledge becomes, as far as various principles and procedures involved in it are concerned, some sort of a relatively established knowledge that can be used for manipulating a more or less similar specific problem in the future.

. . . It is a complete error to suppose that efforts at social control depend upon the prior existence of a social science. The reverse is the case. The building up of social science, that is, of a body of knowledge in which facts are ascertained in their significant relations, is dependent upon putting social planning into effect. It is at this point that the misconception about physical science, when it is taken as a model for social knowledge, is important. Physical science did not develop because inquirer piled up a mass of facts about observed phenomena. It came into being when men intentionally experimented, on the basis of ideas and hypotheses, with observed phenomena to modify them and disclose new observations. This process is self-corrective and self-developing. Imperfect

and even wrong hypotheses, when acted upon, *brought to light significant phenomena which made improved ideas and improved experimentation possible . . . Men obtained knowledge of natural energies by trying deliberately to control the conditions of their operation. The result was knowledge, and then control on a larger scale by the application of what was known.*[89]

The knowledge that human beings have accumulated has its source in those historical specific problems that puzzled and discommoded men, to which they could find some workable solutions. Accumulated knowledge is, therefore, a product neither of attempts to understand existential phenomena as a whole nor of attempts to formulate the laws of behavior of all that falls within them.

Dewey was well aware of the radical difference between the tendencies of contemporary science and the science of the two preceding centuries. Eighteenth- and nineteenth-century science had inherited from theology the habit of formulating comprehensive laws partly because it considered its explanations to be some sort of rivals to theological explanation of the phenomena, and partly because it needed a maturity of outlook to be able to discover the philosophical significance of its own activity.[90] Three hundred years of intense independent activity resulted in an attitude of humility on the part of science. More than any other branch of knowledge, science now is intensely aware of the fact that it knows very little about the mysteries of Man and Nature. Now it admits in all humility that our knowledge of existential phenomena scarcely extends beyond the perimeters of those specific problems on which we have concentrated our attention, and that all the rest that claims to be knowledge is more or less of the nature of a conjecture. The humility shown by science is not reflected in full measure in such disciplines as psychology, economics, political science, history, or sociology. Nevertheless, there too the tendency to undertake deterministic analysis with a view to predicting the behavior of man and the movement of history is certainly on the decline. Even in these disciplines, there is a definite growth of a tendency to concentrate more on the immediate specific problems and to devise *ad hoc* specific remedies for solving them rather than to establish grandiose schemes and to bring about rash innovations on the basis of such schemes.

'Laws' of social life . . . are like laws of engineering. If you want certain results, certain means must be found and employed. The

key to the situation is a clear conception of consequences wanted, and the technique for reaching them.[91]

The act of manipulation is therefore as *specific* an act as the specific problem itself. Specific problems cannot be grouped together under broad generalizations, nor can they be resolved with the help of highly generalized remedies. To say that the low standard of living in half a dozen different societies is due to appropriation of the surplus value by the owners of means of production in those societies is hardly making specific statements about their real problems, nor does a generalized remedy of nationalization of all their productive resources provide a solution. The problem of a low standard of living in different societies can be broken up into a group of specific problems in respect of which every society is different from others, although they all have low standards of living.

From Dewey's point of view, a manipulative effort concentrates upon the specific problem and, through the specific problem, upon the situation of interacting forces that underlies it. It attempts to eliminate that situation or to secure an alternative situation in the place of the one that gave rise to the specific problem. The aim of our manipulative effort is to bring about what Dewey calls the transformation of the existing situation.[92] There are two types of manipulative measures by which a situation can be reconstructed: by diminishing the surplus strength of one or more interacting factors directly responsible for a specific problem, or by constantly controlling the interaction of the various factors with the help of permanently established regulative agencies. The manipulative operations of the first variety are periodic, and those of the second variety are permanent.[93] In the first, the situation is *reconstructed*, that is, the desired interaction of factors is brought about with the help of specific measures especially designed to bring about a desired balance among the interacting factors. As opposed to this, manipulative operations of the second type function through certain established regulative agencies which themselves interact with the rest of the interacting factors and thereby bring about a desired balance in which the specific problem disappears. As opposed to the first type, the second type is not only permanent, but flexible as well. The manipulative operations of the second type keep on constantly balancing the interactive factors and thus vary in their range of regulative control.

The aim of manipulative measures of both types is to produce an equilibrium among the interactive forces that might eliminate the specific problem. All manipulative measures are essentially *ad hoc* measures. They constantly strive to regain an equilibrium of interactive forces, which is continually threatened by the dynamic nature of the factors that go to make the specific problems.

▰▰▰ *Political theory as a theory of the art of control*

The various ideas of Dewey on the problems of manipulation that we have studied in the last section are of considerable significance to Dewey's own political theory. They tend to make political theory a theory of the *art of control*. Thus his political theory either loses its own identity in the face of science, which according to Dewey is the most highly developed and the most dependable technique of control, or it becomes a branch of science, operating in the field of politics. In this section we shall attempt to point out that his political theory, on account of its overwhelming emphasis on manipulation, tends to merge with science.

The traits of natural existence which generate the fears and adorations of superstitious barbarians generate the scientific procedures of disciplined civilization.[94]

That is to say, the hazards and the uncertainties of human existence have been responsible for the growth of both supernaturalism and science. The hostility and the uncertainties of the environment necessitated, on the part of human beings, the attempt to develop such techniques as might give them the command of their environment, and supernaturalism and science are the two extreme stages in this human attempt. The supernatural art of control consists of magic, superstitious rituals, and religions, all practiced in the belief that they will alienate the forces of evil and induce the protection of the forces of good. Science as an art of control has succeeded in developing the most sophisticated techniques and procedures of acquiring control over the environment and of making use of its energies. As opposed to the supernatural art of control, which provided human beings with only a feeling of assurance, science as an art of control has yielded indisputable concrete results.

Nevertheless, when we consider arts of control in the perspective of history, especially with reference to conscious historical attempts to reflect and to state the problems concerning these arts, we find that politics as a science and art of control occupies an intermediary place between supernaturalism and science. There have been periods in history when politics or political science was considered to be more than the mere art of politically organizing the society. Greek political science, for instance, was not confined to the problem of the political organization of society. It was concerned mainly with attainment of what the Greeks called the "good life." Thus Greek political thinkers were compelled to include in their political science a discourse on morality, law, education, economics, aesthetics, and so forth. Greek political science, in other words, came to acquire a very comprehensive notion of *organizing* society that was not coextensive with political organization of the society as we understand it. Such a comprehensive task of organizing the society for the attainment of the "good life," which from our point of view lies beyond the scope of political science, certainly fell within the scope of Greek political science. From their point of view, the threat to human existence was not so much from the physical environment as from the social environment. Consequently, in their discourses on the art of control, they restricted themselves to the art of controlling and managing the society in which the attainment of the good life may be possible.

Apart from the fact that political science has been regarded at one time or another as *the* art of control, what is interesting for us to note is the fact that political reflections were primary sources of the philosophical concepts of all those disciplines, which, like politics, were engaged in the study of organizing and regulating human activity. This came about for two reasons. Historically speaking, political reflections as reflections on the art of control were the first to acquire a philosophical statement. Secondly, the thinkers who borrowed concepts from politics in order to expand other subjects were primarily political thinkers. This reason is explicitly stated in Dewey's own writings. Aristotle's analysis of the psychology of a slave, Hobbes's analysis of human nature in general, the emphasis on "inner freedom" by the German idealists, the emphasis on the pleasure-seeking aspect of human nature by the Utilitarians, and so forth, were all not only the extension of concepts from politics into psychology, but were also expounded in order to support their respective arguments in politics.[95] Similarly, the concept of "person" in jurisprudence[96] and that of the "individual" in classical economics[97] have their sources in politics.

168

However, with the gradual recognition of the fact that science has developed the most efficacious art of control, the interest of disciplines like psychology, sociology, jurisprudence, and economics, the method and technique of science has steadily grown. These disciplines, which in the part were directly or indirectly influenced by the reflections in politics, are now looking to science for a method and technique of controlling factors that operate in their respective fields. As far as Dewey is concerned, his political theory, like the other branches of inquiry in his system of thought, looks to science for guidance in dealing with its problems of manipulation and control.

In its attempt to be guided by science in dealing with these problems, Dewey's political theory loses its identity. There are two reasons for the merger of Dewey's political theory into science.

First, on account of the overwhelming stress on manipulation and control in his political theory, Dewey gives the impression that the functions of science and of political theory, in their respective fields, are identical functions, since they both deal with problems concerning investigation and manipulation. But science occupies a unique position in Dewey's system of thought. Science for him, as we have already seen, is nothing but the art of knowing and doing at its best. It is this unique position that science occupies in his system of thought that is responsible for the disappearance of his political theory into science. Since science has perfected the art of knowing and doing *as such*, political theory, when it adopts the method and technique of science, does not introduce anything extraneous into its own field. From Dewey's point of view, however, political theory's attempt to adopt the method and technique of science is just a different way of saying that political science has gone back to the proper method from which it had aberrated. This therefore makes science and political theory two different expressions of basically the *same* cognitive process, and as this unity of cognitive process is best expressed in science, it is science and its significance to the problems of political investigation and manipulation that ought to receive our attention rather than political theory. Secondly, nowhere has Dewey defined the exact nature of political manipulation. Measures undertaken with explicit intentions of protecting or enhancing the general well-being are not necessarily political—for instance, the manipulative measures undertaken for building roads and bridges, which are just plain manipulative measures. Dewey has no definitive criterion for discriminating manipulative measures that have political significance from those that are devoid of it. In the absence of discriminatory criteria, the identity of his political theory is once again threatened by science. All the manipulative measures undertaken in a society become the concern of his political theory, as his political theory no longer seeks to bring out the *political* significance of manipulative measures that are either proposed or undertaken. It concerns itself with manipulative measures as such. And as an overwhelming number of manipulative measures are undertaken by applied science, Dewey's attention is invariably shifted from political theory to science.

◄▬▬► *The manipulative aspect of Dewey's political theory*

In this section we shall undertake to point out some of the weaknesses of Dewey's ideas on the problems of manipulation and control in politics, discussing: the different purposes of knowledge; the role of beliefs and opinions in manipulation; diversity in the natures of various manipulative operations; the fact that manipulation is not an abstract problem.

In Dewey's system of thought in general, and in the manipulative aspect of his political theory in particular, the *practical* use of knowledge is much exaggerated. For Dewey the entire cognitive effort has its source in obstacles, conflicts, doubts, tensions, and so forth, that one experiences in one's environment, and its purpose is to transform the situations in which they arise. The entire human cognitive effort in his system of thought is therefore well committed to *practical* purposes. Even the aesthetic branch of cognitive effort arises from an attempt through the medium of his own expression to remove the element of discord that exists between a creative artist and his world.[96] On the other hand, when we examine Dewey's ideas on the manipulative aspect of his political theory, we get the impression that he tends to look down upon those stages of knowledge that are not directly consummated in an act of manipulation, that is to say, if the intermediary stages of knowledge, such as investigation, comparison, or prediction, do not directly lead to some sort of manipulative activity, then they are alternatives to manipulative acts themselves. His criticism of prediction for instance is a case in point:

> *We can predict the occurrence of an eclipse precisely because we cannot control it. If we could control it, we could not predict, except contingently.*[99]

170

Now to consider prediction as an alternative to control, as Dewey takes it to be, is certainly farfetched. Prediction is invariably a stage in our knowledge that precedes the undertaking of actual manipulative operations. The engineer who chooses a site for digging a well for the purposes of discovering oil acts on his calculations and his prediction that oil will be found beneath the site that he has chosen. In the investigations and calculations that precede the undertaking of manipulative measures, a stage is invariably reached where with reasonable certainty one can predict the results. In fact the very inducement to undertake a manipulative measure rests on some kind of a belief, as good as a prediction, that it will solve the problem in question.

By making manipulative operations the goal of all knowledge, Dewey seems to overlook the fact that those who contribute to knowledge are usually different from those who put it into practice, from whom they are often separated by centuries. Those who enrich human knowledge can scarcely foresee the future manipulative possibilities of their own contributions. In the absence of such a goal what keeps them going is either social prestige or the joy that any creative work brings with it. The mathematician, the laboratory worker, and the social investigator, who are behind the engineer, the physicist, and the administrator, respectively, think in different terms about the goals of their effort than do the latter. Only in a retrospective analysis can we judge whether a particular body of knowledge is of any practical use or not.

Dewey was opposed to the classification of specific problems as "physical" or "social." For him, all problems were "existential" and the products of innumerable interacting factors. The interacting factors that produce specific problems make them unique as well as dynamic. Such a conception of specific problems, as far as the question of their manipulation is concerned, successfully refutes the criticism that "physical" problems, being uniform and repetitive, are capable of mechanical manipulation, and "social" problems, being unique and changeable, are not capable of manipulation. Nevertheless, what his conception of specific problems cannot refute or afford to ignore is the part played by beliefs and opinions of men.[100]

Here it might be argued on behalf of Dewey that the *recognition* of specific problems that arouse political concern is not a matter of belief or opinion, since specific problems can be recognized independently. Beliefs or opinions play an important part not so much in the appreciation or the recognition of specific problems as in their manipulation. The recognition of the specific problem that the British railways cover only their operational cost and nothing else under the system of state ownership of railways is not prevented by and political belief or opinions. On the other hand political opinions any beliefs become very significant in the attempts to reorganize the British railways either by a process of denationalization or by reducing the wages of railwaymen or by increasing the railway fares. Dewey therefore cannot deny the fact that beliefs and opinions do count in the manipulation of specific problems, if not in the recognition of them, and his acknowledgement of this fact is evident in the following:

> *The key to the situation (that is, the manipulation of specific problems) is a clear conception of consequences wanted, and of the technique for reaching them, together with, of course, the state of desires and aversions which causes some consequences to be wanted rather than others.*[101]

Nevertheless, what is lacking in his acknowledgement is the fact that opinions or beliefs compete with one another to direct our manipulative operations, and they invariably tend to be more or less equally informed. Dewey in his writings invariably visualizes conflicts between beliefs or opinions as conflicts between completely and correctly informed beliefs or opinions, on the one hand, and beliefs or opinions that are as good as prejudices or whims, on the other. When more or less equally informed beliefs or opinions compete with one another for influencing our manipulative operations, there is no other alternative but to subject them to the procedure of trial and error. The very spirit of trial and error implies that we are only a little more certain about the soundness of what we are subjecting to trial than we are of its competing alternative. Its confirmation depends upon the results of the trial.

Two of the basic premises of Dewey's philosophy, namely, the unity of experience and the unity of cognitive process, made him totally oblivious to the fundamental difference between the nature of one type of manipulative measure and another. In the earlier part of this book we analyzed what Dewey meant by the term "experience." We also saw that to him "experience" is the experience of the existential environment and hence it is a single whole or a unity. Similarly, as we have also seen before, cognitive operations, according to Dewey, have a uniformity of purpose, namely, that of removing of obstacles and securing those conditions that the existential experience needs or demands. Such a unity of existential experience, on the one hand, and that of the cognitive operations, on the other, also gives a unity of character to all the manipulative measures.

In the last analysis, all manipulative measures seek to solve specific problems that arise in our existential experience. Consequently, one type of manipulative measure is of the same nature as another.

Such a conception of manipulative measures remained a serious drawback in Dewey's political theory. It stemmed from his conceptions of "experience" and of cognitive process, but its results were actually felt in his political methodology. On the one hand he granted the character of uniqueness to every problem, both in his general theory of inquiry as well as in his theory of political inquiry, and hence insisted on calling every problem a *specific problem*. On the other hand, he maintained that manipulative measures that bring about "existential reconstructions" resolve the specific problems in question. What he therefore recognized was only the plurality of manipulative measures which are undertaken to resolve them. In other words, as far as he was concerned, the question of manipulating *all* kinds of specific problems fell within the same theoretical framework.

While expounding his ideas on the problems of manipulation in politics Dewey acted more like an engineer or a social engineer than a theorist who reflects on the activities of engineers. What interfered with his attempts at reflecting and theorizing about the activities of engineers was his own intensely positivistic attitude towards reflective thought in general.

An engineer who builds bridges and roads might come into conflict with a geometrician because of his belief in the possibility of a straight line. And it is the task of the theoretician to point out that the engineer's belief in a straight line has nothing to do with the geometrical and logical problems that a geometrician encounters when he holds the possibility of a straight line. He might possibly point out that the explanations of the engineer and that of the geometrician on the possibility or impossibility of a straight line imply altogether different presuppositions. He also might point out that their respective presuppositions make them talk two different languages in spite of the fact that they both are engaged in the discussion of a common subject.

Similarly, it was the task of a methodologist like Dewey to point out the difference in the nature of the manipulative operations of a civil or mechanical engineer, on the one hand, and those of a political engineer, on the other. The manipulative operations of a civil or mechanical engineer *directly* bring about the desired changes in the physical situation. For instance, construction of a bridge across a river or diversion of the flow of the river with the help of a dam are examples of civil as well as mechanical engineering. The desired changes in the physical situation are directly brought about by the bridge and the dam. The manipulative operations of the political engineer, however, cannot all by themselves bring about the desired reconstruction of the problematic situation. The success of a manipulative operation such as price-fixing does not entirely depend upon an act of legislation and the proclamation of a severe penalty for the default. Its success depends upon its ability to create corresponding patterns of behavior in the people. Moreover, a civil or mechanical engineer has a clear conception of his target that he wants to reach with the help of manipulative operations. The manipulative operations of a political engineer, on the other hand, are directed towards a more or less hypothetical situation that is expected to come into existence as a result of certain inhibitions and liberations that these manipulative operations introduce. Each manipulative operation of a political engineer imposes certain restrictions on spontaneous activity along with a promise of a greater degree of liberation elsewhere.

Dewey's inability to grasp such a basic difference in the natures of manipulative operations of a civil or mechanical engineer on the one hand and a political engineer on the other made his entire approach to the problems of manipulation in politics unrealistic as well as naive.

Finally, the problems of manipulation in politics cannot be discussed in abstraction. In his political writings Dewey laid considerable emphasis on the uniqueness of specific problems because he considered them to be the products of unique interacting factors. He therefore refrained from making any theoretical generalizations about specific problems excepting that they all have unique and dynamic characters. While expounding his ideas on the problems of manipulation, however, he seemed to undermine the intrinsic relationship that exists between the manipulative machinery of a society and its unique cultural composition. Consideration of manipulative machineries, irrespective of the cultural situation from which they emanate and in which they operate, is meaningless. Equally meaningless is not taking into account the history, the traditions, and the genius of the people who operate the machineries. Dewey's ideas on the problems of manipulation in politics, to summarize, suffered considerably because their exposition, unlike that of specific problems, was undertaken by Dewey at purely an abstract level.

Conclusion

In the foregoing pages we have examined in considerable detail the three aspects of Dewey's political theory that emerge when we consider his political ideas against the background of his ideas on logic, philosophy of science, and methodology. Here, in brief, I propose to mention the various characteristics of Dewey's political theory and their significance to problems of political inquiry.

Conceptual framework

Dewey, as we have already seen, renounced the concept of the state on the ground that it does not help us in the understanding of the peculiarities of political phenomena that surround us. Only the empirical investigation of these phenomena, guided by adequate conceptual tools, he maintained, can help us in the understanding of what they are. He also believed that in order fully to grasp these peculiarities, a political analyst must go beyond the formal structure of political institutions and must take into account the broad social structure within which they function and from which they derive their peculiarities. The conceptual framework that he himself had formulated was capable of making generic discriminations between the peculiarities of a group of more or less similar societies.

In this respect the achievement of Dewey's political theory was mainly negative. This is because he made a far more convincing case against the adoption of *a priori*, causal, and universalistic concepts than in favor of his own conceptual framework. His devising a set of concepts that make generic discriminations possible was more or less an illustration of his own negative argument. Not being a trained political theorist himself, he could not go into the details of his own illustrations, and it would not be proper, therefore, to attach greater importance to them than they deserve. What Dewey failed to emphasize was the possibility of attempting generalizations to the extent that empirical data are available. He had recognized the importance of this in the physical sciences, but did not emphasize it in the study of political phenomena. His preoccupation with the problem of manipulation may be said to be responsible for this.

Political activity as consequential

In his political writings Dewey regarded political activity as both secondary and consequential. It is preceded by such primary activities as social, economic, religious, scientific, and educational activities, which more or less pursue their own specific ends for their own sake. The aim of political activity is to control and regulate the consequences of primary activities. These consequences, coupled with the desire on the part of a people to regulate them, bring political activity into existence.

To a great extent Dewey was correct in pointing out the secondary and consequential character of political activity; nevertheless, he overlooked the fact that not all political activities have both of these qualities. Those political activities that are pursued within well-established political institutions do not distinctly possess the secondary and consequential characteristics of which Dewey speaks. In fact, they lay down the set of regulations for primary activities long before these come into existence. Moreover, it is a mistake to suggest that political activities always organize primary activities and regulate their consequences. Highly organized religious activities, such as the church during the Middle Ages, and highly organized economic activities, such as trade unions and chambers of commerce, often themselves control political activity. The nature of political activity, therefore, cannot be determined without reference to the situation of other activities in a society at any particular time.

Political investigation and the statement of phenomena

In his theory of inquiry Dewey rejected the conventional characterization of a class of problems as moral problems *sui generis*. He believed that all problems are basically existential, but that some of them also acquire a moral dimension by virtue of the fact that their consequences have good or evil effects on the well-being of men. In the investigation and the statement of such problems, no discrimination should be made between one kind of problem and another. What

176

is more, the results of the investigation of problems should be stated *in their own terms.*

Dewey applied similar reasoning to the task of the investigation and statement of political problems. He believed that after Galileo natural sciences have been able to make progress because they had given up the Greek aesthetic-ethical attitude of looking at problems. In political investigation, therefore, he emphasized a similar change of outlook.

The investigation and statement of political problems in their own terms require, first of all, an adequate conception of the scope of political phenomena and the problems that can be fruitfully raised, and, secondly, an adequate set of terms with the help of which statement about the problems can be made. Dewey threw light on the first requirement to some extent, but remained totally oblivious of the second requirement.

The notion of manipulation

Finally, Dewey may be said to have made the determination and resolution of specific problems of politics an integral part of his political theory. For Dewey, as we have already seen, problems arise within an existential situation in the form of doubts, conflicts, and obstacles that are resolved only when the existential situation giving rise to them is altered or reconstructed. Political problems, therefore, are of that nature and call for a similar resolution.

Specific problems of politics, he believed, share the two dominant characteristics of all other problems. Like all other problems, they are unique and dynamic. They therefore call for the recognition of these two characteristics when their resolution is undertaken.

In his emphasis on the manipulative aspect Dewey tends to make of the discipline of political science some sort of policy science. His investigations as well as his statements of specific problems of politics are geared to the ultimate goal of manipulation. Problem resolution considerations are therefore the most dominant characteristic of Dewey's political theory.

Dewey considered the problems of manipulation to be common to all branches of knowledge, as there is a *common* theory of inquiry. Neither his theory of inquiry nor his theory of manipulation recognizes the differences between one branch of human knowledge and another.

These, then, are the principal characteristics of Dewey's political theory that emerge from our analysis of his philosophical and political ideas. Let us now take into account the significance of these ideas to the problems of political inquiry.

Dewey's emphasis on the study of existential situations that give rise to specific problems of politics deserves to be considered seriously. He has rightly emphasized the fact that all specific problems are the products of the interaction of a group of factors—physical, biological, social, and human. This fact is often ignored in conventional political inquiry, in which political problems are examined against a narrow institutional background. Dewey has therefore correctly emphasized the need to go beyond the formal institutions of politics while examining a specific problem. Such an approach, however, is not free from difficulties of its own. This is because political investigation is now required to go beyond the familiar and precise field of political institutions to a wider and more complex field of political phenomena, where over and above the study of political institutions the investigator is required to discover the political significance of semipolitical and nonpolitical factors.

Dewey's emphasis of the need to study specific problems of politics is a salutary warning against any temptation to make unwarranted generalizations. He rightly points out that we approach political phenomena through the specific problems that we confront and that our knowledge does not extend beyond the perimeters of the specific problems investigated. Empirically collected data may help us to make generalizations about a range of specific problems, but there too such generalizations are not valid beyond those specific problems and the group of factors that give rise to them.

Finally, Dewey's emphasis on the need to have a conceptual framework for the investigation of political phenomena is particularly welcome at a period when political theorists are engaged in the task of rejuvenating political theory. His political writings clearly point out the fact that the much needed empirical investigation cannot be undertaken without the help of adequate tools of inquiry. His own attempts in this direction have been both limited and unsatisfactory; nevertheless, he has indicated a fruitful area for investigation and the need for the methodological equipment required in order for us to undertake it.

NOTES

Notes to Introduction, pp. 1–7

[1] P. A. Schilpp, ed., *The Philosophy of John Dewey* (Chicago: Northwestern University Press, 1939), pp. 337–368.
[2] Sidney Ratner, foreword to the volume, *The Philosopher of the Common Man: Essays in Honor of John Dewey to Celebrate His Eightieth Birthday* (New York: G. P. Putnam's Sons, 1940), pp. 205–219.
[3] Paul Ward, *Intelligence in Politics* (Chapel Hill: University of North Carolina Press, 1931), p. 50.
[4] Herbert Schneider, in *A Bibliography of John Dewey*, written in collaboration with M. H. Thomas (New York: Columbia University Press, 1939), complains that sufficient interest is not taken in *The Public and Its Problems*. (See his introduction, p. xiii.)

Notes to Chapter 1, pp. 9–22

[1] John Dewey, *Philosophy and Civilization* (New York, Minton, Balch and Company, 1931), p. 3.
[2] John Dewey, *Context and Thought* (Berkeley: University of California Press, 1931), p. 214.
[3] *Ibid.*, pp. 214–215.
[4] Sidney Hook has expressed it as follows: "Just as there is a 'method behind madness' so there is a 'meaning behind nonsense.' Dewey's hypothesis is that even in a crazy patchwork quilt of metaphysics, particularly if it wins acceptance, we can find some response to the same difficulties and predicaments of life which are at the basis of political, cultural, and social struggles." Sidney Hook, *John Dewey: An Intellectual Portrait* (New York: The John Day Company, 1939), p. 44.

[5.] John Dewey, *Reconstruction in Philosophy* (New York: Henry Holt and Company, 1920), p. 18.

[6.] John Dewey, *Philosophy and Civilization*, pp. 3–4.

[7.] See page 36 in Chapter 1.

[8.] See page 147 in Chapter 4.

[9.] John Dewey, *The Quest for Certainty* (New York: Minton, Balch and Company, 1929), p. 6.

[10.] *Ibid.*, pp. 7–8.

[11.] *Ibid.*, p. 21.

[12.] John Dewey, "Psychology as Philosophical Method," *Mind, 11* (April 1886), 153–173.

[13.] John Dewey, "The Vanishing Subject in the Psychology of James," *The Journal of Philosophy, 37*, 22 (October 1940), 589.

[14.] John Dewey, "From Absolutism to Experimentalism," in *Contemporary American Philosophy*, ed. G. P. Adams and W. P. Montague (New York: The Macmillan Company, 1930), vol. 2, p. 24.

[15.] *Ibid.*, p. 25.

[16.] P. A. Schilpp (ed.), *op. cit.*, p. 17.

[17.] *Ibid.*, p. 17.

[18.] John Dewey, "The Need for a Recovery in Philosophy," in *Creative Intelligence: Essays in the Pragmatic Attitude* (New York: Henry Holt and Company, 1917), p. 8.

[19.] *Ibid.*, p. 9.

[20.] "We may borrow words from a context less technical than that of biology, and convey the same idea by saying that habits are arts. They involve skill of sensory and motor organs, cunning or craft, and objective materials. They assimilate objective energies, and eventuate in command of environment. They require order, discipline, and manifest technique. They have a beginning, middle and end. Each stage marks progress in dealing with materials and tools, advance in converting material to active use." John Dewey, *Human Nature and Conduct: An Introduction to Psychology* (New York: Henry Holt and Company, 1922), p. 15.

[21.] It would be interesting to note Dewey's emphasis on the objectivity of aesthetic experience. Dewey expresses it as follows: "The rhythm of loss of integration with environment and recovery of union not only persists in man but becomes conscious with him; its conditions are material out of which he forms purposes. Emotion is the conscious sign of a break, actual or impending. The discord is the occasion that induces reflection. Desire for restoration of the union converts mere emotion into interest in objects as conditions of realization of harmony. With the realization, material of reflection is incorporated into objects as their meaning. Since the artist cares in a peculiar way for the phase of experience in which the union is achieved, he does not shun moments of resistance and tension. He rather cultivates them, not for their own sake but because of their potentialities, bringing to living consciousness an experience that is unified and total." *Art as Experience* (New York: Minton, Balch and Company, 1934), p. 15.

22. John Dewey, *The Quest for Certainty*, p. 239.
23. John Dewey, *Creative Intelligence*, p. 11.
24. John Dewey, *Experience and Nature* (New York: W. W. Norton and Company, 1929), p. 43.
25. John Dewey, *Logic: The Theory of Inquiry* (New York: Holt, Rinehart and Winston, 1964), see pp. 67–69.
26. *Ibid.*, pp. 379–380.
27. *Ibid.*, pp. 3–4.
28. John Dewey, *Experience and Nature*, pp. 84–85.
29. *Ibid.*, p. 88.
30. Dewey does not maintain in any way the existence of *the* beginning or *the* ending. He only maintains that there is a certain way in which a thing ends for something and begins for something else. In his words, a "thing which is a close of one history is always the beginning of another." *Ibid.*, p. 85.
31. *Ibid.*, p. 84.
32. John Dewey, *The Quest for Certainty*, pp. 140–145.
33. John Dewey, *Logic: The Theory of Inquiry*, p. 416.
34. John Dewey, *The Quest for Certainty*, pp. 172–173.
35. John Dewey: *Logic: The Theory of Inquiry*, p. 111.
36. John Dewey, *Experience and Nature*, pp. 7–15.
37. *Ibid.*, p. 19.
38. M. Oakeshott, *Experience and Its Modes* (Cambridge, England: Cambridge University Press, 1933), p. 14.

Notes to Chapter 2, pp. 23–38

1. John Dewey, *The Quest for Certainty*, p. 93.
2. *Ibid.*, pp. 94–95.
3. *Ibid.*, p. 99.
4. *Ibid.*, p. 105.
5. *Ibid.*, p. 196.
6. *Ibid.*, p. 69.
7. *Ibid.*, pp. 172–173.
8. *Ibid.*, p. 179.
9. John Dewey, *Philosophy and Civilization*, p. 40.
10. For this position, Dewey acknowledges the support given to his theory by Heisenberg's principle of indeterminacy. ". . . We have depended," says Dewey, "upon the general pattern of experimental knowing. . . . We gratefully acknowledge the support given . . . by

one of the definite conclusions reached in recent physical science. For this one result is of a crucially decisive nature. It is known technically as Heisenberg's principle of indeterminacy." *The Quest for Certainty*, p. 201.

Heisenberg's principle, based on the indeterminable position of electrons, declared that the interaction of the agent's effort to know with the subject matter "prevents an accurate measurement of velocity and position of *any* body." (*Ibid.*, p. 202.) This interaction is considered both in the case of touching a big object and in seeing a minute ray of light and measuring it. According to Dewey, the logical and philosophical import of Heisenberg's principle is far greater than it is commonly supposed to be. In the light of this principle, ". . . what is known is seen to be a product in which the act of observation plays the necessary role. Knowing is seen to be a participant in what is finally known." *The Quest for Certainty*, p. 204.

However, although Dewey appeals to Heisenberg's principle, it is neither the inspiration nor the authority for his theory of knowledge. His theory springs, instead, from his anxiety to get rid of the "spectator theory of knowledge." This he achieves by making knowing a partner in what is finally known. As a matter of fact, Heisenberg's principle of indeterminacy is of no great relevance to Dewey's theory. This is because the former mainly considers the impossibility of measuring the position and velocity of a body that is disturbed as a result of the interaction between the agent's effort to know and the subject matter itself. For Dewey the same interaction brings in properties that enable both knowing and controlling what is known. The results of interaction for them are just opposite, because the interaction that produces indeterminacy for Heisenberg produces knowledge for Dewey.

11. John Dewey, *The Quest for Certainty*, p. 223.
12. *Ibid.*, p. 225.
13. *Ibid.*, p. 225.
14. *Ibid.*, p. 226.
15. *Ibid.*, p. 231.
16. John Dewey, *Logic: The Theory of Inquiry*, p. 488.
17. John Dewey, *The Quest for Certainty*, pp. 216–217.
18. John Dewey, *Logic: The Theory of Inquiry*, p. 116.
19. *Ibid.*, p. 492.
20. See Bertrand Russell's essay on Dewey in *The Philosophy of John Dewey*, ed. P. A. Schilpp, pp. 139–140.
21. John Dewey, *Logic: The Theory of Inquiry*, p. 495.
22. *Ibid.*, pp. 494–495.
23. *Ibid.*, p. 496.
24. In his ethical theory, Dewey develops the unity of motives and con-

sequences by denying the dualism of character and conduct. To him, ". . . the key to a correct theory of morality is recognition of the essential unity of the self and its acts." John Dewey and J. H. Tufts, *Ethics* (New York: Henry Holt and Company, 1908), pp. 318–319.

25. "Judgment which is actually judgment (that satisfies the logical conditions of judgment) institutes means-consequences (ends) in *strict conjugate relation* to each other." John Dewey, *Logic: The Theory of Inquiry*, p. 496.

26. John Dewey and J. H. Tufts, *Ethics*, p. 269.

27. *Ibid.*, p. 269.

28. *Ibid.*, p. 247.

29. *Ibid.*, pp. 244–245.

30. John Dewey, *Experience and Nature*, p. 340.

31. *Ibid.*, p. 341.

32. *Ibid.*, p. 343.

33. *Ibid.*, p. 343.

34. John Dewey, *The Quest for Certainty*, p. 265.

35. Dewey objects to use of the term "value-judgment" for a product of personal preference. He says, ". . . there is nothing whatever that methodologically (*qua* judgment) marks off 'value-judgment' from conclusions reached in astronomical, chemical, or biological inquiries. . . . Evaluative judgments cannot be arrived so as to be warranted without going outside the value field into matters physical, physiological, anthropological, historical, socio-psychological, and so on. Only by taking facts ascertained in these subjects into account can we determine the conditions and consequences of given valuings, and without such determination, 'judgment' occurs only as a pure myth." John Dewey, "The Field of Value" in *Value: A Cooperative Inquiry*, ed. R. Lepley (New York: Columbia University Press, 1957), p. 77.

36. John Dewey, *The Quest for Certainty*, p. 267.

37. M. J. Oakeshott, *Experience and Its Modes*, p. 266.

Notes to Chapter 3, pp. 39–93

1. John Dewey, *op. cit.* in *Contemporary American Philosophy*, vol. 2, p. 20.

2. George Herbert Mead, *Movements of Thought in the Nineteenth Century*, ed. Merritt H. Moore, (Chicago: The University of Chicago Press, 1936).

3. John Dewey, *Freedom and Culture* (New York: G. P. Putnam's Sons, 1939), pp. 83–84.

4. "The obnoxious state was closely bound up in fact and in tradition with other associations, ecclesiastic (and through its influence with the family), and economic, such as gilds and corporations, and by means of church-state, even with unions for scientific inquiry and

with educational institutions. The easiest way out was to go back to the naked individual, to sweep away all associations as foreign to his nature and rights save as they proceeded from his voluntary choice and guaranteed his own private ends." John Dewey, *The Public and Its Problems* (New York: Henry Holt and Company, 1927), p. 88.

5. John Dewey, *Freedom and Culture*, pp. 105–106.

6. John Dewey, *Liberalism and Social Action* (New York: G. P. Putnam's Sons, 1935), p. 16.

7. *Ibid.*, pp. 42–43.

8. See "The Political Philosophy of Instrumentalism" by Hu Shih in *The Philosopher of the Common Man*, ed. Sidney Ratner, p. 208.

9. John Dewey, "Kant and Philosophical Method," *The Journal of Speculative Philosophy, 18* (April 1884), pp. 162–174.

10. *Ibid.*, pp. 170–171.

11. John Dewey, *Contemporary American Philosophy*, vol. 2, p. 18.

12. In an autobiographical note tracing his own intellectual genesis, Dewey writes with considerable feeling about Morris, as follows, "I have never known a more single-hearted and whole-souled man—a man of a single piece all the way through; while I long since deviated from his philosophic faith, I should be happy to believe that the influence of the spirit of his teaching has been an enduring influence." *Contemporary American Philosophy*, vol. 2, p. 18.

As a mark of his gratitude, Dewey christened his third child "Morris." This child was born at Ann Arbor, the place where Dewey succeeded Morris to the Chair of Philosophy. Unfortunately, the child died two years later, and Dewey never fully recovered from this blow. See *The Philosophy of John Dewey*, P. A. Schilpp, ed., p. 24. For Dewey's tribute to Morris, also see R. M. Wenley, *Life and Work of George Sylvester Morris* (New York: The Macmillan Company, 1917), pp. 308–326.

13. John Dewey, "The Psychological Standpoint," *Mind*, vol. 41, (January 1886), pp. 1–19 and "Psychology as Philosophic Method," *Mind*, vol. 42, (April 1886), pp. 153–173.

14. Interesting parallels can be found between Dewey's intellectual development, on the one hand, and the development of psychology, on the other. The phase of rational psychology in psychology has a parallel in Dewey's early idealist position. The behaviorist and the experimental phases in psychology have their parallels in Dewey's naturalist and experimental theory of knowledge. And social psychology has its parallel in Dewey's social philosophy, which takes into consideration cultural contexts of every problem.

15. John Dewey, "The Psychological Standpoint," *Mind*, vol. 41, (January 1886), p. 10.

16. See Chapter 4, pp. 113–118, 126–129, 151–160.

17. After a lifetime of criticism of Kant, on the occasion of the two

hundredth anniversary of Kant's birth in 1924, Dewey started taking a more human interest in Kant's personality, although his criticism of Kant did not diminish. The greatest shortcoming of Kant appeared to him to be his "ancestral piety," as opposed to the defects of Herbert Spencer, at the other extreme, who totally disregarded all the ideas of his predecessors that did not come near his own.

"He (Kant) was extraordinarily sensitive to the ideas of every author he studied. He responded to Hume, Shaftsbury, Burke, and Rousseau as well as to thinkers with whom he was congenitally much more sympathetic. To raw experience, to experience in mass, he was remarkably insensitive. Even his marked proclivities for social and political reform in the direction of republican freedom and equality, seems to be conditioned by his intellectual response to Rousseau and other writers, rather than to be a direct response to what was going on about him." J. Ratner, ed., *Character and Events* (New York: Henry Holt and Company, 1929), p. 64.

[18] John Dewey, preface to *German Philosophy and Politics*, rev. ed., (New York: G. P. Putnam's Sons, 1942), pp. 5–6.

[19] See Jane M. Dewey, "Biography of John Dewey" in *Philosophy of John Dewey*, ed. P. A. Schilpp, pp. 25–26.

[20] To cite Mead's own words, "The former (Rousseau) gave a popular vogue to its (the French Revolution's) doctrines; the latter (Kant) incorporated its principles into a speculative system." George Herbert Mead, *Movements of Thought in the Nineteenth Century*, p. 51.

[21] *Ibid.*, pp. 37–42.

[22] See page 47, this chapter.

[23] John Dewey, *German Philosophy and Politics*, first ed. (New York: Henry Holt and Company, 1915), p. 20.

[24] John Dewey, *Philosophy and Civilization*, p. 291.

[25] Isaiah Berlin, *Historical Inevitability* (London: Oxford University Press, 1955), p. 78.

[26] *Ibid.*, pp. 33–34.

[27] John Dewey, *German Philosophy and Politics*, first ed., p. 23.

[28] For a short discussion of the Kantian distinction between the empirical and the *a priori* aspects of ethics, see H. J. Paton, *The Moral Law: or Kant's Groundwork of the Metaphysics of Morals* (London: Hutchinson's University Library, 1953), pp. 13–14.

[29] John Dewey, *German Philosophy and Politics*, first ed., p. 25.

[30] *Ibid.*, p. 48.

[31] B. Bosanquet, *The Philosophical Theory of the State* (London: Macmillan and Company Limited, 1951), pp. 110–114.

[32] John Dewey, *German Philosophy and Politics*, first ed., pp. 51–53.

[33] An admirable comparison of the temperaments and early influences on James and Dewey is that of Professor Ralph Barton

Perry. It is as follows: "These differences are no doubt related to the general philosophical temper of the two men, as well as to their early influences. James is more conciliatory and hospitable to ideas, Dewey more systematic. The interest of James is strongly metaphysical and religious, that of Dewey, social and logical. Both men feel the influence of Darwin and of modern experimental science, but while James springs from British empiricism crossed with voluntarism and fideism of Renouvier, Dewey has his roots in Hegel and neo-Kantism. James is interested in content, while Dewey's preoccupation with method amounts in effect to a naturalistic panlogism, in which content *is* method. To James ultimate vision is intuitive, while to Dewey it is discursive. Or, while James *is* percipient, artistic, and religious, Dewey elaborates ideas *about* perception, art, and religion. With James the essence of life and experience can be grasped only in the living and in experiencing, and this conviction springs from the abundance and vividness of personal living and experience; whereas with Dewey the essence of things emerges only upon reflection, and this conviction springs from his characteristic and perpetual thoughtfulness. This must not be taken to imply that Dewey would abandon life for thought but that his ideal of life is *thoughtful* living." Ralph Barton Perry, *The Thought and Character of William James* (Boston: Atlantic-Little, Brown and Co., copyright 1935 by Henry James), vol. 2, p. 515.

34. "One will understand the philosophy of James better if one considers it in its totality as a revision of English empiricism, a revision which replaces the value of past experience, of what is already given, by the future, by that which is mere possibility." John Dewey, "The Development of American Pragmatism," *Studies in the History of Ideas* (New York: Columbia University Press, 1925), vol. 2, pp. 336–367.

35. The following is an extract from Dewey's letter to James on December 19, 1903. It clearly indicates Dewey's anxiety about meeting the criticism of the pragmatic conception of truth.

"I have something brewing in my head on what I call to myself 'Truth As Stimulation and As Control,' a commentary in effect upon your (James's) 'Sentiment of Rationality,' to point out that in certain situations truth is that which liberates and sets agoing more experience, in others, that which limits and defines, which adjusts to definite ends. *It seems to me this will straighten out some objections to pragmatism, its seeming over-utilitarianism* (my italics, ed.) (the 'control' side) and provide a place for the aesthetic function *in* knowledge—'truth for its own sake,' harmony, etc. (the liberation side). And I believe this has a bearing on the indeterminate character of experience, and hence upon freedom, etc. Schiller from this point of view overdoes relatively the control side of truth, its utility for *specific* purposes, not making enough of the tremendous freedom, possibilities of new growth, etc., that come from developing 'intelligence' that works along for a time according to its *own* technique, *in abstracto* from preconceived and pre-experienced ends and results . . . I am getting to another documentary letter, but 'truth for its own sake' has upon complete pragmatic principles, it seems to me, not only a justification, but an absolutely indispensable function, without which the last word would be with an 'environment' which finally determines what is and what isn't useful; and it makes little difference whether this 'environment' is called 'matter' or a complete system to thought-relations, or Experience *per* Bradley or *per* Royce. . . . " Ralph Barton Perry, *The Thought and Character of William James*, vol. 2, pp. 525–526.

[36.] See Chapter 2, p. 29.

[37.] In a biographical sketch of Dewey, Miss Jane Dewey writes as follows: "James's influence on Dewey's theory of knowledge was exercised not by the Pragmatism, which appeared after Dewey's theory had been formed, but by chapters in *The Principles of Psychology* dealing with conception, discrimination and comparison, and reasoning. Dewey had frequently recommended these chapters to students as a better introduction to the essentials of a pragmatic theory of knowledge than the *Pragmatism*." *The Philosophy of John Dewey*, ed. P. A. Schlipp, p. 23. Also see in this connection Dewey's autobiographical sketch, "From Absolutism to Experimentalism," in *The Contemporary American Philosophy*, ed. G. P. Adams and W. P. Montague, vol. 2, p. 23.

[38.] John Dewey, "What Does Pragmatism Mean by Practical?," *The Journal of Philosophy*, vol. 4 (1908), p. 94. In this passage, Dewey has cited William ᵀames, *Pragmatism: A New Name for Some Old Ways of Thinking* (New York: Longmans, Green and Company, 1907).

[39.] Ralph Barton Perry, *The Thought and Character of William James*, vol. 2, pp. 528–529.

[40.] Professor Perry divides verification into four classes: (1) verification by perception, (2) verification by consistency, (3) verification by operation, and (4) verification by sentiment. The Jamesian conception of verification was a combination of the third and fourth types. Verification by operation (subsequent utility) was common to James and Dewey, but verification by sentiment was confined to James.

"Satisfactoriness (personal) of an idea," and "*agreeableness* of an hypothesis" were regarded by James as the verification of an idea or hypothesis. The problem of verification was also connected by him with the human will: "The proof of an idea by its immediate pleasantness or by its tonic effect upon the will." Ralph Barton Perry,

Present Philosophical Tendencies (New York: Longmans, Green and Company, 1916), pp. 208–209.

41. See Chapter 1, p. 16.
42. See Chapter 1, p. 18.
43. See Chapter 2, p. 25.
44. John Dewey, *Liberalism and Social Action* (New York: G. P. Putnam's Sons, 1935), p. 43.
45. John Dewey, *Philosophy and Civilization*, p. 294.
46. John Dewey, *The Public and Its Problems*, p. 197.
47. John Dewey, *German Philosophy and Politics*, first ed., p. 44.
48. *Ibid.*, p. 66.
49. *Ibid.*, p. 62.
50. "The Idea of a Universal Cosmopolitical History," in *Kant's Principles of Politics*, ed. and tr. W. Hastie (Edinburgh: T.N.T. Clark, 1891), p. 11.
51. *Ibid.*, p. 9.
52. *Ibid.*, p. 7.
53. *Ibid.*, pp. 8–9.
54. John Dewey, *German Philosophy and Politics*, first ed., pp. 64–65.
55. B. Bosanquet, *op. cit.*, pp. 255–256.
56. Professor Georg Simmel defined *Kultur*, in its deepest sense, as ". . . the accomplishment of the soul through the development of all germs and possibilities inherent in it, provoked by the objective creations the spirit of humanity has produced." See *Georg Simmel: The Conflict in Modern Culture and Other Essays*, ed. K. Peter Etzkorn (New York: Teachers College Press, 1968).
57. The term *Kultur* in German, on account of its metaphysical and political accretions, cannot be regarded as synonymous with the term "culture." The above-mentioned analysis attempts only a general comparison between the functions of these two terms as found in English and in German.
58. Kant, *op. cit.*, ed. and tr. W. Hastie, p. 20.
59. Sir Philip Hartog in his admirable paper, "Kultur as a Symbol in Peace and in War," provides a fairly reliable evidence of the origin of the term *Kultur* in the German language. Sir Philip writes as follows: "The word *Culture* (as it was originally spelt), the Latin *cultra*, was introduced into Germany from France; and thanks to Johann Cristoph Adelung (1732–1806), a typical German scholar of the universal type, the date of its introduction can be fixed with some precision. In the first edition of his dictionary, the *Grammatisch-Kritisches Warterbuch der Hochdeutschen Mundart, Culture* does not appear in the volume published in 1774, containing the letter C, nor does it under the letter K. In the second edition of the volume containing C, published in 1793, *Culture* appears and is defined as follows: 'The en-

nobling or refining of the whole spiritual and bodily powers of a person or people; so that the word connotes not only the enlightenment (Aufklarung) and ennobling of the understanding by delivering it from prejudices, but also the polishing (Politur) the ennobling and refining of the moral qualities (der Sitten).' " Sir Philip Hartog, *The Sociological Review*, vol. 30, no. 4 (Oct. 1938), p. 320.

60. Charles A. Beard, *The Nature of Social Sciences* (New York: Charles Scribner's Sons, 1934), pp. 159–162.

61. Sabine's views on the empirical method in politics is given in his paper, "What Is Political Theory?" in *Journal of Politics*, vol. 1, no. 1 (Feb. 1939), pp. 1–16.

62. See Chapter 1, p. 21.

63. John Dewey, "The Philosophy of Thomas Hill Green," *Andover Review*, vol. 11 (April 1889), pp. 337–355.

64. *Ibid.*, p. 339.

65. John Dewey, "The Metaphysical Assumptions of Materialism," *Journal of Speculative Philosophy*, vol. 16 (1882), pp. 208–213.

66. John Dewey, *op. cit.* in *Andover Review*, p. 346.

67. *Ibid.*, p. 346.

68. *Ibid.*, p. 344.

69. John Dewey, "Green's Theory of the Moral Motive," *Philosophical Review*, vol. 1 (1892), pp. 593–612.

70. John Dewey, "Self-Realization as the Moral Ideal," *Philosophical Review*, vol. 2 (1893), p. 663.

71. *Ibid.*, p. 653.

72. It must be pointed out here that the complete identification of the self with self-realizing activities was subsequently modified by Dewey in the revised edition of *Ethics* (1932). The following passage clearly indicates his acknowledgement of an antecedent self: ". . . Every . . . choice sustains double relation to the self. It reveals the existing self and it forms the future self. That which is chosen is that which is found congenial to the desires and habits of the self as it already exists." Dewey and Tufts, *Ethics* (New York: Henry Holt and Company, 1908), p. 317.

73. Other parallels can be drawn between the principal ideas of Green's and Dewey's political philosophies. Green's "common consciousness of common good," for example, has its counterpart in Dewey's associated community, consciousness of the indirect consequences which affect the general well-being and seek to regulate them. Furthermore, Green's thesis on the scope and limits of state action as that of "hindering the hindrances" to a good life has its counterpart in Dewey's conception of political action, which aims at eliminating external obstacles to the fullest development of the individual's personality and participation. The quality of state action both in Green and in Dewey

primarily remains negative or indirect. As far as positive action is concerned, Green leaves it to the moral initiative of the individual, whereas with Dewey it becomes some kind of a communal responsibility. Communal responsibility includes the responsibility for education, research, and the publication of facts about all aspects of the society, the exchange of ideas, the inculcation of an experimental attitude, and the simultaneous abrogation of dogmatism of all shades and forms.

However, we are prevented from undertaking an extensive analysis of these parallels between Green and Dewey by the following:

First, in Dewey's writings there is no direct or indirect evidence of his attempt to reconsider the problems that Green raised. The relationship that exists between Dewey and Kant does not exist between Dewey and Green.

Second, Green's frame of reference of ideas is totally different from Dewey's; Green's common consciousness of common good, for example, is worked out within the framework of the problem of rights and duties. For Green, the problem of rights and duties presupposes the common consciousness of common good, whereas Dewey's communal consciousness of the indirect consequences affecting the general well-being has the quality of Locke's "inconveniences" in the enjoyment of natural rights in the state of nature. There are no natural rights in Dewey's political philosophy, and the consciousness of the indirect consequences affecting the general well-being does not require any *a priori* standards like natural rights. With Dewey, the indirect consequences affecting the general well-being and therefore requiring political regulation are to be found in the plain commonsense experience. In this respect, then, the frame of reference of Dewey's communal consciousness of the direct consequences is radically different from Green's.

74. John Dewey, *The Ethics of Democracy*, in University of Michigan, Philosophical Papers, second series, no. 1 (Ann Arbor: Andrews and Company, Publishers, 1888), pp. 1–28.

75. *Ibid.*, pp. 4–7.

76. *Ibid.*, p. 9.

77. *Ibid.*, p. 7.

78. *Ibid.*, p. 9.

79. *Ibid.*, pp. 17–18.

80. *Ibid.*, pp. 21–22.

81. *Ibid.*, p. 2.

82. John Dewey, *The Public and Its Problems*, p. 77.

83. *Ibid.*, p. 84.

84. John Dewey, "Austin's Theory of Sovereignty," *The Political Science Quarterly*, vol. 9 (189ː), pp. 1–52.

85. John Dewey, "The Motivation of Hobbes's Political Philosophy," in *Studies in the History of Ideas*, vol. 1 (May 1867), pp. 88–115.
86. *Ibid.*, p. 107.
87. *Ibid.*, p. 88.
88. *Ibid.*, p. 91.
89. *Ibid.*, p. 111.
90. *Ibid.*, p. 114.
91. *Ibid.*, p. 88.
92. John Dewey, *Freedom and Culture*, pp. 109–110.
93. John Dewey, *Reconstruction in Philosophy* (New York: Henry Holt and Company, 1920), pp. 188–189.
94. *Ibid.*, p. 205 (my italics).
95. *Ibid.*, p. 203.

Notes to Chapter 4, pp. 94–178

1. Harold Laski, Review of *The Public and Its Problems*, *Saturday Review of Literature* (October 15, 1927).
2. Walter Lippmann, *Public Opinion* (New York: The Macmillan Co., 1922), p. 25.
3. Harold Laski, *op. cit.*, p. 198.
4. William Benett Munro, Review of *The Public and Its Problems*, *The Yale Review*, vol. 17 (1928), pp. 610–612.
5. *Ibid.*, p. 611.
6. See pp. 91–92 in Chapter 3.
7. William Benett Munro, "Physics and Politics—An Old Analogy Revised," *American Political Science Review*, vol. 22, no. 1 (1928), p. 6. For Dewey's use of this phrase, see *The Public and Its Problems*, p. 193.
8. William Benett Munro, *op. cit.* in *American Political Science Review*, p. 3.
9. *Ibid.*, p. 10.
10. *Ibid.*, p. 6.
11. John Dewey, *The Public and Its Problems*, p. 199.
12. W. E. Hocking, Review of *The Public and Its Problems*, *Journal of Philosophy*, vol. 26, no. 13 (June 1929), pp. 329–335.
13. *Ibid.*, p. 329.
14. *Ibid.*, p. 330.
15. *Ibid.*, p. 329.
16. In his article "Political Science in the United States," Charles Merriam has written as follows: "Political philosophy inevitably involves the interrelation of general philosophy with the narrower field of political philosophy of John Dewey, whose pragmatism in general philosophy and liberalism in political philosophy were of outstanding influence." UNESCO, *Contemporary Political Science*, New York: Co-

lumbia University Press, 1950), p. 240.

17. This is quoted from a letter written by Dewey to Hu Shih, as reprinted in *The Philosopher of the Common Man*, ed. Sidney Ratner, p. 211.

18. See Charles E. Merriam, "Political Science in the United States," in *Contemporary Political Science*, UNESCO, pp. 232–248.

19. John Dewey, *The Public and Its Problems*, p. 6.

20. John Dewey, *Logic: The Theory of Inquiry*, p. 507.

21. John Dewey, *The Public and Its Problems*, p. 10 (my italics).

22. John Dewey, "Psychology and Philosophic Method" (Berkeley: The University Press, 1899). This was subsequently reprinted, with minor changes, under the title of "Consciousness and Experience," in *The Influence of Darwin on Philosophy* (New York: Henry Holt and Company, 1910), p. 267.

23. *Ibid.*, pp. 244–248.

24. *Ibid.*, p. 243.

25. John Dewey, *Human Nature and Conduct*, p. 15.

26. *Ibid.*, p. 52.

27. John Dewey, *Freedom and Culture*, pp. 6–7.

28. John Dewey, *Democracy and Education* (New York: The Macmillan Company, 1916), p. 22.

29. John Dewey, *School and Society* (Chicago: The University of Chicago Press, 1913), p. 44.

30. "The underlying and generative conditions of concrete behavior are social as well as organic: much more social than organic as far as the manifestation of *differential* wants, purposes, and methods of operation is concerned. . . . the desires, aims and standards of satisfaction . . . are themselves socially conditioned phenomena." John Dewey, *The Public and Its Problems*, pp. 103–104.

31. John Dewey, *The Public and Its Problems*, p. 9.

32. John Dewey, *Freedom and Culture*, p. 18.

33. See the following for a cross-section of studies which have made the concept of power a central theme in contemporary political science: George Catlin, *The Science and Method of Politics* (New York: Knopf, 1927). Harold Lasswell, *Politics: Who Gets What, When, How* (New York: McGraw-Hill, 1936). C. Wright Mills, *Power, Politics and People* (New York: Ballantine Books, 1963). Floyd Hunter, *Community Power Structure: A Study of Decision Makers* (New York: Doubleday and Company, 1963). Robert Dahl, *Who Governs? Democracy and Power in an American City* (New Haven: Yale University Press, 1961).

34. J. W. Garner, *Political Science and Government* (New York: American Book Company, 1928), pp. 46–53.

35. "Thinking by itself without any observation or consideration of in-

stances seemed capable of finding out the true meanings of words, and this process in some indefinable way was held to give information as to the nature and relations of things to which words referred. The application of this to political inquiries is almost painfully evident." Further, ". . . The inquiry is however doomed to sterility because words do not have meanings in the universal sense at all; they simply have uses." T. D. Weldon, *The Vocabulary of Politics* (London: Penguin Books, 1953), p. 19.

I must mention here that I do not find Mr. Weldon's argument altogether sound. Political thinking may be without conscious observation, but what finally comes out as the product of thinking is some form of reflection on the historical settings in which thinking is undertaken. No thinking can take place *in vacuo*. Even in the most metaphysical political philosophies, we can find a connection with their historical settings.

Moreover, words have meanings as well as uses. Historical political philosophies had undertaken the search for the meanings of words, because that is invariably the first state of reflection. In the process of reflection, words help us to concentrate. What is necessary is to distinguish between the search for the meanings of words and the meanings that are attributed to words from time to time.

Mr. Weldon's argument, in the last analysis, implies that as words have *uses*, some agreement must be reached on their uses. But what is forgotten in this emphasis is the fact that words are after all our media and tools for understanding tangible and intangible reality, the character of which cannot be permanently determined by agreement on the uses of words. Some agreement, however, ought to be reached as to the way in which a particular word can be used. At the same time, adequate freedom must be provided to people who wish to challenge from time to time the assumption that everything implied by word symbols is not conveyed by their accepted uses.

[36.] John Dewey, *The Public and Its Problems*, pp. 8–9.

[37.] John Dewey, *Experience and Nature*, p. 91.

[38.] In one of his earlier papers, Dewey maintained that the particular water with which the experimenter deals is as unique as Abraham Lincoln, that physical events do not recur for the sake of comparison. They are *reproduced* for the second time or for as many times as desired. Such a reproduction is brought about by experimentation, which controls the effective conditions of events. John Dewey, "The Evolutionary Method as Applied to Morality," *Philosophical Review*, vol. 11, no. 2 (March 1902), pp. 109–111.

[39.] John Dewey, *Reconstruction in Philosophy* (New York: Henry Holt and Company, 1920), p. 189.

[40.] John Dewey, *The Public and Its Problems*, p. 6.

41. *Ibid.*, p. 27.
42. *Ibid.*, p. 31.
43. R. H. Lowie, *The Origin of the State* (New York: Harcourt Brace and Company, 1927), p. 2.
44. *Ibid.*, p. 1.
45. John Dewey, Review of *The Origin of the State*, Columbia Law Review (1928), p. 253.
46. John Dewey, *The Public and Its Problems*, p. 23.
47. ". . . there is no sense in asking how individuals come to be associated. They exist and operate in association. If there is any mystery about the matter, it is the mystery that the universe is the kind of universe it is." *Ibid.*, p. 23.
48. " 'Society' . . . is either an abstract or collective noun. In the concrete, there are societies, associations, groups of an immense number of kinds, having different ties and instituting different interests." *Ibid.*, p. 69.
49. Walter Lippmann, *The Phantom Public* (New York: Harcourt Brace and Company, 1925), pp. 55–56.
50. *Ibid.*, p. 156.
51. *Ibid.*, p. 42.
52. *Ibid.*, p. 20.
53. *Ibid.*, p. 16.
54. John Dewey, *The Public and Its Problems*, p. 35.
55. See Chapter 2, p. 24.
56. John Dewey, *The Public and Its Problems*, p. 39.
57. *Ibid.*, p. 47.
58. *Ibid.*, p. 62.
59. *Ibid.*, pp. 57–58.
60. *Ibid.*, p. 47.
61. *Ibid.*, pp. 202–203.
62. John Dewey, "The Economic Basis of the New Society," in *Intelligence in the Modern World*, ed. Joseph Ratner (New York: The Modern Library, 1939), pp. 431–432.
63. See Chapter 1, p. 20.
64. G. H. Sabine, "What Is Political Theory," *The Journal of Politics*, vol. 1, no. 1 (Feb. 1939), pp. 1–16.
65. G. H. Sabine, "The Pragmatic Approach to Politics," *The American Political Science Review*, vol. 24, no. 4 (Nov. 1930), pp. 865–885.
66. G. H. Sabine, *op. cit.* in *The Journal of Politics*, p. 15.
67. *Ibid.*, p. 5.
68. *Ibid.*, p. 5. In his preface to *A History of Political Theory* (New York: Holt, Rinehart and Winston, 1965, p. v), Sabine took the same position with regard to the factors of bias and predilections operating in political theory. "Taken as a whole" Sabine wrote, "a political

theory can hardly be said to be true. It contains among its elements certain judgments of fact, or estimates of probability, which time proves perhaps to be objectively right or wrong. It involves also certain questions of logical compatibility respecting the elements which it tries to combine. Invariably, however, it includes valuations and predilections, personal or collective, which distort the perception of fact, the estimate of probability, and the weighing of compatibilities. The most that criticism can do is to keep these three factors as much as possible distinct: to prevent preferences from claiming the inevitableness of logic and the certainty of fact."

69. G. H. Sabine, *op. cit.* in *The Journal of Politics*, p. 5.

70. In one of his earlier papers, namely "Descriptive and Normative Sciences" (*The Philosophical Review*, vol. 21, 1912, p. 438), Sabine expressed his disapproval of Husserl's thesis that normative sciences rest on theoretical judgments that are grounded in facts, hence the possibility of investigating normative and descriptive subjects together. To Sabine, the possibility of reducing investigation to a unity comes only from its normative side: "The true methodological reason for abolishing the distinction is not that all sciences are descriptive but rather that all are normative." *Ibid.*, p. 450.

71. G. H. Sabine, *op. cit.* in *The Journal of Politics*, p. 6.

72. "The sciences which are usually called normative—especially the humanistic sciences—are those in which the place of valuation is too clear and distinct to be overlooked." G. H. Sabine, *op. cit.* in *The Philosophical Review*, p. 450.

73. ". . . all logical forms (with their characteristic properties) arise within the operation of inquiry and are concerned with control of inquiry so that it may yield warranted assertions. This conception implies much more than that logical forms are disclosed or come to light when we reflect upon processes of inquiry that are in use. Of course, it means that; but it also means that forms originate in operations of inquiry." John Dewey, *Logic: The Theory of Inquiry*, pp. 3–4.

74. John Dewey, *Logic: The Theory of Inquiry*, p. 496.

75. G. H. Sabine, *A History of Political Theory*, p. vi.

76. See Chapter 2, p. 36.

77. The term "rational dogmas" has been used here in order to indicate the use of intellectual authorities for the purposes of reasoning which are themselves not questioned. The use of such unquestioned intellectual authorities is fairly widespread in political reasoning. The following are some illustrations: liberty, equality, neutral rights, general will, economic determinism.

Dewey's comments on Plato and Aristotle invariably give the impression that they used rational dogmas for the purpose of their reasoning. Such a claim can certainly be disputed. For the purposes of illustrating his thesis on the authoritative and the experimental phase

THE POLITICAL THEORY

in political reasoning, however, I have refrained from criticizing his contention.

78. T. D. Weldon, *op. cit.* , pp. 88, 97.

79. John Dewey, "Traffic in Absolute," *The New Republic* (July 1917), p. 281.

80. John Dewey, *Freedom and Culture*, p. 102.

81. John Dewey, *Liberalism and Social Action*, p. 45.

82. *Ibid.*, p. 73.

83. Lionel Trilling, *The Liberal Imagination* (New York: The Viking Press, 1950), p. 34.

84. John Dewey, *Problems of Men* (New York: Philosophical Library, 1946), pp. 107–108.

85. The term "political authority" is used here in order to indicate political authority as it exists in Western democratic societies.

86. John Dewey, *Experience and Nature*, p. 91.

87. "It is a truism that mathematics is the method by which elements can be stated as terms in constant relations, and be subjected to equations and other functions of transformation and substitution. An element is appropriately represented by a mathematical variable; for since any variable falls within some equation, it is treated as a constant function of other variables. The shift from variability to constancy is repeated as often as is needed. It is thus only *pro forma* that the variable is variable. It is not variable in the sense in which unique individualized existences are variable. The inevitable consequence is the subjection of individuals or unique modes of variation to external relations, to laws of uniformity; that is to say, the elimination of individuality. Bear in mind the instrumental nature of the relation of elements, and this abrogation of individuality merely means a temporary neglect—an abstracted gaze—in behalf of attending to conditions under which individualities present themselves." *Ibid.*, p. 122.

In this passage Dewey gives the impression that what he means by "variables" and "constants" is not what is normally meant. The normal use is as follows: "Suppose X (variable) is equal to 4 (constant)." For him instead, a relational proposition is a *constant*. It is a constant which indicates an invariable relationship between two or more variables or unique objects and events. Unique objects or events in relation to one another are variables. For the purposes of analysis of the characteristics of specific problems I have used "constants" and "variables" in Dewey's sense of the terms.

88. John Dewey, *Logic: The Theory of Inquiry*, p. 452.

89. John Dewey, "Social Science and Social Control," *The New Republic* (July 1931), pp. 276–277.

90. John Dewey, *Freedom and Culture*, pp. 84–85.

91. John Dewey, *The Public and Its Problems*, p. 197.
92. John Dewey, *Logic: The Theory of Inquiry*, pp. 499–500.
93. The example of manipulative operation of the first variety is to be found in tariff policy as country balances its exports and imports. Tariff policy is therefore its manipulative instrument for mitigating specific problems connected with overproduction, unemployment, crises in price mechanism, deficit in the balance of payments, and so forth. An example of a manipulative operation of the second variety is to be found in a permanently established institution such as a hypothetical economic council that is supposed to have its branches spread all over the country's economy. Its branches are supposed to keep the council in touch with day-to-day developments in the country's economy and implement its proposals.
94. John Dewey, *Experience and Nature*, p. 60.
95. John Dewey, *Freedom and Culture*, pp. 108–109.
96. Different meanings of the term "person" in jurisprudence have been derived from the notion of the term "person" prevalent in politics at different times: that of Maitland—"corporate personality," "a right-and-duty-bearing unit;" that of Gierke—"organism possessing a will;" that of Michoud—"subject of rights and duties;" and so forth. See John Dewey, *Philosophy and Civilization*, pp. 145–148.
97. The notion of the isolated, self-sufficient "individual," as conceived by Locke, and further emancipated from the ties of different associations by the French Revolutionaries, became the basis of classical economics. See John Dewey, *The Public and Its Problems*, pp. 187–190.
98. The reader is referred to Bertrand Russell's criticism of this emphasis on the practical use of knowledge in *The Philosophy of John Dewey*, ed. P. A. Schilpp, pp. 155–156.
99. John Dewey, "Science and Social Control," p. 277.
100. Prof. F. A. Hayek is one of the exponents of the view that the data of the social sciences reside in the opinion and/or the beliefs of men: "They (the facts of the social sciences) differ from the facts of the physical sciences in being beliefs or opinions held by particular people, beliefs which as such are our data, irrespective of whether they are true or false, and which, moreover, we cannot directly observe in the minds of the people but which we can recognize from what they do and say merely because we have ourselves a mind similar to theirs." F. A. Hayek, *The Counter-Revolution of Science* (Glencoe, Illinois: The Free Press, 1952), p. 28.

I do not think that Professor Hayek's contention is altogether sound. "Facts" of social science can be said to rest on an empirical and publicly observable basis in varying degrees.

Professor Hayek's contention seems to be directed against the "scientism" of Comte, Marx, Hobhouse, and Dewey. As far as Dewey is concerned, I do not think that his contention is valid at all. Dewey was not in favor of collecting facts but in resolving specific problems. Both the scope and the purpose of his inquiry were declared in advance. Within a broad empirical framework of inquiry and the manipulation of specific problems, Dewey seems to acknowledge the directive functions of opinions and beliefs. What he does not acknowledge, however, is the fact that opinions and beliefs are the sole data of specific problems.

101. John Dewey, *The Public and Its Problems*, p. 197.

SELECTED BIBLIOGRAPHY

Biographical References*

Thomas, Minton Halsey and Herbert Schneider, *A Bibliography of John Dewey, 1882–1939*. New York: Columbia University Press, 1939.

Thomas, Milton Halsey, *John Dewey: A Centennial Bibliography*. Chicago: The University of Chicago Press, 1962.

Writings of Dewey Given Special Emphasis in This Study

Art as Experience. New York: Minton, Balch and Company, 1934.

Characters and Events: Popular Essays in Social and Political Philosophy (ed. Joseph Ratner). New York: Henry Holt and Company, 1929.

Democracy and Education: An Introduction to the Philosophy of Education. New York: The Macmillan Company, 1916.

Ethics (with J. H. Tufts). New York: Henry Holt and Company, 1908.

Essays in Experimental Logic. Chicago: The University of Chicago Press, 1916.

Experience and Nature. New York: W. W. Norton and Company, 1929.

Freedom and Culture. New York: G. P. Putnam's Sons, 1939.

German Philosophy and Politics. New York: Henry Holt and Company, 1915.

Human Nature and Conduct: An Introduction to Psychology. New York: Henry Holt and Company, 1922.

Individualism, Old and New. New York: Minton, Balch and Company, 1930.

* Thomas (1962) is an excellent bibliography of writings of and on Dewey.

Intelligence in the Modern World: John Dewey's Philosophy (ed. Joseph Ratner). New York: The Modern Library, 1939.

Knowing and the Known (with A. F. Bentley). Boston: The Beacon Press, 1949.

Liberalism and Social Action. New York: G. P. Putnam's Sons, 1935.

Logic: The Theory of Inquiry. New York: Henry Holt and Company, 1938.

Philosophy and Civilization. New York: Minton, Balch and Company, 1931.

Problems of Men. New York: Philosophical Library, 1946.

Psychology. New York: American Book Company, 1891, 3rd. rev. ed.

The Public and Its Problems. New York: Henry Holt and Company, 1927.

The Quest for Certainty. New York: Minton, Balch and Company, 1929.

Reconstruction in Philosophy. New York: Henry Holt and Company, 1920.

The School and Society. Chicago: The University of Chicago Press, 1913.

Studies in Logical Theory. Chicago: The University of Chicago Press, 1903.

Writings on Dewey

Archimbault, R. D. (ed.), *Dewey on Education: Appraisals.* New York: Random House, New York, 1966.

Geiger, G. R., *John Dewey in Perspective.* New York: Oxford University Press, 1958.

Hook, Sidney (ed.), *Philosopher of Science and Freedom.* New York: The Dial Press, 1950.

Schilpp, P. A. (ed.), *The Philosophy of John Dewey.* Chicago: Northwestern University Press, 1939.

INDEX

abstractions
    role of, 18
activism in D's thought, 4, 46–47
ADAMS, G. P., 188 *n.*
ADELUNG, JOHANN CRISTOPH, 189 *n.*
analysis
    factual-causal, evaluative, 142 ff.
analytic dualism, 68 ff.
antecedent self
    D's change in position, 190–191 *n.*
antidualism in D
    of subject vs. object, 13 ff.
anti-individualism in D, 41, 113
ARISTOTLE, 24, 80, 107, 111, 153, 169
ARNOLD, MATTHEW, 65
Art as Experience, 14, 181 *n.*
associated living, 127–128
association
    in definition of "society," 92–93
    indirect moral reference of, 98
AUSTIN, 79, 80, 83, 84, 93
"Austin's Theory of Sovereignty,"
    6, 83, 89, 190 *n.*
authority in politics, 158 ff.
    vs. authority in science, 158–160

BACON, 10, 49, 50, 152
BARKER, 5
BEARD, CHARLES A., 68, 69, 70, 189 *n.*
beginnings, related to endings (D),
    181 *n.*
behavior, conditions of, 192 *n.*
behaviorism, as unable to accom-
    modate cognitive activity, 56
BENTHAM, 40, 52, 80, 110, 154
BERKELEY, 47
BERLIN, ISAIAH, 51, 185 *n.*
BOSANQUET, 43, 54, 65, 68, 185 *n.*,
    188 *n.*
BRADLEY, 187 *n.*
British philosophy
    empiricism, 12, 17, 40, 47, 49, 55,
        72, 186 *n.*
    idealism, 43
    utilitarianism, 40, 52, 152

British Labor Party, 154
BURKE, 185 *n.*

the CAIRDS, 42, 43
CATLIN, GEORGE, 6, 117, 192 *n.*
causal explanations, specific and
    general, 111
causality, 16 ff.
    and sequential order, 21 ff., 163 ff.
Chicago school in philosophy, 57
Civilization vs. *Kultur*, 61 ff., 66–67
    distinction in Marx, 67
classical economists, D's criticism
    of, 115 ff.
classless society, as reconstructive
    concept, 103
cognitive activity, 56 ff.
    ideas or hypotheses as tools, 59
    trial and error as procedure, 59
cognitive experience, as conscious
    and discriminating, 59–60
COLE, 5
common inquiry, *see* inquiry
COMTE, 52, 197 *n.*
community, D's idea of, 71
comprehensive method
    concern of Hobbes and D, 86
    in *The Public and Its Problems*,
        3, 94 ff.
concepts
    as consciously formulated, 103 ff.
    demands imposed by rational
        techniques, 91
concepts, *a priori*, 119 ff.
    as indispensable to idealist, 67 ff.
    see also concepts, universal
concepts, generic
    and associated living, 127
    "consequences, perception, and
        organization," 126–127
    discriminatory functions of, 93,
        120 ff., 134 ff.
    functions tested, 135 ff.
    as hypotheses, 91

201

concepts, generic (cont.)
"power," 117
"public," 134
in retrospective analysis, 127–128
vs. universal concepts, 93
concepts, reconstructive
as precise propositions, 103
concepts, universal
as criticized by D, 91 ff.
position of *Reconstruction in Philosophy*, 91
position of *The Public and Its Problems*, 95–96
consciousness
in D's philosophy, 113
divine and human (Green), 74
as subject for psychology, 42
consequences as concept for discrimination, 134 ff.
Context and Thought, 10, 180 n.
continuously planning society, 145
contractualists, on growth of political organizations, 128
control
of consequences, 139–140
as dependent on knowing, 20
and prediction, 171
scientific vs. supernatural, 167
in theory of knowledge (D), 20
COOK, W. W., 146
Creative Intelligence, 15, 181 n.
critical intelligence, 56–57
cultural medium, adequate, 79

DAHL, ROBERT, 117, 192 n.
DARWIN, 186
data-objects distinction, 134
democracy
accidental nature of (Maine), 82
as condition of making and testing hypotheses, 151 ff.
as condition of morality, 90
defense of, 82, 90, 154–155
Democracy and Education, 115, 192 n.
DESCARTES, 10, 49
determinateness (Austin), D's admiration of concept, 83–84
"The Development of American Pragmatism," 55, 186 n.
DEWEY, JANE M., 49, 57, 185 n., 187 n.
DEWEY, JOHN, *see* other headings

discriminatory operations in politics, 47, 59–60, 93, 120 ff., 134 ff.
dogmas, religious and rational, in science and politics, 151–152

EASTON, DAVID, 6
EINSTEIN, 157
empirical method in politics, 189 n.
see also experimentation
ends, natural vs. practical, 17
environment
conflict inducing reflection, 113
D's conception, 112 ff.
and education, 115
and human wants, 115
interdependence with psychophysical mechanism, 113–115
and motives, 116–117
epistemological dualism in political philosophy, 67–68
epistemology, *see* political epistemology, theory of knowledge
ethical theory, D's, 32 ff., 182–183 n.
ethics of obligations absent, 71
and Green's ethical values, 72 ff.
naturalistic treatment in, 37–38
Ethics, 33, 34, 35, 78, 86, 183 n., 189 n.
"The Ethics of Democracy," 79, 80, 81, 82, 89, 190 n.
"The Evolutionary Method as Applied to Morality," 121, 193 n.
experience
aesthetic, as objective, 180 n.
and the concept of divine consciousness (Green), 74
D's concept of, 11 ff.
as of the environment, 13
primary vs. cognitive levels, 19 ff.
sources of D's concept, 12
totality of, D's concept criticized, 21
Experience and Nature, 15, 16, 17, 18, 19, 35, 36, 86, 94, 121, 161, 162, 167, 181 n., 183 n., 196 n., 197 n.
experimentation in politics
democracy as condition, 151 ff.
vs. experimentation in science, 152–154, 193
as principal political value, 7
existence, nature of, 15

Liberalism and Social Action, 2, 40,
41, 60, 156, 184 *n.*, 188 *n.*, 196 *n.*
LIPPMANN, WALTER, 7, 95, 130, 131,
191 *n.*, 194 *n.*
LOCKE, 14, 43, 47, 66, 97, 100, 102,
128, 152, 154, 197 *n.*
logic, as functional tool, 16
Logic: The Theory of Inquiry, 16,
31, 32, 33, 111, 147, 149, 162, 166,
181 *n.*, 182 *n.*, 192 *n.*, 195 *n.*,
196 *n.*, 197 *n.*
LOWIE, R. N., 125, 126, 128, 194 *n.*

MACHIAVELLI, 110
MAINE, 79, 82, 83, 90
MAITLAND, 197 *n.*
manipulation in politics
and discrimination, 47
equilibrium of, periodic vs. permanent, 166–167
examples of measures, 197 *n.*
and specific knowledge, 163 ff.
as test of knowledge, 164 ff.
transformation as aim of, 166
see also political manipulation
MANNHEIM, KARL, 48
MARX, 40, 47, 52, 67, 110, 142, 143,
144, 145, 146, 197 *n.*
determinism criticized (D), 143 ff.
materialism, as incomplete, 73
MEAD, G. H., 40, 49, 183 *n.*, 185 *n.*
means-end relation, 183 *n.*
mechanistic approach
in Maine, D's criticism, 79–81
reconciled with organistic, 81 ff.
MERRIAM, C. E., 6, 99, 105, 191–192 *n.*
"The Metaphysical Assumptions
of Materialism," 73, 74, 189 *n.*
metaphysics, naturalistic (D), 94
methodological framework, 3
*see also The Public and Its
Problems*
Michigan, University of, 43
MICHOUD, 197 *n.*
MILL, J. S., 40, 52
MILLS, C. WRIGHT, 117, 192 *n.*
mind
as active (D), 26
Greek theory of, 11
MITCHELL, W. C., 146
MONTAGUE, W. P., 180 *n.*
MOORE, MERRITT H., 183 *n.*

moral aspects
to all problems (D), 69 ff.
to political problems, 82
nonqualitative formulation, 32 ff.
moral choice (Kant), 51
moral reference, associations, 98
"moral state" vs. "economic society," 61 ff.
MORRIS, G. S., 12, 42, 43, 72
relationship with D, 184 *n.*
"The Motivation of Hobbes's Political Philosophy," 83, 85, 87,
88, 190–191 *n.*
MUNRO, W. B., 95, 96, 97

NATHANSON, JEROME, 3
natural law, 102
natural rights (Locke, D), 190 *n.*
Nazi Germany, 48
"The Need for a Recovery in Philosophy," 13, 14, 180 *n.*
New Deal period, 156
"new" society, 6 ff.
NEWTON, 49, 50, 51
Newtonian atom, as rational dogma of democracy, 153
NIETZSCHE, 110
normative vs. descriptive
"arbitrary unity" in D, 146 ff.
in enquirer's end-in-view, 148

OAKESHOTT, M. J., 22, 38, 181 *n.*,
183 *n.*
objects and events, as processes
(D, from Hegel), 46
OLIPHANT, HARMAN, 146
opinion, in political knowledge
(Sabine) 171, 172, 194–195 *n.*
OPPENHEIMER, 125
organicism
from Hegel (D), 4, 45–47
from Liebniz (D) vs. Maine's
atomistic philosophy, 79–80
and mechanistic reconciled, 81
in methodology, 81
organization
in associated living, 127–128
concept for discrimination, 134
organizations and the scope of
political phenomena, 124 ff.

"society"
 as plurality of associations, 92
 as universal concept (D), 92–93
 vs. "state," 65, 92
Sophists, 10
sovereignty (Austin), 83–84
SPENCER, HERBERT, 43, 52, 185 n.
standards
 in D's ethical theory, 33
 reflection on ends pursued, 34
state
 a priori nature of concept, 118 ff.
 as association, 97 ff.
 attacked by D, 5 ff.
 as coordinator, 93
 Garner's definition, 120
 and individual, 183–184 n.
 moral qualities of, 98 ff.
Studies in Logical Theory, 86
subjectivity of belief, 36

theory of knowledge (D), 4 ff.
 as basis of common inquiry, 30
 characteristics summarized, 25
 as experimental, 25 ff.
 Green's influence, 73 ff.
 and indeterminancy, 182 n.
 James's influence, 187 n.
 knowing, as participant in what
  is finally known, 181–182 n.
 knowledge as control, 20
 presuppositions in, 74–75
 "problems" vs. "objects" in, 26
thinking
 phases of, 28
 as verifiable, 28
THURNWALD, 126
"Traffic in Absolute," 155, 196 n.
transformation, as aim of manipulation, 166
trial-and-error procedure
 cognitive experience in, 59–60
 and democracy, 154–155
 in positive action, 156
 in retrospective analysis, 155

source of principle, 83
trial-and-error rationalism, 59 ff.
 reaction to Kant, 61
TREITSCHKE, 48
TRILLING, LIONEL, 157, 196 n.
truth, pragmatic conception de-
 fended, 186–187 n.
TUFTS, J. H., 183 n., 189 n.

uniform behavior, and relational
 propositions in science, 162 ff.
unity in conduct, D vs. Green, 76
universal concepts, *see* concepts

valuation, process of, 36–37
"value-judgment," D on, 183 n.
values
 determination of, 78
 and facts, correlativity of, 146 ff.
 and hypotheses, 149 ff.
 interaction and, 78–79
 and political investigation, 68 ff.
 in politics, summarized, 7
 source of, in knowledge, 35 ff.
"The Vanishing Subject in the Psychology of James," 12, 180 n.
VEBLEN, THORSTEIN, 146

WALLACE, 42, 43
WALLAS, 6, 110
WARD, PAUL, 3, 179 n.
WELDON, T. D., 119, 153, 193 n., 196 n.
welfare state, as reconstructive
 concept, 103
WENLEY, R. M., 43, 184 n.
"What Does Pragmatism Mean by
 Practical?" 58
"What Is Political Theory?," 146
WOODBRIDGE, 58
World War I, 48
World War II, 41, 48